# FREEDOM AND
# KARL JASPERS'S PHILOSOPHY

# FREEDOM AND KARL JASPERS'S PHILOSOPHY

ELISABETH YOUNG-BRUEHL

NEW HAVEN AND LONDON
YALE UNIVERSITY PRESS

Designed by Nancy Ovedovitz and set in VIP Times Roman type.
Printed in the United States of America by The Alpine Press, Inc., Stoughton, Mass.

**Library of Congress Cataloging in Publication Data**

Young-Bruehl, Elisabeth.
  Freedom and Karl Jaspers's philosophy.

  Bibliography: p.
  Includes index.
  1. Jaspers, Karl, 1883–1969. 2. Liberty.
I. Title.
B3279. J34Y68      193      81-40436
ISBN 0-300-02629-3      AACR2

10  9  8  7  6  5  4  3  2  1

# CONTENTS

127559

# PREFACE

My students tell me that they want to learn "how to think." Their lives, our world, the past and the future, present them with imponderables—for they are without orientation, they do not know where and how to begin to ponder. There are ideologies and "isms" of many sorts for them to take up, live with, sometimes live *in*. But there are also forms of questioning that tell them how fleeting and history-bound ideologies can be; there is metacriticism and there are descriptions of how an ism becomes a "post-ism." Most alluring for many of them is the possibility that the many and various isms of our day can be synthesized, that a grand eclecticism or dialecticism will produce an amalgam of Marxism, psychoanalysis, structuralism, hermeneutics, linguistics, feminism, and so forth.

But beneath the rare air of theory and metatheory and critical theory, immediate and pressing questions stand with frightening solidity. There are nuclear weapons and power plants—overwhelming technologies; there are starvation, overpopulation, colossal economic imbalances, diminishing natural resources; there are decaying and corrupt political processes, the specters of totalitarianism, terrorism, and racial, ethnic, and sexual oppression. While theories are woven and rewoven, many people ask what is to be done without receiving an answer—while much is done blindly or shortsightedly. Theories of the relation or relations between theory and practice advanced to provide an answer are inadequate.

After the Second World War many European writers, labeled "existentialist," turned their attention to the realities of everyday life with the clear sense that philosophers had been looking in another direction, finding the realm of human affairs unserious. The German philosopher Karl Jaspers was one of these, but he, like most of the others, rejected the label. "The public creates its own phantoms," he wrote in the 1950s. "Thus, today it takes as existentialism that which Sartre has effected, and subsumes under it all others who have spoken of existence and have a relation to Kierkegaard. The suggestion of such a phenomenon is so great that assistant professors of philosophy write books on a topic which they claim to see as a whole, which they already can historically summarize and whose assumptions they can trace back through the centuries. . . ."[1] Jaspers was distressed to see his own thinking effort, his own effort to relate thinking and doing, his own effort to philosophize in the world and not from above the world, turned into an ism. He knew very well that when *Geistesgeschichte,* the history of ideas, envelops philosophical activity, all concern for *how to think* will be lost as the contents of thoughts are catalogued, compared, given genealogies, classified.

Existentialism, like many another ism, has lost its power to excite controversy; as an ism it is now datable: it was a phenomenon of the postwar decade. But this power of existentialism's was in many respects a false power in the first place—and its loss is no real loss. The public phantom has disappeared. One can hope that this leaves space for the possibility of recovering the thinking activity of Jaspers and others for our time.

A thinker's thinking activity is invisible in itself; what can be recovered are the traces of the activity, the spoken words and the written words of the thinker. Though these traces are not the thinking per se, they are what teaches us how to think. They are exemplary. No words should be taken as the last words, the only example, or even the ultimate example; but those words which present—as Jaspers's do—a profound awareness of different modes of thought and the relations between those modes and lived lives (modes of living) are particularly important in times of intellectual disorientation.

Over many years of work as a psychiatrist and a philosopher, Karl Jaspers developed a repertoire of thinking procedures. In the tradition that stems from Aristotle, procedures of the sort Jaspers developed would have been called dialectics. Students of philosophy trained within this ancient tradition learned to argue with and from good opinions, *endoxoi,* arranged to reveal both sides of an issue, or all sides of an issue. They learned to find the first principles of disciplines and inquiries. They learned the art of making distinctions. Of course, these procedures, with centuries of use, could and did degenerate into scholasticism, as they had in Aristotle's own time served eristics. Jaspers was well aware that for our time, the techniques of dialectic could not simply be revived. Forms, once emptied of meaning, cannot simply be refilled as old bottles with new wine.

For his time, Karl Jaspers knew philosophy had to be revived and reoriented, not given over to more fruitless argumentation; he took this need as a challenge. After the Second World War, while Germany was still materially and spiritually in chaos, Jaspers wrote a somber letter to his former student Hannah Arendt. He expressed his hope that she would agree, as she certainly did, with his statement of the thinker's task: "Philosophy must become concrete and practical, without for a moment losing sight of its origin."[2] Jaspers dedicated himself to an effort for which his academic training in psychiatry and his self-education in philosophy had not prepared him. He began to pay careful attention to politics, painfully aware that he had once been slow to see the dangers of National Socialism. Like many Germans who detested Hitler, Jaspers had expected the Nazis to pass quickly from power; the error both made Jaspers careful and gave him a deep sense of urgency.

Even before Hitler's chancellorship, Jaspers had wanted to address his philosophizing to a wide audience, to write—in the best sense of the word—popularly. But his first effort to do so, in 1931, through a small book called *Die geistige Situation der Zeit* (*Man in the Modern Age* in English), was neither concrete nor practical. After the war, with his new sense of philosophy's task, Jaspers commented frequently on public affairs, giving lectures, radio broadcasts and, from his last home in Basel, Switzerland, television interviews. Thousands heard his *Die Schuldfrage* (*The Question of German Guilt*) in 1946 and took his televised philosophy course—"Philosophy Is for Everyman"—in 1967. Jaspers's *The Future of Mankind*, first published in 1958, is one of the few books by a philosopher that thoroughly and far-sightedly confronts the "unthinkable" possibility of nuclear war. When in the 1960s Jaspers wrote *The Future of Germany*, a book about the reappearance in German political life of former Nazis which questioned whether Germany's democracy would survive party oligarchy, the controversy was so violent that Jaspers's answers to his critics filled a second book. Until his death in 1969, at the age of eighty-six, Jaspers was a model of political integrity and philosophical independence, a true European and a philosopher engagé. In his work and in his life, freedom and communication became the ideals by which he was guided.

This study of Karl Jaspers is divided into two major parts: "The Philosophy of Freedom" and "The Freedom of Philosophy." If Jaspers's development as a thinker, his intellectual biography, were my subject, the order of the parts would have to be reversed: Jaspers turned from psychiatry to philosophy and then from philosophy to politics.[3] If I had intended to introduce Jaspers's work in the context of twentieth-century philosophy and for students of contemporary philosophy, it would be logical to organize my work around the three divisions of Jaspers's own *Philosophy*: world orientation, existential elucidation, and metaphysics.[4] But this is a study of *how* Jaspers thought, and it treats his thinking procedures, developed over many years, as facets of a whole. Jaspers did not construct a philosophical system, but he thought systematically. The distinction is crucial. Jaspers did not take up the vexed question of theory's relation to *praxis* because he did not have *a* theory or *a* philosophy; he viewed philosophy as an activity, philosophizing.

In order to indicate how Jaspers's thinking was and is of a piece, I have placed an introductory overview before the two main chapters. This introduction, "The Common Room," presents Karl Jaspers's philosophical terminology and his basic themes by means of a series of thought-figures. In his works there are many recurring patterns: relations of two and three elements, relations of levels or planes or modes of thinking, and corresponding thought-movements: linkings and bridgings of the elements, seeking the ground of oppositions, transcending, leaping, opening and, most importantly, foundering. The introduction is, so to speak, topographical; it illustrates movements over systematic terrain. The terrain is familiar—it is the perennial world of philosophy—but the movements and the terminology are peculiar to Jaspers's own journey toward what he referred to as "boundary situations."

The focus of the two major chapters that follow the introduction is this question, posed at a boundary: "We stand at the brink of the abyss, both in the mind and in existence. The question is: what now?"[5] Chapter 2 explores this brink situation in existence; chapter 3 in the mind. The former deals with Jaspers's concept of political freedom; the latter with freedom of the mind. Both chapters gesture toward the always undefined "freedom of Existenz." Voyaging over the philosophical terrain, we discover: "what seemed an abyss becomes space for freedom; apparent Nothingness is transformed into that from which authentic being speaks to us."[6] The Renaissance explorers found, not a pit of monsters at the Atlantic's edge, but the New World; Jaspers found, not the abyss of nihilism at thinking's edge, but space for freedom.[7]

Jaspers's emphasis is on *now*—the moment in which all the past is gathered, becomes contemporary, and in which the future is born. The growth of concern for history and for ideologies—the two phenomena which characterize philosophy at the turn of the century, with their emphases on the past and on the future—the "no longer" and the "not yet"—do not overshadow Jaspers's concern with the now. We live in a new age, comparable in its demands and possibilities to the Promethean age, to man's first emergence from darkness.

What is new about this age, in all . . . areas of the world, is that man becomes conscious of Being as a whole, of himself and his limitations. He experiences the terror of the world and his own powerlessness. He asks radical questions. Face

to face with the void he strives for liberation and redemption. By consciously recognizing his limits he sets himself
the highest goals. He experiences absoluteness in the depths
of selfhood and in the lucidity of transcendence.[8]

Each of these new, boundary situations poses challenges; and
man is his own challenge as he faces these situations.

Chapter 2 deals with the challenges of the contemporary
boundary situations represented by totalitarianism and nuclear
weapons; it takes up the alternative possibilities of political
freedom and political unfreedom. In the third chapter, possibilities for meeting the challenges of broken traditions, lost
authorities, the decline of institutional religions, and the
"death of God" are discussed. Three alternatives are posed:
authentic modern science or pseudoscience; philosophical
freedom versus dogmas, doctrines, fixations, or "shells";
philosophical faith or revelation and traditional metaphysics or
"playful metaphysics."

The first discussion is concerned with Jaspers's philosophy
of freedom, the second with the freedom of philosophy. Of his
philosophy of freedom, Jaspers wrote:

> . . . its strength lies not in solidified thought, not in an
> image, form, thought-figure, not in visuality—all of these are
> mere tools—but in enabling the historic Existenz to live up
> to it. . . . this is a philosophy of freedom, and, by the same
> token, of the will to limitless communication.[9]

The philosophy of freedom appeals for "participation in what
thought-figures bring to mind."[10] Crucial in such philosophizing is the avoidance of absolutizations or hypostatizations,
which "void freedom as well as the need *to round out thoughts
with action* by the thinking Existenz."[11] The opposition of
freedom and unfreedom in the political realm must not become
a two-character melodrama, a schematism; it is the thoughtful
presentation of possibilities given the realities of a changing
situation; it is a communicative appeal. Mere schematism covers a sliding away from the issues, an avoidance of boundary

situations, a refusal to "round out thoughts with action." A philosophy of freedom preserves the space for action, for realizing freedom.

Of the freedom of philosophy, Jaspers wrote:

> It is the freedom of philosophy that shows in the thought we call encompassing—neither object nor subjective "I" but involving both at once, connecting them and encompassing both, splitting into two and in the split fulfilling itself.[12]

The freedom of thought-movement is the correlative to the freedom of action—inner action is correlative to outer action.

Freedom in the political realm requires freedom of thought, and freedom of thought without political freedom is hidden and easily withers away. The two meet in communication, in unrestricted speech and interaction, in the notion that philosophy is for Everyman.

Jaspers presented no programs; he presented spaces, possibilities—and the example of his own choices, his own life.

In the introduction to this study of Nietzsche's philosophical activity, Jaspers defined a presentation as that study which "attempts to efface its own thinking in favor of that which is presented: it must not use its subject as an occasion for any philosophizing of its own. Such thinking is a constant endeavor to yield completely to the thinking of another person; it is thinking which seeks simply to present what someone else has thought."[13] This is an indication of Jaspers's manner of creative listening. "To philosophize with Nietzsche is an exercise in possibility."[14]

The attempt to draw together possibilities presented in and by Jaspers's philosophizing takes its cue from this definition of presentation. And it is guided by Max Weber's method as a historian, here described by Jaspers:

> . . . in order to grasp reality, we must see the possibilities. In the present, a formulation of the possibilities is the area, the space in which I gain certainty concerning what I decide; without possibility, I have no freedom; without a vision of

the possibilities, I act blindly; only knowledge of the possibilities enables me to know what I am actually doing. Analogously, Weber employs the category of "objective possibility" in his historical appraisal of past situations. The historian considers a situation. His knowledge enables him to construct the possibilities of the day. By these constructions he first measures the possibilities of which the protagonists were aware. And then, by the possibilities, he measures what really happened, in order to ask: for what specific reason did a particular possibility among several materialize? The historian turns happening back into possibility in order to find the critical factor in the decision which brought it about.[15]

When Jaspers explored thought-possibilities and action-possibilities in philosophical works and political analyses, the specific reason for his choices and his appeals was almost always the same: this is the path of freedom, for freedom. When Jaspers turned away from a path, it was with Kant's often-employed conditional in mind: if this is so, then freedom cannot be saved (*so ist Freiheit nicht zu retten*).[16]

Kant's consideration of freedom is multidimensional: in Jaspers's description, it "unfolds like spokes radiating from a center." The center, transcendental freedom, Kant disclosed as mere possibility.[17] The spokes are: the spontaneity of the understanding; the freedom of reason in the ideas; freedom in action; and the "free play" of contemplation. Jaspers reexplored each of these dimensions—freedom in world orientation, in existential elucidation, and in "playful metaphysics"—in a way that eliminates any fixation, any objectification or stratification. The concept of freedom is "sheer motion."

Jaspers did not define freedom. He indicated dimensions, he opened spaces or appealed for the opening of spaces, in which freedom can appear, in which Existenz can manifest itself communicatively and know freedom as the gift of self. With the hope that this example of freedom in and for philosophizing will speak to my students' desire to learn "how to think," I dedicate this study to them.

# ONE
# THE COMMON ROOM

## 1. TRANSCENDING AND THINKING

### Subject and Object

I can easily say "I think." But who or what is this "I"? The history of modern philosophy presents an array of possible ways of conceiving the subject: as a thinking substance opposed to extended substance (Descartes); as a tabula rasa on which experiences of the world are written (Locke); as a monad containing and potentially capable of realizing the world (Leibniz); as a bundle of sensations (Hume).

Kant's conception of the subject marked a new departure. The threefold distinction of the empirical subject, open to psychological investigation, the logical subject, the "I think," and the subject as the source of freedom is the background for Jaspers's fourfold conception of "the modes of the encompassing that we are." Jaspers distinguished *Dasein* (the empirical subject), *Bewusstsein überhaupt* (consciousness at large), and *Geist* (spirit) as immanent modes of the encompassing that we are from the transcendent mode, Existenz. The immanent modes reflect "the basic experiences of finding ourselves in the world":

I *exist* in my environment, among temporal and spatial forces, in success and failure. *I am a thinking person.* I have thoughts of compelling validity in consciousness at large. A world of the mind is discovered and produced by me; *I have imagination.*

The objective entirety arising from these three origins is the *world.* Yet it does not fully answer the question how I find myself in the world, for I am aware of my freedom that lets me come to myself as possible *Existenz*. In this awareness I come to be sure of *Transcendence,* the power from which I receive the gift of myself, in my freedom. I am not self-made. I did not create myself.[1]

The dichotomy of subject and object is fundamental to the immanent modes—the subject faces on *Welt*, the world. The dichotomy is fundamental for what Jaspers called "world orientation"; all "objective thinking," all knowing, all science, is *of,* intentional. But Jaspers's philosophizing is a ceaseless attempt to transcend the dichotomy, to think nonobjectively, to illuminate and, ultimately, to "read the ciphers" of what is not Welt, Transcendence. The expression of this attempt in language is never adequate because language is a general medium; language is the transcending thinker's means of "appealing" to others.

Jaspers's schemata of the modes of the encompassing grew from a series of thought-movements, guided by Kant's distinctions, that trace "the basic experiences of finding ourselves in the world." The starting point is the following reflection:

> The fact that I (the subject) am directed upon a thing (the object), considering it (intentionally), constitutes the prime phenomenon of conscious experience. 'Intentional' consciousness has something before it to which it is mentally related in a manner incomparable to any other relationship in the world. The fact that it is absolutely commonplace does not make this irresistible prime phenomenon any less puzzling. It cannot be clarified through anything else, rather it is itself the medium of all clarification in the world. . . . In the subject-object dichotomy neither side exists without the other.[2]

The subject and the object can each be thought without the other; they can be detached, but only for "thinking across their conjunction."[3] Each time we reach the extreme of the detachment, a "dialectical reversal" takes place. On the one hand, if we try to conceive of the objective world independently we end with the realization that it is, indeed, we who conceive it. On the other hand, the subjective conceived out of context, in isolation, is empty, "nothing"; it reverts "to the reality of existence and . . . becomes an object and a factual part of the encompassing objective world."[4] The objective world always appears "disjoint," there is a "multiplicity of [subjectively approached] worlds which exist and meet in the one objective world."[5] The multiplicity can be moved through but never embraced; there is a "universal mobility of standpoints"[6] (and empathy is our way of moving into each), but there is no single standpoint "outside," no fixed Archimedean point.

The world is my world, and I am worldly. This does not mean that the world springs full-blown from the brain of man (what Jaspers termed the psychological-anthropological misunderstanding of Kant); nor does it mean that the methodological premises of cognition are the premises of the *existence* of possible objects of experience (the methodological-epistemological misunderstanding of Kant).[7] Consciousness is the *medium* of all things. "To analyze existence is to analyze consciousness."[8]

But another possibility exists for thought. "The being of things is unaware of itself; but I, the thinking subject, know about it. When I conceive of this being in the abstract, the way it is independently of being an object for a subject—that is to say, not as a phenomenon for something else—I call it 'being in itself.' "[9] This being-in-itself is a thought-possibility, what Jaspers termed a boundary concept. Any thought *of* it would turn it into an object. But as a possibility, it keeps us from taking any objective being as absolute: "it is conceivable that there are things which are not conceivable."[10] This is a boundary which thinking sets for itself and which it cannot cross—and yet, by thinking its limit, thinking appeals for a crossing of the limit.[11]

## The Analysis of Consciousness and Unanalyzable Existenz

So far, these reflections leave us with "three inseparable poles for the being I find myself in,"[12] subjective being, objective

being, and being-in-itself. All three "spring from the thinker's
existence."[13] Another series of possibilities is presented—
possibilities for the analysis of the thinker's existence.

Psychological investigation can yield a "diagram of consciousness in reality,"[14] of empirical consciousness, of the
"particularities of matter, living body and soul."[15] Consciousness can also be described as formal consciousness at large:

> In objective consciousness I have the modes of objective
> being as categories; I understand what definite being I en-
> counter, and I know that cognition of all mundane existence
> is possible in generally valid form. My consciousness at
> large is interchangeable with that of anyone else who is my
> kind, even though not numerically identical.[16]

Thirdly, consciousness can be analyzed as historic, as undergoing transformations—by anthropologists, analytical psy-
chologists, intellectual historians.[17] This approach was set in
the context of a metaphysics, of course, by Hegel—the stages
of Geist are repeated in the individual spirit.

Each of these three possibilities is adopted by Jaspers; each
is taken as a mode of "the encompassing which we are." But it
was Jaspers's conviction that none of these analyses of consciousness took him to the heart of the matter: "Constructions
of existence will not take me to being."

Jaspers took a position in relation to these constructions
analogous to Kierkegaard's in relation to Hegel's explanation
of existence in terms of pure thought as "thought without a
thinker." Kierkegaard felt that Hegelian philosophizing forgot,
"in a sort of world-historical absent-mindedness,"[18] what it
means to be a human being, what it means to decide, to act, to
identify with an existential possibility. In Jaspers's words:

> I not only want to know what exists, reasoning pro and con;
> I want to know from a source beyond reasoning, and there
> are moments of action when I feel certain that what I want
> now, what I am now doing, is what I really want myself. I
> want to be so that this will and this action are mine. My very
> essence—which I do not know even though I am sure of

it—comes over me in the way I want to know and act. In this
potential freedom of knowledge and action I am "possible
Existenz."[19]

This wanting, this being related to one's own potential, is the
condition portrayed with spectacular virtuosity by Johannes
Climacus—"John the Climber"—"a humorist, content with his
situation at this moment, hoping that something higher may be
granted him. . . ."[20] Kierkegaard does not grant Climacus this
something higher, because to grant it would be to take away his
freedom—and ours as readers. In Jaspers's terms, to go beyond relating to one's potential, to actualize possible Existenz,
is to be transformed in a way that can be communicated only
through "appeals" (for Kierkegaard, through "indirect communication"). "Existenz is gained in time, *by our own decisions.*"[21]

For Kierkegaard, the something higher is bestowed upon
man, as a kind of grace; it is the gift of faith. Man does not so
much leap as he is lifted into identity with what is thought, out
of the despair of self-alienation, out of the contradictoriness of
being finite and infinite, temporal and eternal (as characterized
by Hegel, "unhappy consciousness"). For Jaspers, there is the
possibility of another kind of thinking on the way to being,
beyond the constructions of existence:

> Constructions of existence will not take me to being. They
> can only help me get there by a leap; and the approach that
> may enable me to take this leap is not existence analysis any
> more; it is elucidation of Existenz.[22]

"To conceive the meaning of possible Existenz is to break
through the circle of all modes of objective and subjective being."[23] It is to relate to the thought-possibility of being-in-itself
in another way. We can think being-in-itself negatively—as
neither subjective being nor objective being. "Possible Existenz may perhaps open the positive way. . . ."[24]

It is in myself alone that I know a being that not merely appears to, but is for itself—one in which being and being

known go together. My own being differs radically from any being of things because I can say "I am." But if I objectify my empirical existence, this is not the same as the I-in-itself. I do not know what I am in myself if I am my own object; to find out, I would have to become aware of myself in some other way than cognitive knowledge.[25]

This other way is the elucidation of Existenz. It is only through self-relation that being-in-itself can be positively approached: Existenz is "what relates to itself, and thus to its transcendence."[26]

In this terminology—"a being that not merely appears to, but is for, itself"—there is an obvious echo of Hegel's terminology. Hegel's Geist, in the stage of self-consciousness, can fully know itself only when it is recognized by another self-consciousness: "Self-consciousness exists in itself and for itself in that, and by the fact that, it exists for another self-consciousness; that is to say, it *is* only by being acknowledged or recognized."[27] And for Jaspers, Existenz *is* in communication with Existenz. But at this point Jaspers introduces the idea of "trains of thought that involve no cognition,"[28] of elucidative thinking, not as an end in itself but as a way to *approach* being-in-itself. Not reconciliation, overcoming self-alienation, transcending the subject-object dichotomy, but something further is involved: "To meet in communication is to break through the thought that made the break-through possible."[29] To turn self-consciousness (in its meeting with another) into an end, or an absolute, is a falsification: "Consciousness and the Existenz that appears to itself in consciousness are not everything."[30] The identity of Being and thought cannot be declared; thinking can prepare for the "positive way" only by its own failure.

But to see how Jaspers worked out this positive way toward being-in-itself, the way through existential elucidation, we must step back again to the movement from world orientation to elucidation, from objective thinking to nonobjective thinking, which Jaspers called a fundamental operation.

## Thinking as Inner Action

Language has many words which do not denote objects and are not definable either, or whose definition, if there is one, will not preserve the essence of what lies in them, words like freedom, choice, decision, resolve, probation, loyalty or fate. The very language empowers our philosophizing to get into the existential elucidation which, *qua* language, it has already performed.[31]

The clues or guidelines for nonobjective thinking are present in the objective medium of language; the possibility of communication, appealing, is given. The impetus for communicating the incommunicable is summarized in the following sentence: "The apparent impossibility of communicating what lies *at* the source does not exclude the possibility of communicating *from* the source."[32] No proposition can present *philosophical* truth (which is distinguished from other levels of truth, correspondent to the levels, or modes, of our immanent existence—these will be discussed below); but philosophizing's task is to gain insight into the ways of truth's communicability, to elucidate our communicative medium existentially.

No proposition can grasp philosophical truth because it is not "something"—not objective, not even ideally so. Truth is not something independently existing which we struggle to reach, truth is "our revealing struggle." Transcending is not a result; it is an action. There is no transcendental situation or condition.

To further clarify the distinction between objective thinking and transcending thinking, we will look now at Jaspers's notion of "inner action" and see how it is manifest in communication, in inter-action. We return again to Kierkegaard, whose Johannes Climacus gives the following description of inner action.

When I am deliberating, it is my task to think every possibility; but when I have decided, and consequently acted in-

wardly, a change takes place so that it is now my task to
ward against further deliberation, except in so far as something requires to be undone.[33]

Kierkegaard's example (which Jaspers also adopted) is
Luther's appearance before the Diet of Worms—"Here I
stand, I can do no other."

This inner action is not simply choice; it is, so to speak,
self-choice. It is a response to the Pindaric challenge "become
what you are!" Possibilities are entertained, like guests in the
mind; we can circulate among them (the "rational mobility" of
empathizing), engage them, size them up. But the existential
problem is to identify with a possibility, to actualize Existenz
in and through it. For Kierkegaard, however, what men find
when they attempt to commit themselves "with entire subjective passion"[34] is that they have been seduced—by themselves. The conditionality of existence (the condition of "unhappy consciousness") is surpassed only with God's grace; to
hope otherwise is vain.

In Jaspers's view, "unconditional religious action" implies
that Existenz gives up its personal freedom—man becomes an
instrument—and that transcendence is, in some form (however spiritually attenuated), materialized—God speaks or appears, or God's witnesses and interpreters are taken as authorities. He opposes to it the possibility of moral action.

The difference is that in one case God is hidden, *that his very
concealment requires the freedom of Existenz as a condition
of all truth in time.* Existenz attains itself in the darkness of
transcendence without receiving objectively certain demands and answers from transcendence.[35]

Inner action, which precedes and determines external action,
is the affirmative and enhancing, or negative and inhibiting,
position taken toward impulses; it is "intervention in my inner
existence." The inner action of conceiving transcendence is
called "active contemplation"; it "allows freedom to discover

ways to relate to the hidden transcendence.'' This inner action is, so to speak, self-communication.

''Philosophical truth is a function of communication *with the other and with myself;* it is the truth I live by and do not merely think about. . . .''[36] This is because the truth of existential thought never lies in its contents as such, but rather in what happens to the thinker in the thinking of it. Thought is unfettering. And ''if philosophizing is my way to unfetter myself, to make freedom possible and real, I can ask whether my thoughts will speed or retard my quest.''[37] The form that this questioning takes is: ''what thoughts are needed to make the most profound communication possible?''[38] These quotations stand at the center of Jaspers's endeavor—transcending thinking does not lift the thinker out of the world, it takes him into the world, into communication with others, transformed.

The thoughts which are needed are not the thoughts which can be fitted together to make a doctrine, like the bricks of a wall—a wall separating the believers and the nonbelievers, the initiated and the uninitiated, the ''warriors of the faith'' and their critics, their enemies and their potential converts. ''Existential philosophy has to keep consciousness free for possibilities; it must call for space and see to it that there is no loss of tension.''[39] Existential philosophizing does not lead to insights to have and to hold; it leads to a point that calls on us to turn around, so as to reenter existence more surely and clear-sightedly, and it leads back. Existential philosophizing leads the way for the realization of Existenz, and it also brings about ''an existential brightening of the gloom in which I had to find my way to transcending.''[40] ''Thought sets the stage'' and then reflects on the performance. By philosophizing's light, ''I am a different person for the experience'' of transcending, for the inner action, for the ''shift in the posture of my consciousness.''[41] ''Life is nothing without thought.''[42]

Philosophical thought unfetters, it makes space for freedom, for the clear articulation of Existenz. This space Jaspers also referred to as the ''common room''—the room for existential communication.

## Philosophical Systemizations and Communication

Jaspers's work is a net of systemizations, schemata, and recurrent thought-patterns; but Jaspers did not create a philosophical system. Philosophical forms are such that "if I think them through, they make me produce my thinking. They act upon my inwardness, my freedom. They give shape to my thinking and must therefore be complemented by reality."[43] The space opened by philosophical forms, and the movement of thought in that space "creates in the thinker the reality he thinks about."[44] And this reality *is* "original existential communication."[45] By thinking, we make a space for meeting communicatively—and the communication is what, so to speak, fills the space: communication's thinking is the thinking of communication.

"Truth is not a property, but something that is present as *we* search for it."[46] To put this in terms of a criterion for truth: "a thought is philosophically true to the extent which its thinking promotes communication."[47] Thus "uncommunicativeness in a philosopher is virtually a criterion of the untruth of his thinking."[48]

Jaspers's philosophizing is a testament to the potential of Existenz for realizing itself in communication; as he put it in the introduction to his *Philosophy,* "I wanted to show the thinking space where this could happen."[49]

The significance of Jaspers's dedication to communication will come up clearly if we make a comparison. Philosophers who take seriously Nietzsche's effort to give the mind power as an internal agent, a transformer of the self, and a transvaluator of all values, often speak of some kind of inner action. The late Heidegger, for example, conceived of thinking as acting. Such conceptions reflect feelings of powerlessness in the world and feelings of powerlessness before the irreversibility of actions in the world—the fact that what has been done cannot be undone. Jaspers, particularly after Hitler came to power in Germany, did not thus confuse mental processes and worldly action. Although he internalized action and spoke of inner action, he did not abandon plurality; he never left the mind in solitary confinement. His commitment to action is not—as we shall see—that of a man of action speaking from within a political plurality, but it is also not the dream of a solitary thinker. Internal communication is always conceived as a prelude to talking with another.

## 2. THE SPATIAL IMAGE AND HISTORICITY

### Objective Thinking and Spatial Images

The image of spaces opening functions in each of the three modes of transcending—world orientation, existential elucidation, and metaphysics. Spaces are necessary for realizing, actualizing, performing, meeting, appearing: for all human action, inner and outer. Without space, there is no freedom: there is no objective freedom in existence, no freedom of the mind; there is no realization of Existenz; there is no relating to transcendence.

"To think objectively means to think in spatial images. . . . Not until we approach Existenz do we come to something absolutely non-objective."[50] We will take up again the contrast between objective and transcending thinking with this statement as a starting point.

### Nonobjective Thinking and Temporality

The detachment in thought of the subject and the object is always incomplete; it leads to dialectical reversals in which the detached object is shown to be *for* a subject and the detached subject is shown to be *of* the world. "We always live and think within a horizon. But the very fact that it is a horizon indicates something further which again surrounds the given horizon."[51] The immanent modes of the "encompassing which we are," when thought through, are found to be within the encompassing of Existenz; the immanent mode *Welt* is found to be within the encompassing mode transcendence.

No definable concept—which would presuppose some kind

of objective being—can express the being of Existenz. Covering Existenz with a concept would make it invisible—we would be faced with the problem Kierkegaard posed himself in the *Concept of Irony*: how to describe the elf wearing the magic cap that when worn makes the wearer invisible. When we "approach Existenz," through the horizons of the immanent modes, the spatial imagery of objective thinking must be abandoned; and the key to this is that "time is the phenomenality of Existenz."[52]

But here again Jaspers makes a distinction: between objective time (time, in Kantian terms, as a form of intuition) and "existential time." Existential time is, so to speak, a boundary between objective time and timelessness, between lived time and the mystical *nunc stans*. Existenz itself is described as "floating," "in suspension," between intramundane and extramundane being (*in der Schwebe*).

> In acts of original freedom, in all forms of absolute consciousness, in every act of love . . . my temporality—not forgotten, but accentuated, rather, as decision and choice—is simultaneously broken through to eternity: existential time as a phenomenon of true being becomes both inexorable time as such and its transcendence in eternity.[53]

This is Jaspers's way of expressing the paradox that we are worldly, temporal beings but that we exist in time in such a way that this existence is itself the phenomenon of "timeless self-being." We are historically determined—we live in a particular time, and we are bound by our own pasts ("I can never start afresh")[54]—but "if I am certain of my Existenz, I do not see myself as just empirically given."[55] We live in conditions and are conditioned, but we are also, as possible Existenz, unconditional. Existenz stands ready to "saturate" every given with possibility.

"What is time then? As the future it is possibility; as the past it is the bond of fidelity; as the present it is decision."[56] In this formulation, the past, so to speak, lends a force of continuity and commitment, while the future pushes in with novelty; the two meet head-on; but the present is not thereby erased; it is accentuated.[57] Man is not ejected from the world by this collision; he discovers that in the present there is an aspect of eternity.

This perplexing dynamic, as we shall see in detail later, plays a central role in Jaspers's metaphysics. We indicate it here, with the following quotation:

> Remembrance and foresight alone give me access to being. If I grasp the cipher in both, they become one. What I remember is present as a possibility that can be regained in foresight. What I see in foresight is empty unless it is remembered also. The present no longer remains simply the present; if I read the cipher in a foresight permeated by remembrance, it becomes present eternity.[58]

Either depreciation of the past and/or the future or accentuation of them implies distortion of the present—it becomes either all or nothing; men are left with either an eternity-less present ("cipherless objectivity") or an empty timelessness.

Jaspers elaborated a schema of "concepts of Existenz" which stands, so to speak, between a categorical scheme of *a* mode of subjective immanence (a scheme for Dasein like Heidegger's, a scheme for consciousness at large like Kant's, a scheme for Geist like Hegel's, for example) and a chaotic, irrational silence or a mystical silence. The concepts of freedom, communication, historicity, boundary situations, and so forth are not static or fixed in number; they are as mobile as the time which is the phenomenon of Existenz which they constitute.[59]

## A Thought-Pattern, with Examples

How does spatial imagery give way in nonobjective thinking? It does not simply give way to temporal imagery. This would be the case if, for example, Jaspers had followed Nietzsche in the elimination of transcendence, in his inversion of Platonism.

Philosophically, Nietzsche's view of becoming must be understood as a way of thinking in which all determinateness is transcended and in which space itself and all forms of objective being are absorbed by time, while time becomes synonymous with being itself, so that it alone is left, as it were . . . the actuality of temporality becomes absolute.[60]

The concept of Being was restored or approximated by Nietzsche through the notion of "the eternal recurrence of the same."

The direction Nietzsche took is exemplified in attempts to recreate the world in the realm of the inner sense, time. The elevation of temporal imagery—the elevation of music as the true reality—culminated in Rilke's *Gesang ist Dasein* ("song is being"). Rilke absorbed the spatial world into this invisible realm (*Weltinnenraum*)—*Erde, ist es nicht dies, was du willst: unsichtbar / in uns erstehen?* ("Earth, isn't this what you want: invisibly / to arise in us?")[61]

Jaspers's attempt was not to vanquish the spatial realm but to saturate it—objectivity—with existentiality: "As I seize upon time in decision, I seize upon space in the fact that the moment's decision is no shriveled point. It is *a world,* rather, which I fulfill because it is not just a world but the presence of transcendent being."[62] When Existenz fills a space, the space appears to Existenz as the expression of the nonobjective. (As language, an objective medium, appeals to Existenz as the phenomena of thought.)

This pattern recurs in Jaspers's work: spaces are opened by the thinking and acting man, they are filled with his existential reality (as the common room, for example, is filled in communication) and with intimations of his transcendent source; they close when his "performance of the existential possibility" ends; and they must be reopened ("there is no other freedom than the freedom I have won for myself"—freedom is won and can be lost; it is not independently existing, constantly existing, or an attribute of something else).

Below are examples of this pattern from each of the modes of transcending thinking:

1. Jaspers's basic political axiom (adopted from Kant) was: an individual's "freedom depends on the freedom of everyone else."[63] Existential freedom is manifest in the political realm only insofar as the objective conditions of that realm leave space for it. This means, in the terms of the political realm itself, that laws (boundaries, *nomoi*) must protect political spaces—as, for example, the right to assemble protects the space where men meet to talk, exchange views, plan. Kant illustrated his notion of "unsocial sociability" with the following metaphor, which is applicable to this notion of reciprocal freedoms:

> Just as trees in a forest, by trying, each one, to take air and sunlight from others, compel each other to seek both air and sunlight above them and so achieve a fine, straight growth; while those who let their branches grow as they please develop a stunted, crooked growth.[64]

(If the give and take of this *agon* itself gets out of hand, of course, the metaphor fails—the self-correcting processes of nature and of men differ considerably.) In existence, laws protect men from abuses of objective freedom; but they also leave room for existential freedom. "I have not come to myself until the world in which I can establish possible communication has come to itself with me. . . . The measure of my self-being is my neighbor's self-being, and finally that of all men."[65] Both political intercourse and existential communication take place in the world.

2. Man is the creature who breaks with nature to make a world within the world, man is the "acting creature" within the world. Men may review their history, "adopt" it inwardly. "The individual fulfills his sense of historicity" (*geschichtliches Bewusstsein*) by "broadening into this immense space" of history.[66] On the other hand, he "truthfully fulfills it only by putting it into effect here and now," that is, by joining together with others in communicating and acting. Present existential acting fulfills this "immense space"—making concrete the sense of historicity. Similarly, philosophizing man

enters into the immense space of past philosophies, knowing them as present thought-possibilities; without the reality of present thinking, there is only intellectual history. The "unfathomable tradition" of metaphysical thought, for example, tells the thinker in the language of metaphysical objectivity what his ties to the tradition let him experience as his own present reality. Philosophizing does not accept the tradition or any part of it as authoritative; it adopts the tradition inwardly in order to think freely.[67]

3. Existential freedom appears in the political realm "like an alien element"—like a *pneuma* breathed into a body, giving it life. "A man will make a political factor of his own Existenz, so to speak, will risk combining it with political action."[68] For Jaspers, the career of Max Weber was paradigmatic; through him, even though his political involvement was limited, "the philosophical Existenz became visible to others."[69] Public life alone can put a man in touch with "the power on which all existence somehow depends"[70]—the power of and from individuals joining together in action. When a man takes the risk of entering the political realm, "all he can do is act with others."[71] Unless it is ceaselessly filled with acting individuals joining together, the political space grows solid, impenetrable—ultimately totalitarian, given the technological capacity of modern men.

4. The "living space" of Existenz is the mind's freedom. This living, or thinking, space is also the common room. The objectivities which bear witness to the thinking space are called, collectively, cultural objects. Cultural objects are "created among the realities of life,"[72] and they have significance only in relation to those realities. Philosophical works are testaments to the entrance into the world of the "world" of the mind: "The significance of entering into the world constitutes the value of philosophy."[73] Any cultural activity for its own sake—art for art's sake, for example—lacks this worldly relation. On the other hand, any cultural activity which aims to *be* reality—Schopenhauer's claim that music is reality, Schlegel's *Universalpoesie*, for example—is a reversal

of the Platonic view without abandoning the disjunction of art and reality: the world and the world of the mind suffused through it are, in their distinct ways, the stages of the "performance of the existential possibility."

5. Jaspers sought forms[74] to produce a "room-making, dialectically daring, never-fixating kind of thinking" (as he described Nietzsche's thinking): "philosophical thought is freedom, and except for freedom it is nothing."[75] Freedom is not thinking's product, nor is it thinking's attribute. Thinking has no product, no terminus. It is a present performance which is satisfying as such but which is also "never finished as a temporal phenomenon."[76] Thinking is a motion "from self-abandonment to self-recovery . . . from dispersal to the unity of my self, from existence to being."[77] This motion fills the space opened, marked off, by philosophical forms.

6. As the political space is secured by laws, so the thinking space is secured by forms, structures, and systemizations (which are to be distinguished from systems, or architectonics). Within these forms thinking plays with possibilities; but if there is only play, "aesthetic noncommitment" characterizes thinking. Inner action is the affirmation or denial of possibilities. As laws become constrictive and merely negative when they are disconnected from a people's active will to freedom, so philosophical forms become coercive and unproductive of thinking when they subsist, empty of thought-movements. They become "shells" (*Gehäuse*). "The unique power of definition, or rational form, may, when the philosophy is elaborated in the work, destroy the philosophy's power to transcend the rational form"[78] (or to extend the analogy, destroy the form's capacity to generate philosophy's power as political action, interplay, generates political power). Abandoned thought-spaces, like empty theaters, echo and grow silent—with the first moment of the new performance, the space is transformed, recreated.

7. The pattern of (1) room-making, (2) performance or fulfilling, (3) reflection and sustaining, recurs in Jaspers's metaphysics. Existenz

creates its own space in the pure categories of logical transcending; . . . fulfills that space with the movement of existential relations to transcendence; . . . and ascertains the
language of an objectiveness that is present and vanishing at
the same time, in reading ciphers.[79]

In formal transcending, Existenz finds that the methods of absolutizing one of the traditional categories (e.g., substance) or
setting two such categories in opposition (the method of *coincidentia oppositorum*) or making one category self-referring
(e.g., the category cause in the notion of *causa sui*) lead to the
same limit we have encountered before. Namely, any conceivable being is among other beings in the world, and is *for a
subject*. Formal transcending by means of categories opens a
space in which Existenz relates to transcendence in a nonob-
jectifiable way. Of this relation (which, Jaspers indicated, is
never equivocal, never fixed) we have no *knowledge*; but
reflecting on it, Existenz "reads the ciphers" of transcendence. (We will return to this idea in chapter 3.)

## Thought-in-Motion and Action

These examples show that nonobjective thinking is "sheer
motion." Jaspers's "philosophy of freedom" appeals to what
is perhaps our simplest image of freedom—unrestricted motion. The freedom to move about and meet is fundamental to
political freedom; thought unbounded by fixed forms or
ideological needs is free thought.

Kierkegaard "adopted" Aristotle by drawing his logical
forms into the subject: "When Aristotle says that the transition
from possibility to actuality is a *kinesis* this is not to be understood logically, but with reference to historical freedom."[80] In
Jaspers's thought also there is a kinesis involved in both inner
and outer action, in the realization of Existenz. But the kinesis
is unending—there is no final state that we may call "self,"
and there is no hypostatization that we may call "freedom."
And the movement that is Existenz actualizing is always tied to
the world, to existence in the world;[81] this tie is the historicity

of Existenz. Historicity is, as Jaspers once beautifully expressed it, "hard, free becoming in an impervious material."[82]

We can turn again to a contrast which shows the significance of Jaspers's conception. Historicity, in the late work of Heidegger, connotes a passive "happening-to," a pure receptivity to Being. From such a conception, a political theory cannot arise, for history is, finally, not a story of deeds but a function of Being (*Seingeschichte*). Jaspers's conception is the opposite: *through* inner action and action in the world, men demonstrate that they are not merely worldly creatures, that they are historically situated and conditioned but not without the possibility of unconditionality and freedom.

## 3. EXISTENZ AND EXISTENCE

### Concepts of Existenz

Conceptions which are pure motion are called "concepts of Existenz." Jaspers's schema of these concepts is based on Kant's categories of the understanding. Both "require the medium of time," but objective time, as we have seen, is to be distinguished from existential time. With reference to Kant's relational categories, for example, Jaspers set forth the following concepts:

> The rules of reality are causal laws; whatever happens has its cause or effect in the course of time. Existential reality, on the other hand, is self-originating as it appears to itself in time—in other words, it is free. . . . Substantiality is temporal inertia, the quality of enduring, of being neither increased nor decreased, while Existenz begins and vanishes in the phenomenality of time. . . . The mutual causality of substances, the Kantian reciprocity or community, confronts communication between self-beings. . . .[83]

The concepts of Existenz—freedom, historicity, communication, and so forth—are not the formal conditions of objectivity or of the subject-object dichotomy itself. The mysterious root of intuition and understanding which Kant sought in his mediating schematism of imagination is, so to speak, on a different level from the Existenz which Jaspers appealed to with his concepts—his existential schematism. The existential schematism mediates between the inexpressible self-certainty of Existenz (as opposed to the certainty of objective knowledge) and elucidative reason.

> Reason without content would be mere understanding, with no basis as reason. And, as the concepts of understanding are empty without intuition, so reason is hollow without Existenz. Reason is not itself as mere understanding, but only in the acts of possible Existenz. . . . Existenz becomes clear through reason, reason only has content through Existenz.[84]

The concepts of Existenz are the focus of the interdependent clarifying of reason and the fulfilling of Existenz itself.

We will take one concept—that of a boundary situation—as an illustration, and we will use it also to make one more approach to the notion of nonobjective thinking.

## Boundary Situations

> Whenever I imagine a situation, I see it as the relative location of things, as their topographical arrangement in space. This spatial perspective conception makes me think of a situation as a reality for an existing subject who has a stake in it. . . . existence means to be in situations.[85]

Situations can be known to a certain extent; the sciences approach situational existence from many angles, either formulating its typicality or determining its uniqueness. But situations exist by changing,[86] and one of the factors in the change is consciousness itself. If any situation becomes wholly transparent, a man can stand outside of it: "unshakeably, I view the positive objects of my valid cognition."[87] This selfless and solitary viewing can be either an end in itself or a preliminary—"having tried to know regardless of my situation, I . . . turn it into my object again, only to learn that there are indeed situations I *cannot get out of,* situations I *cannot see through as a whole.*"[88] These situations are boundary situations, which can only be elucidated.

> Situations like the following: that I am always in situations; that I cannot live without struggling and suffering; that I cannot avoid guilt; that I must die—these are what I call boundary situations.[89]

We see here another version of the dialectical reversal that comes about if we detach the object from the objectifying subject; nonobjective thinking begins here with what Jaspers called "consummate knowing." "I now draw a line between the being of the world, which I can knowingly leave as a mere specific dimension of being [i.e., as consciousness at large], and Existenz, which for me is not something to contemplate and get out of, but something to be or not to be."[90] In this version of the "dialectical reversal," another level is reached: it is not just the realization that all objects are *for* subjects, it is the realization that the consummately knowing subject (the "pure eye") cannot leap out of itself. Situations in which the subject is involved are not transparent to it: "there is no surveying this being-in-situations."[91] The level that is reached is existential elucidation: "to experience boundary situations is the same as Existenz."

For Kant, transcending from understanding to reason is the source of the antinomies. Jaspers incorporated the doctrine of the antinomies into his discussion of ideas and Geist (as we shall see later), but he also posited "antinomies of self-being." In boundary situations these antinomies come into play: the apparent, phenomenal self is not the whole. The empirical self and the Existenz which feels itself somehow dependent on transcendence, the made self and the "given" self, are forever incomprehensibly related, but neither is reducible to the other. "Freedom is tied to dependence, communication to loneliness, the sense of historicity to universal truth, and my own possible Existenz to the phenomenon of my empirical existence."[92] Antinomies, unlike contradictions, cannot be resolved, overcome; they cannot be bridged in thought or, except for brief and particular moments, in existence.

Situations are indicated spatially; the subject is among the things of the world, part of the topography. Surveying a situation—standing like a painter before a landscape—is possible, but at this boundary questions arise (because *I* stand there) which have no immediate and definitive answers.

> Awakening to myself, in my situation, I raised the question of being. Finding myself in the situation as an indeterminate possibility, I must search for being if I want to find my real self. But it is not until I fail in this search for intrinsic being that I begin to philosophize. This is what we call philosophizing on the ground of possible Existenz, and the method used is transcending.[93]

Illumination of the situation is the starting point; when possible Existenz encounters, with eyes open, a boundary situation, the vague sense of motion—"I can see the situation only that keeps transforming me along with itself, a motion that carries me from a darkness in which I did not exist to a darkness in which I shall not exist"[94]—forces us to pose the questions whither? whence? why? When we ask these questions of the world, the antinomies arise; when we ask them of ourselves, the antinomies of self-being arise.

### The Movement from Existence to Existenz

At boundaries, the dialectical reversal implicit in detaching subject and object takes on a new dimension; we look, so to speak, through opposites to their ground. The relation between the opposites and their ground—between subject and object and Existenz and transcendence—is antinomical; it cannot be objectified.

We present some examples of these movements, to indicate the recurrence of this pattern in Jaspers's work:

1. In world orientation, either the subjective or the objective can be identified with being and a conclusive world orientation achieved on the basis of the identification. If it is thought that

nothing can be except as an object—the subject is an object among others—and nothing but objects can be known (by natural science), the thought is positivistic. Opposed to positivism is idealism; "a view of the world in which being is identified with the being of the mind as understood and explored in the intellectual sciences."[95] Jaspers rejected neither possibility; he showed their interdependence in searching for the ground. Existenz. Again the model is the relation of intuition and understanding (intuitions without concepts are blind, concepts without intuitions are empty) to reason. "Without positivism, the objective and substantial realization of possible Existenz lacks a body; without idealism, it lacks scope."[96] The relation of philosophy and science is thus: science without wisdom is meaningless, wisdom without science is unreal.

2. In a mental situation in which "in objective knowledge of objects, the actual meaning of being, and thereby essentiality and interest, cease,"[97] a breakthrough to the subjective may seem necessary—as it was for Kierkegaard. On the other hand, in a mental situation in which "in the endless reflection of subjectivity, in the merely speculative movement of thought, the object, and with it its content, has disappeared,"[98] a breakthrough to the objective may seen necessary—as it was for the young Schelling and for the "back to the things themselves" phenomenologists. Both directions of thought, in dialectical tension, point to another level, another possibility:

> The task of actually taking hold of Being is fulfilled by the symbol (the metaphor or the cipher-status). . . . The cipher is neither object nor subject. It is objectivity that is permeated by subjectivity and in such a way that Being becomes present in the whole.[99]

3. The language of science, objective language, is comprehensible to all—for all men, regardless of their determinate situations, share consciousness at large. If this language is taken as an ideal (as it is by many of Wittgenstein's heirs), Existenz is jeopardized—there is no appeal. On the other

hand, if "that within that passes show" (as Hamlet called the heart of hearts) has no access to the world through speech, it may become completely unintelligible, emptily silent.[100] Existenz is realized in communication. Expressed in terms of the dialectical pattern: "Without mundane contents, existential communication has no phenomenal medium; without communication, such contents are senseless and void."[101]

4. As indicated above, Existenz becomes clear through reason, and reason has content only through Existenz. Jaspers, rather than opposing reason and faith, developed a concept of "philosophical faith." Philosophical faith is the mean between Kierkegaard's faith through grace and Nietzsche's atheism— both extreme positions, tenable only by "exceptions."[102] And philosophical faith is consistently opposed to revelation as well as to any form of "conclusive world orientation" (or secular faith). Existenz becomes clear through reason; through imagination it becomes "perceptible . . . , so to speak, as beauty." But imagination's visualizations can be merely playfully entertained: "there is always a difference between the noncommittal world of *possibility* and an immersion in existential *reality*."[103] Philosophical faith is committed. Expressed dialectically: "without imagination, faith will not unfold, and without faith, imagination will remain unreal."[104] Imagination mediates between intuition and understanding (this is "objective imagination"); but imagination is also the "eye of Existenz."

## Transcending as Opposed to Operating with Fixed Antitheses

As these examples show, Jaspers's procedure of balancing opposites, finding their ground and exploring the ground in its antinomical relation to the opposites, is consciously opposed to the procedure of turning upside down, inverting a traditional, or a predecessor's, disjunction. The method of transcending reveals the interrelations of (for example) "spirit and flesh, understanding and sensuality, soul and body, duty and inclination, being and appearance, thought and action"[105] on each of its steps—world orientation, existential elucidation, and metaphysics. Oppositions are posed to bring to light an entirely different plane of being, a middle term that does not flatten out the opposites but elucidates their origin.

Jaspers did not speak of a leap from doubt to faith or a "leap to tradition" (both are to be found in Kierkegaard's thought, the latter being analogous to Dostoyevsky's Slavophilism) or a leap from necessity to freedom (as for Marx) or from old values to new in an inversion of Platonism (as for Nietzsche). Jaspers treated opposites as, in themselves, complexly structured, contradictorily conceivable; and the ground reached is reached indirectly, without once-and-for-all resolutions.

Transcending fixed positions, as opposed to both inversion of fixed positions and "accommodation to various philosphies, as if there were various philosophies among which it is necessary to choose,"[106] is also a method that prevents resting within the embrace of an ideology. This is (as we shall see in detail below) particularly important for Jaspers's political thinking. In 1931 Jaspers claimed that "the old antitheses—known respectively as individualism and socialism, liberal and conservative, revolutionary and reactionary, materialistic and idealistic" were no longer appropriate for our situation.[107] The fourth pair on Jaspers's list, materialistic and idealistic, has already been discussed, but we will take the other three as illustrations of Jaspers's method:

1. "Both starting from Hegel, Marx and Kierkegaard take opposite paths. Marx finds the salvation of man in society. Kierkegaard in the individual. Kant's thinking takes in both possibilities."[108] And Jaspers here followed Kant—but without abandoning Hegel's historical insights. The individual in existential communication and action with others is Jaspers's concern—though the phrase "kingdom of ends" is not really appropriate, for Existenz in its unconditionality is not comprehensible within the confines of the means-ends distinction, as we shall see below.

2. Two opposed "process ideologies" share a common assumption: that of a fixed path. Freedom, by the one, is viewed

as the inevitable result of human forward progress—the liberal position.[109] Freedom, by the other, is viewed as a primal, natural condition, irrevocably lost in an inevitable (and increasingly socialized and politicized) decline—the conservative position. There is no road to or from freedom for men to travel on; freedom *is* "man's road in time."

> What shall freely happen can not be shifted to events or institutions or causal or contextual relations open to e.g., sociological analysis. Freedom dwells in depths that make all these relations look superficial. It can issue only from the individual, from many individuals who transcend outward communal forms and really meet one another in man-to-man communication.[110]

3. In 1931, with both the National Socialists and the Communists in mind, Jaspers compared the "language of mystification" and their "languages of revolt." The former is used to maintain the fiction that the status quo of the life order (the apparatus for satisfying material necessities) is absolutely valid and, furthermore, equivalent to the public interest or the utmost welfare of the community. It is assumed that there is such a thing as a general interest, the interest of a fictional all-embracing man writ large, and that there is such a thing as public opinion (which Jaspers referred to as a "false pathos of the human average"),[111]

> . . . an authority of a method or system which is held consecrate because it is reputed to promote the general interest—and it is upon this method or system in one of its multifarious forms that responsibility in the last resort accrues. Each individual is a tiny wheel with a fractional share in the decision, but no one effectively decides.[112]

On the other hand, there is a language of revolt which "appeals to all sorts of obscure impulses, justifying them with the one aim of justifying disturbance and revolt."[113] Neither of these languages has anything in common with communication or appeal to Existenz, though they have much in common with each other in their refusal to acknowledge individual responsibility.

## The Foundering of Transcending Thinking

The dialectical procedure in world orientation and existential elucidation culminates in "formal transcending" (which depends upon both imagination and faith, as we have seen). We will show how Jaspers applied this method to the categories of freedom in order to return again to freedom as a concept of Existenz.

If transcendence or being-in-itself is conceived as free, it is made finite—in situations, subject to conditions. Taking the immanent modes of the encompassing as guidelines, we can think of freedom and nature, freedom and the intellect, freedom and the idea, in approaching transcendence. The identification of nature and freedom is inconceivable—it was Kant's insight that "our understanding is quite incapable of conceiving in one two things that . . . are radically separate: intelligible freedom and phenomenal necessity."[114] Transcendence can be, so to speak, thought toward, in the tension of freedom and nature. If we identify freedom and intellect, transcendence can be thought toward as *Logos* or *Demiourgos;* in the first case, transcendence is the "generally valid latticework for articulating all that exists," categorical totality; in the second case, the master builder, confronting a material which he shapes, is "only a notion without any reality to correspond to it" (and such it was for Plato).[115] If we identify freedom and the idea, transcendence is not a categorical totality but an entirety including all ideas—but ideas, like categories, lie in the reality of a finite creature, man.[116] In either case, true transcendence is lost to an immanent conception. Thinking of transcendence as Existenz itself would attribute to transcendence properties of dependence, for Existenz is itself in communication with another, and "transcendence is that being that needs nothing else to be itself."[117]

Transcendence is not, for Jaspers, freedom; it is what makes freedom possible for Existenz, for the intellect and for the spirit. Absolutization of the categories of freedom yields an anthropomorphized deity (in contrast to either a logicized deity or a naturalized one). Thinking freedom through each of the modes of encompassing, identifying it with each, and foundering on the ultimate unthinkability of the identity "makes room for the cipher language of transcendence and thereby consciously and systematically prevents its materialization."[118] Formal transcending keeps the Godhead concealed. But the thinking toward it in formal transcending affects Existenz inwardly. In this concerned thought, in this inner action, boundary situations appear to Existenz. Ultimate questions are posed.

> In the world there is no bridging the antitheses of subjective and objective being, of being as thought and being as reality, of free being and extant being, and so forth. Nor can my thinking grasp them in one thought, as possibly one. They must be conceived as overcome, to reach the being where all questions cease, and yet they cannot really be overcome. This limit, this failure of thought, is formal transcending.[119]

Neither to objective cognition nor to fleeting conceptions of antitheses overcome is freedom given. In world orientation, being is extant, objective, valid; there is no freedom yet. In transcendence there is freedom no longer. "Nothing but Existenz in temporal existence can be free."[120] Freedom is the beginning and the end, the alpha and omega, of existential elucidation. Between the not yet and the no longer of the thought-motion of transcending there is freedom—revealed to Existenz in its own action, the paradoxical presence of eternity in existential time.[121]

Goethe remarked, with reference to the *Tranzendental-philosophie* of his time and its—to him, ominously—elaborate means of providing reason with abstract-systematic escape routes from the duties of the day, "It is now about twenty years since the whole race of Germans began to 'transcend'; should they ever wake up to this fact, they will look very odd to themselves."[122] He was equally opposed to the excessive abstract systematics of the contemporary physics—Newton's. The same uneasiness was later expressed by Nietzsche: "Man ought not to know more of a thing than he can creatively live

up to."[123] Goethe called for propriety; Nietzsche for correspondence of "taste and ability."[124] In Jaspers's thinking, the
notion of the foundering, or shipwreck, of transcending thinking marks the unbreakable connection between transcending
dialectics and situations. It prevents Existenz, the "master of
thoughts," from the oddity of awakening to find itself the ser-
vant of its own child of the soul.


## 4. THE SHAPE OF PHILOSOPHIZING

### The Essential Systematic of Philosophizing and Existenz

The essential systematic in philosophizing would not be an
edifice on cornerstones, but a globe adrift in space—a globe
which ceaselessly contracts and expands *ad infinitum*, will
take asymmetric forms and then lose them again, has no absolute center but different centers at different times, and
must be upheld by a center that is no longer inside the globe,
but in the self-being that conceives it.[125]

In this image Jaspers presented the mobility of his philosophizing: the center shifts with the shifts from one mode
to another of the immanent modes of the encompassing, while
an external center, Existenz, the transcendent mode of the encompassing that we are, upholds the whole.

If the external center were denied and Existenz eliminated,
there would be only what Nietzsche referred to as the
"perspectivist sphere." In Nietzsche's words, probably
adopted in this description by Jaspers, "the subjective sphere
is constantly growing or declining; the central point of the
system is constantly shifting."[126] Nietzsche's conception is that
the interpretation of the world from different perspectives is a
function of the will to power; the net of relations between units
of power *is* reality. But a perspectivist sphere also results,
without professed elimination of transcendence, from the
psychological and methodological misunderstandings of Kant
mentioned above, from the idea that "I am *in* the totality to
which everything real and valid for me must belong."[127] Not

transcendence itself but access to the transcendent mode of the encompassing that we are, Existenz, is eliminated.

The recognition that the essential systematic of philosophizing cannot become a system, that the unity of knowledge is an idea, is a turning point. We seek universal knowledge and the premises of objectivity, reaching consciousness at large: then "absolute consciousness is reached by transcending this universal back into temporality—a temporality which, without ceasing to be empirical, has, in that double transcending, acquired a new unconditionality it did not have before."[128] (This is, as we have seen, existential time.)

The return to the world of "knowledge and planning," of the duties of the day, of causes and effects, means and ends, is the return of a transformed thinker. "Humanity demands that purposeless self-determination and undesigning ascertainment should take us to an effective foundation and guidance of all we do."[129] This purposeless self-determination is inner action, realization of possible Existenz; undesigning ascertainment is the reflection upon the performance of the existential possibility.

Unlike the return of Plato's philosopher to the burdens of kingship after his sojourn in the bright realm of the ideas, the return of Existenz as absolute consciousness is based on the experience of *not*-knowing, reaching the limits of knowing, and of *self*-certainty. The returning thinker has no model, no final insight; rather he has *potential* forms in which all realized knowledge is enclosed like a step or an articulation. The "ceaseless flow of mundane events and free choices"[130] that is our situation in time is the starting point of philosophizing, not that from which we must escape in order to philosophize. Practical philosophy, which is "an attempt to get our bearings in the entirety of realities and possibilities,"[131] looks for bearings neither in the beyond nor in the facts of the matter but through an original sense of being. Possibilities are unlimited for Existenz in communication; and, "in our world, linked fellowship seems like the true reality."[132]

## The Axial Period and Adoption

Our bearings in our situation come from the origin—the individual's Existenz and mankind's origin. Of the former, in its worldly appearance, we have existential concepts; of the latter, we have an ideal. As Jaspers developed his cosmopolitan vision after the Second World War, he postulated an "Axial Period" of human history, the period of cultural flowering in Greece, Persia, Palestine, India, and China, culminating in about the fifth century B.C. He viewed this period as the "incarnation of an ideal axis around which mankind in its movement is drawn together."[133] It is the "spatial-temporal localization" of the spiritual reality of humanity. Present communication among the peoples who share this common origin would be "the only unity truly attainable to us humans";[134] it would be the unity upon which any political unity would rest. This unity is also the "goal of history"—a goal which is, for us, as an idea. The idea of unity, of the One underlying historically manifold origins and developments, is a point of reference which we return to again and again in renaissances. "The interpretative contemplation of history becomes a determination of man's will."[135]

Present philosophizing is shaped by adopting inwardly the traces of mankind's unitary origin and the traditions springing from it. For example, in metaphysical thinking ("adoptive metaphysics"):

> . . . we must try to unearth the buried language [transcendence] has acquired over thousands of years. But the way to adopt this language is identical to that in which our present is adopted as a real presence. . . . It is fulfillment from tradition by the self-becoming Existenz of the individual who hears the language of the world which is entered by all being that comes to matter to him.[136]

Past metaphysical experiences of hearing the language of transcendence—the ciphers—are incarnate in philosophical systems, objectifications. These incarnations, like the incarnation of the ideal axis, are exemplary, not binding on us. The "immense space" of human history, the "common room" of communication, the "thinking space" of Existenz—these are opened for freedom, for present action, present communication, present reason.

## Against Closed Forms and Isms

Jaspers's philosophizing was open to the past; he saw the tradition of philosophizing as neither something to be overcome nor something to be destroyed, as neither a history of errors nor an aberration. But he realized that in our situation, we have broken with the tradition. "We stand at the brink of the abyss, both in the mind and in existence. The question is: what now?" His philosophizing was his way of carrying out Nietzsche's command: "to impregnate the past and beget the future, let that be the present for me!"

But the key to this endeavor—in existence and in the mind—was flexibility, openness. Jaspers's potential forms, his interdependent systematics, his dialectical methods, and so forth allow him to focus on one mode, one level, one type, of the subjective or objective spheres; to establish one center; to describe the view, so to speak, fom there and then to shift to another focus. These analyses are always en route, and they always refer to the concepts of Existenz, which are sheer motion. They move under the auspices of the transcendent modes—the center outside the sphere.

The negative answer to the question "what now?" is: no more closed rooms. In political terms, as we shall see, this means opening the way in the world for existential action and communication, for reason. In the mind, it means, for example, no more isms. Concentration on Dasein can end in psychologism; concentration on forms of judgment or categories of the understanding can end in logicism; concentration on Geist can end in idealism or historicism.[137] Positivism, vitalism, scientism, pragmatism, phenomenalism—on and on. The value of a schematism of modes like Jaspers's (and he is careful to point out that the *Grundwissen* is a schematism, a theory, and not a fundamental ontology) is that no facet of our lives and situations can be singled out to the neglect of the others and no one can be said to be the origin of the others.

There is no final positive answer to the question "what now?" But there is the notion of Existenz as the "positive way"—which we shall explore more fully in the two chapters that follow.

JASPERS'S SYSTEMATICS

| | Modes of the encompassing that we are | Levels of truth (modes of expression) | Types of purposive action | The encompassing that Being itself is: | |
|---|---|---|---|---|---|
| | | | | Phenomena | Ciphers |
| Immanent modes: | Dasein | pragmatic (persuasion) | technological cultivational | unorganic nature organic nature | { ciphers of nature { ciphers of history |
| | Bewusstsein überhaupt (categories of: objectivity at large, reality, freedom) | cogency (rational argument) | { educational { political | psyche intellect and will (spheres of mind: knowledge, ethos, art, religion) | } ciphers of rational being |

| Transcendent Modes: | | | |
|---|---|---|---|
| Geist (ideas: rational, ethical, aesthetic) | conviction (communication guided by ideas) | | ciphers of man and ciphers of existence as a whole |
| Existenz | philosophical faith (communication in loving struggle) | unconditional action | ciphers of transcendence and ciphers of being-in-foundering |

Existential relations to transcendence: defiance and surrender, rise and fall, diurnal law and nocturnal passion, the wealth of diversity and the One.

# TWO
# THE PHILOSOPHY OF FREEDOM

## 1. PHILOSOPHY AND POLITICS

### Action and Contemplation Are Not Opposites

Jaspers conceived of contemplation not as simply viewing, solitary spectating, but as "ocular inspection, adoption, ascertainment, inner action."[1] That is, it is spectating but also relation to tradition (adoption); ascertainment (not objective certainty, but the certainty of self-being: "as Existenz results from the real act of breaking through mundane existence, existential elucidation is the *thinking ascertainment* of that act");[2] inner action (intervention in inner existence, self-formation without end), which is always related to the interaction of communication. Thinking prepares the way for action, reflects upon the act, ascertains it, and relates the thinker not only to himself but to others. Thinking without action is empty ("mere contemplation") and action without thinking is blind (random, unselfeducative, without unconditionality).

Jaspers spoke of active contemplation as the "source of the clarification and purification of self-being by the consciousness of transcendence. . . . it allows freedom to discover ways to relate to the hidden transcendence."[3] Active contemplation prepares the way, opens a space, and appeals for an unconditional act of relation to transcendence or invocation of transcendence.

> Unconditional action . . . is an expression of self-conscious Existenz doing in phenomenal existence, with reference to its transcendence, what it considers essential for all eternity.[4]

Such unconditional action (incomprehensible in terms of ends-means categories) is a seed or germ of a world. Human affairs are truly human when man breaks with the natural world—man alone is, in Aristotle's phrase, πραξέων τινῶν ἀρχή,[5] the source of actions—or when man's condition of being able neither to accept sheer existence nor to escape from it is overcome in a free reconciliation. That man is neither an unfree animal nor an absolutely free god, that he "breaks from nature" but remains a worldly being, is the possibility of his unconditionality, of his freedom to create a world in the world. Politics is, in Jaspers's terms, part of world orientation, and "world orientation as a whole creates the space, so to speak, in which we act in the world."[6] It is this space where Existenz appears, where men meet and communicate, where the common room can come to be, where a world is created.

> Since the world is its stage, its material, its condition, its encompassing, and, in time, its ultimately conquering reality, the world's being is to Existenz as its own being.[7]

This existential commitment to the world distinguishes Jaspers's philosophizing from the French literary movement known as Existentialism. Jaspers regarded Existentialism as an "absolutization of self-elucidation, making it the sole theme of philosophizing"[8]—to the exclusion of world orientation and metaphysics. The Existentialists' worldlessness, or world-alienation (their lack of world orientation), and their elimination of transcendence—the simultaneous loss of world and transcendence is not coincidental, as we shall see below[9]—left only the groundless "I" that said no and its ultimately meaningless *engagement* (in contrast to Jaspers's own practical philosophy, which aimed to "make our every action conscious and meaningful").[10] For example:

> The force of Sartre's ontological analysis has been to lead us to the conclusion that bad faith [inauthenticity] is the inescapable human condition . . . Sartre, who throughout his career has in his actions affirmed the value of reflective

lucidity as the highest value, has provided an ontological
analysis that undermines this value.

> If all values are ultimately unjustifiable, then there is no rea-
> son to suppose that it is any better or more valuable to be
> lucid than to be involved in self-deception.[11]

The only criterion that remains for judging an action is authenticity, but the moral imperative to act authentically is without
foundation.

Jaspers rejected both action without philosophizing and
philosophizing without reference to human affairs—but the latter is to be found not in the great philosophers but only in school
philosophy.

> No great philosophy is without political thought, not even the
> philosophy of the great metaphysicians. . . . In its political
> appearance a philosophy shows what it is.[12]

The complement of this important statement—"in its political
appearance philosophy shows what it is"—is Jaspers's statement about his own experience: "I came to feel that it had
taken my political involvement to make my thought fully conscious, down to its metaphysical roots."[13] Metaphysical origins show in the world; it is only from acting in the world on
their foundation that they are made fully conscious.

> Philosophical thinking occurs in movements that accomplish
> and confirm an ethos so that the effects of the philosophical
> thought extend into our private and political lives, thus
> showing what it is. The thought proves true if it encom-
> passes our everyday actions as well as those of the exalted
> moment of its birth.[14]

The upward transcending movement from world orientation
through existential elucidation to metaphysics is incomplete
without its complement: philosophizing affects the thinker; it
brings him to "recognize, to train, to buttress and secure an
inner posture that will shape judgment in concrete situa-

tions."[15] Neither the image of a philosophical system with metaphysical roots and practical flowerings (Descartes's image) nor that of a philosophical system with practical roots and metaphysical flowerings (attributed to Aristotle by Descartes) is adequate both because of claims to completeness, totality, and because of the stasis.

The interrelation of thought and politics that Jaspers strove for is Kantian:

> [Kant's] philosophy is political because he wants thought to be an element of politics. His political thought is philosophical because it is bound to free reason and hence to the experience of transcending.[16]

But for Jaspers, this interrelation is not bound to the tradition in which philosophy is virtually identified with contemplation—the tradition which Kant both participated in and destroyed: for Jaspers, "thinking is as the thinker does."[17]

"Philosophical thought follows the appearance of Existenz in the world."[18] But this is possible because philosophical thought has led to the limits of mundane existence: "from the situations in the world, it leads to 'boundary situations'; from empirical consciousness, to 'absolute consciousness'; from actions qualified by their purposes, to 'unconditional actions.' "[19] Thought prepares the way and then reflects, follows upon the act of going that way—the act in which Existenz is realized—and appears in the world. Both thought and action are unending, moving, performing.

Philosophical thinking conceived as preparatory and reflective in this way is not higher as an existential mode, and the philosophical life is not one set apart from the world. The traditional distinction between the contemplative and the active life is abandoned; and with it the distinction between the philosopher and the many, or between the few philosophers and the many. "Philosophy," Jaspers claimed, "is for every man." And this—this possibility—is what it most deeply shares with politics: both are essential for being human and for humanity's being.

## Great Politics and the Suprapolitical Element

Political thinking that is tied to existential elucidation and metaphysics is of a scope similar to that of what Nietzsche called "great politics."

> Nietzsche provides no constructive whole like Hegel's and no practical political technique like Machiavelli's. Instead his thinking derives from an all-encompassing concern for the being of man. . . . It is no longer mere politics, but philosophy, on the basis of which, within the wealth of possibilities but without rational principle, opposing and contradictory ways can be tied solely under the guidance of the idea of saving and advancing humanity's being. . . .[20]

Jaspers always tied his political analyses to this all-encompassing concern—as is indicated by the German title of *The Future of Mankind (Die Atombombe und die Zukunft des Menschen)*.

Jaspers's thinking differs from Nietzsche's in that "existential philosophy is the present conception, on the grounds of adopted tradition, of the possibilities of a transcendently related humanity."[21] This is a mobile conception, differing from both the elimination of transcendence (nihilism) and the fixed identification of transcendence with "will to power."

Jaspers's thinking is also without fixed rational *principle*, but reason itself controls the other facets—ethical *idea* and willingness to sacrifice (*Opfermut*)—of what Jaspers called the suprapolitical element, without which there is no politics fit for man. It is the suprapolitical element in politics that makes man, each man, responsible "for human freedom and the rights of man."[22] One indivisible ethical idea must guide men in their private and their public lives: the two cannot be separated; man's personality is the same in every sphere of his life. Individuals must be ready to make sacrifices, and nations must be ready to sacrifice their absolute sovereignty voluntarily (*die freiwillige Einschränkung der Staatssouveränität*). Reason is the sine qua non for politics "on a grand scale," that is, politics "oriented toward the entirety of human events, and acting, thinking and speaking so as to gain the confidence of mankind."[23]

It is reason which reveals to man the sameness, the grounds for communication, in the diversity of opposing and contradictory ways, the diversity of traditions and historical backgrounds. It is reason that grasps the idea of the "origin and goal of history": the idea was incarnate in the Axial Period from which all historical people are derived, and to which they are heirs; it is susceptible of incarnation in the future of mankind. Jaspers is the philosophical heir of Kant's cosmopolitan intent in an age in which new impetus to unity comes from the double threat of technological destruction and totalitarianism, an age only superficially unified into a "global village" by technology. Reason sets the essential tasks for politics: the liberation and self-determination of *all* peoples (*Freilassen, Selbstbehauptung*) and the creation of a new world order. These are analogous to the tasks of individual revolutionary peoples in the past: liberation through rebellion and constitution writing (the latter being rarer of accomplishment than the former). Reason provides no constructive whole and no practical political technique but goals worthy of reflecting concern for "humanity's being."

Jaspers's faith in reason clearly reflects his years under Max Weber's influence. From the beginning of the First World War, which ended Jaspers's apolitical youth, to 1933, which awakened him to the limits of Weber's political vision, he was a Weberian. What Jaspers abandoned in 1933 was not Weber's "cosmopolitan intent" but the form it took, namely, Weber's conviction that Germany had a special mission in the world as the alternative to both Russian and Anglo-Saxon hegemonism. Germany was to become the true home of a truly liberal political life. Jaspers had always been skeptical about Weber's Prussianism and his soldierly respect for Bismarck, but he was slow to reject "the military mind in politics." During the twelve years of the Third Reich, Jaspers, banned first from university administration, then from teaching, and finally from publishing, was politically inactive by necessity. Mentally, he withdrew from Germany of not only the Third Reich but also the Second Reich as he looked for a German tradition lost since the end of the seventeenth century. As his disillusionment with nationalism grew, so did his cosmopolitanism. In his first postwar public appearance outside Germany, at the 1946 Rencontres Philosophiques in Geneva, Jaspers delivered a speech expressing his hope for European federation. When this ideal, longed for by Europe's leading intellectuals, proved unattainable, Jaspers concentrated his attention on the slow steps that might—in a distant future—bring about federated structures in Europe and in other parts of the world. In action and in thought, his maxim was: aim for that which expresses humanity in its unity.

### Political Thinking, Empathizing, and Cipher-Reading

World orientation, existential elucidation, and metaphysics are politically manifest as political thought, imaginative surveying (as what Kant called empathy and as ideation), and cipher-reading. For political people "a small thing . . . , yet prerequisite of everything else, is to *think*; to look around us; to observe what is going on; to visualize the possibilities; to clarify the situation in the directions that emerge . . ."[24] This small thing is no small task. Jaspers, ascribing to political thinking an importance quite different from that usually ascribed by philosophers, traditionally given to distinguishing the political from the theoretical life—the *bios politikos* and the *bios theoretikos*—claimed that "to be able to think politically denotes the attainment of so high a level on the human scale that we can scarcely expect anyone to reach such a level."[25] In our political situation, two unprecedented phenomena make this prerequisite thinking even more pressing: "the atom bomb, as the problem of mankind's very existence" and "the threat of totalitarian rule with its terroristic structure that obliterates all liberty and human dignity . . . . By the one we lose life, by the other a life that is worth living."[26] We can analyze the situations in which these two problems confront us, but to understand the situations is an unending task in which analysis gives way to existential elucidation and cipher-reading. Neither gives practical solutions. This is so in the latter case because, though we have a certain knowledge of totalitarian regimes and their terroristic structures, "what could be expected under totalitarian rule baffles the imagination, because its nature seems humanly impossible and is accordingly not believed in reality."[21] Nonetheless, it is only imagination which can "open our eyes to the deepest abysses as well as the highest potentialities of human life."[28] The unprecedentedness of the situation, its novelty in human affairs, renders existing objective guidelines for analysis inadequate, in addition to the fact that

> intellect always predicts the negative only. It knows what is doomed. . . . Man adds something new to the world, something not adequately comprehensible in terms of what went before, not even in retrospect. Nobody can foresee what men are capable of. . . .[29]

It is by imagination that we range over a situation, viewing it from many perspectives, illuminating it: doing, so to speak at a distance, what Nietzsche called "real dialectic," actually living through many perspectives.[30] It is by imagination that we hold ideas; Kant, considering the inconceivable beginnings of human history, spoke of engaging in exercises which imagination in the company of reason may take for the recreation and health of the mind, but not as serious business, of "venturing on pleasure trips." We can have no *knowledge* of the origins of human history, but we have ideas. This imagination which travels in the company of reason—this imaginative reasoning—is not the "random imagination" of empirical existence (what Jaspers called Dasein) by means of which, as Spinoza mockingly remarked, "man strives to lose his mind,"[31] the imagination which concocts fantasies. It is the imagination by which man as Geist strives to expand; it is the imagination which, in Jaspers's terms, becomes the "organ of Existenz." The idea of the common origin of historical mankind is an idea of imaginative reason. The organ of Existenz also "sees" doctrines and myths—ideas taken as knowable—of mankind's origins (such as the Christian myth of the Fall or the Greek myth of Prometheus) as well as of nature, of rational being, of the deity, as ciphers.

Political freedom is the objective condition in which a man is free "who can be a cipher to himself, as distinct from the empirically existing man whose cipher is his natural being or his consciousness at large, not his being human."[32] The importance of this "being human" is impossible to underestimate if it is recognized that

> our humanity is not, properly speaking, real, but exists only under certain conditions, and when these are in abeyance the savagery of animal selfishness manifests itself as life seeking to maintain itself at any cost to others. . . . The sphere of influence of political activity appears today to be nothing less than the field on which the nature of humanity is to be historically decided.[33]

But again, abstractly outlining conditions which can save and advance humanity's being is, in itself, not sufficient; cipher-reading, existential elucidation, and political analysis in world orientation are all of a piece. If political analysis does not tie thinking to the world—if the prevailing political situation is not taken into account—the result may be nothing more than a "job-lot of idealism" (as Woodrow Wilson's accomplishment at the Peace Conference of Versailles was termed). "Nothing but full clarity concerning a situation which is perpetually changing and regenerating itself under stress of action can make action purposive and effective."[34]

Clarity is not a possession, and its source—philosophical faith—"is no possession . . . it confers no secure knowledge, but gives certainty in the practice of life."[35] But again, this is not objective certainty; it is the certainty of self-being, of the human *Ursprung*.

> From philosophical thinking arises the conscience that makes me responsible for what I allow to enter myself, for

what I concern myself with. What I read, see, hear, what work I do, the possibilities of knowledge and feeling that I encourage, how I choose and how I keep my distance—none of all this is indifferent; everything takes on reality in what I am and become.[36]

Humanity itself thus takes on reality. Philosophical thinking enables man to be human in the practice of life, "to keep faith, on grounds of absolute consciousness; to take the long view, though living wholly in the present; to be able to wait; to go in for self-education, fitting oneself for ends unknown; to take time to reflect; to decide resolutely, to dare . . . "[37]

Jaspers saw both the insufficiency of traditional (political) concepts and room for freedom in situation which is perpetually changing and regenerating itself under stress of action, a situation hedged with possibilities categorized as unthinkable and thus going unthought (atomic catastrophe and totalitarian terror are greeted with a *Nichtwissenwollen,* a do-not-care-to-know). In the face of unprecedented rates of change and unprecedented problems man is challenged to self-transformation, challenged to take on humanity. If our notions of war and violence fail us in a boundary situation, if our notions of political forms fail us when we try to understand totalitarianism, if we are not to resort to accepting revealed answers or ideological final solutions, then we must find ways of communicating to which concepts are auxiliary, that is, means of appeal.

The fact that we interpret reality and ourselves, *and are human only by doing so,* confronts us with an abysmal dilemma—for interpretation never comes to an end. . . . There is no halt, except by sticking arbitrarily to one interpretation. Or is there a halt after all—not a barrier, but an escape from the vortex of indefinitely reversible interpretations? We can find such a halt either in divine revelation, if we believe in it—then the infinite movement of history grows from the interpretations of this revelation, which is the original reality—or we find it in reason, which on the ground of historic existence, in communication with others, enters upon the endless historic movement of intensified communication even with utter strangers.[38]

A revelation is authoritative for a believer, for a restricted circle of human beings; on the other hand, "in rational communication there is a *common authority* to be clarified only in communication itself";[39] an authority potentially common to all; an authority in obedience to which no person need sacrifice his or her humanity.

## 2. POWER AND COMMUNITY

### Purposive Action and Unconditional Action

Not everyone can be a [scientist]. But as a matter of principle each human being shares in politics and philosophy. . . . Everyone desires to know what he really wants. . . . Philosophy is the thinking that enables man to ascertain what exists and what he wants, to grasp his meaning, and to find himself from the source. Politics, for the purpose of bettering human existence, takes its bearing from power—in which, fundamentally, everyone shares, though he may not know it.[40]

Thinking and sharing power, being somehow involved with politics, belong to everyone. We have seen how Jaspers held that philosophy is for Everyman. We turn now to the idea that everyone has a share in power; and to the relation of "man, the only acting being" and the power arising when men act together.

Jaspers distinguished *"instinctive action*, still without reflection proper . . . , taken with instinctive sureness and with the unquestioning naiveté of a will that simply grabs," from *"purposive action* . . . , [in which] I am aware of the ends of my underlying drives . . . and [in which], moreover, I have interposed a series of calculated arrangements between the drive and its satisfaction, to relate the end to certain means."[41] Purposive action in which the end is immediate and particular and

self-interested is *vital action;* there is no search for a final goal
or end, no ultimate "what for?"[42] Actions of all three types are
tied to situations in the world.

But here is a fourth type. When a man acts with an eye to
eternity, doing what he considers essential for all eternity,
when no mundane purpose is sufficient for the act even though
it may serve a mundane purpose and when the act is illuminated as an assurance of being, the act is unconditional.

> Unconditional action is . . . possible only if I have *left* the
> world, so to speak, and am now *re-entering it.* Mundane ac-
> tion, along with all existence, has then acquired a symbolic
> character that does not make the world unreal but allows it
> to be irradiated from its depths. It becomes possible, then,
> for reality to be relative and yet a matter of total present
> commitment, for relativization not to make it indifferent but
> rather to preserve its weight. The tension in existence—that
> I act as if existing reality were absolute, and am aware at the
> same time that as mere reality everything is nothing—this
> tension is the truth of unconditional action in the world.[43]

Out of this tension arise two directions for unconditional action: it can be dedicated to realization in the world, or it can be
the expression of a negation of the world. Similarly, unconditionality can be lost if a man "loses himself in the world,"[44]
and it can be lost in fleeing the world, losing the world. To
maintain the tension, to live in the tension, to sacrifice freedom
neither to worldliness nor to a political or a religious entity, is
to be free existentially.

## Unconditionality and Spectating

Since antiquity, philosophers have seen pleasure, wealth, and
power as conditions inhibiting contemplation. In a famous
simile attributed in antiquity to Pythagoras, life is like a festival
to which some men come to win fame in the games, some to
make money selling their goods, and some simply to admire
the works of art, the performances, and the speeches. The
spectator is the most free man (*liberalissimus;* ἐλευθεριώ-

 τατος) because he is removed from the turmoil of the crowd, from the pursuit of fame and wealth. The freest pursuit is spectating. For Jaspers, as we have seen, the freedom to travel in imagination, to move about and see from many points of view, and to read the world as a cipher-script is more than mere spectating, for there is a transformation worked in and through mental freedom. Furthermore, "disquiet about losing myself even in the most abundant existence"[45] gives a negative intimation that "something else may be present in human acts, something that will retrieve them from temporal endlessness into the self-being which I ascertain in action."[46] But this something is not another way of life, like the bios theoretikos, but unconditionality—present *in human acts*. In action which is merely instinctual or merely purposeful, man may "deteriorate as possible self-being and suffer from a sense of nonbeing";[47] in action which is *unconditional*—though its medium is existence, purposeful action—self-being is ascertained. Self-being is revealed not to contemplation but only in willing and acting.

If removal from the turmoil of life is taken as an ideal permanent condition, we speak of ataraxy. Jaspers described ataraxy as "the impersonal calm of an independence that has become insubstantial," as "point-like autonomy."[48] Ataraxy is the "formalization, and thus the petrification, of freedom . . . , retaining an Existenz that cannot be disturbed because it rests on nothing."[49] The ataraxic man withdraws from communication into empty silence, he is "like a nonbeing." Ataraxy differs from unconditional acts that transcend existence—religious asceticism, or suicide; it is a nonact. It is neither leaving the world absolutely nor leaving it while remaining in it; it is an attempt to *be* a world, a sealed-off unit.[50] The ideal of ataraxy implies apathy, not-sensing, and autarchy, sovereignty of the will within the little world.

The notion that freedom is internal—related neither to the world nor to transcendence—and consists of self-sovereignty was foreign to Jaspers (as was the derivative ideal of sovereignty of the will *in* the world and the ideal of national sovereignty, as we shall see below). He called such freedom "isolating." Freedom in the world is among men, and existential freedom is in communication.

At the opposite pole from isolation and removal from the realm of human affairs is absolutization of the political realm. Unconditionality can be lost in endless calculating and planning, the absolutization of mundane purposes in unlimited management.

A political realist considers that everything man does is politically relevant, that everything man does can be known and reckoned with. "A psychology of human motives evolves, so does a sociology of situations, interrelationships, social structures, types of power and organization. In this political science and psychology, the suprapolitical element disappears. Everything that we call suprapolitical is then mere human reality, political material, sub-political, a calculable factor of political thinking. . . . . 'Politics, as Napoleon said, 'is destiny.' "[51] (In other forms, political realism declares that might is right, or as in the Hindu theory of *Kautilya*, right is what succeeds.)[52]

The stance of the political realist—the claim that everything man does can be known and reckoned with—implies an imaginary point outside, from which a supposed knowledge of what will necessarily happen is achieved. But ironically enough from this point, a man may equally as well proclaim man's impotence as his omnipotence: "whoever talks of the inevitable says more than he can know and feeds the passions of the nihilist, who waits for the moment of catastrophe to bring him the indirect suicide he desires or absolute power by force."[53]

Reason, equated narrowly with political realism, may be considered authoritative, and so may common sense. That common sense by which we concretely have a feeling for "an ethos of undefined rules"[54] in a given societal context and by which we generally have a feeling for something common to all men as they orient themselves in their world can be considered as the "court of last resort." It becomes the source of convincing (not abstract and blind to reality) solutions to problems. But if common sense is thus made authoritative, then in situations that are unstable, in which existing orders and conventions are radically questioned, it will prove inadequate: "in a crisis, more is needed than common sense."[55] Unlike imagination, "common sense is blind both to the very worst and to the very best. . . . the saving decisions in extremity, on the small scale as well as in history at large, come from a depth that common sense cannot attain."[56] What swept away the fixed common sense of the modern world was the radical alteration in the conditions of life brought about by modern technology. Jaspers referred to this alteration as a "world historical leap . . . so great that it can hardly be compared with any previous one; only the inventions of fire and tools are adequate parallels."[57] On the other hand, if common sense is not an authority but a path, then in such situations it is essential. Common sense, as a path, demands (in Kant's formulation) three movements: "First, think yourself; second, think in every other person's place; third, always think in agreement with yourself."

Neither removal from the turmoil of life into the little world of the "I" nor entering into the world blindly (or with eyes shaded by scientific or realistic or commonsense spectacles) and claiming that the world is all there is, for better or for worse, leaves room for the human possibility Jaspers called unconditionality. Neither self-being without experience nor existence without self-being, neither abstention from action nor avoidance of the possibilities of action by false claims to knowledge, leaves room for human freedom. Neither removal from the political realm nor absolutization of it takes into account the responsibility that falls to every man because he has a share in power, the responsibility of seeing that power remains *shared*, is checked by being shared, and "achieves what is right."

Every human being is fated to be enmeshed in the power relations he lives by. This is the inevitable guilt of all, the guilt of human existence. It is counteracted by supporting

the power that achieves what is right, the rights of man.
Failure to collaborate in the struggle for power, for the sake
of serving the right, creates basic political guilt and moral
guilt at the same time. Political guilt turns into moral guilt
where power serves to destroy the meaning of power—the
achievement of what is right, the ethos and purity of one's
own nation. For wherever power does not limit itself, there
exists violence and terror, and in the end the destruction of
life and soul.[58]

## Types of Purposive Action

Jaspers distinguished three types of purposive action—action
in which the actor is aware of the ends of his underlying drives
and in which he interposes a series of calculated arrangements
between the drive and its satisfaction, in order to relate the end
to certain means. The first, political action, is:

> . . . what we call action with reference to the will of other
> human beings whose activity plays a part in the making of
> our world. In this sort of action we arouse and shape the
> will of those who work with us, and we work against
> opposition—that is, against the resistance we meet in the
> form of the human will.[59]

Freedom in the political realm can, in effect, be ascertained by
asking how this arousing and shaping is accomplished. If,
among those whose wills are involved, there is both
"acknowledgment of the cogent accuracy of knowledge" (of
political realities, economics, military situations, and so forth)
and acknowledgment of what Jaspers called unconditionality,
then the result is "joint understanding."[60] The result is communication of facts *and* existential communication, "appeal to
freedom," and hence "communicative demands"—not commands to be unquestioningly obeyed. If neither kind of
acknowledgment is present, then the result is "demands that
are enforceable by means of suggestion, persuasion, or violence."[61] The difference is between a spontaneous unity of
wills for the attainment of ends encompassed by a guiding (in

itself purposeless) reason and an unstable unity of wills that are "like motors" in a centrally directed machine. In the former case, purposive action is permeated by unconditionality, it is the medium of existential action; and in the latter case, purposive action is a means to an end under the conditions of "temporal endlessness"—that is, no final end is ever defined, for every time a "for this" is declared another "what for?" rises up. "In purposive action I should like to know a final goal, though I can never find one; but *unconditional acts need no such goal, since they express a being.*"[62] Freedom is "a matter of action, of the original self-certainty that makes me stop asking for the objective reasons that can be wholly conclusive. . . . just to talk about it takes another way of visualization."[63] The ends-means categories of purposive action cannot encompass this freedom in action. "Everything existential lies outside the realm of my purposive volition or nolition."[64]

When Jaspers stated that the aim of politics is the establishment, consolidation, and preservation of freedom, he did not thereby state a final purpose.[65] Objective freedom, political freedom, is "historically manifold, and nowhere quite reliable . . . we find it in ancient English liberty, in Dutch and Swiss liberty, in the liberty of the French Revolution, in that of the Scandinavian states, even in that of Bismarck's pseudoconstitutional Germany, and in American liberty."[66] There is no formula for freedom, no simple set of conditions under which it is secure.

> Freedom is the most-used word of our time. What it is seems obvious to all. Every country, every people, every individual wants to be free; the whole world seems as one in claiming and asserting freedom. Yet there is nothing more obscure, more ambiguous, more abused.[67]

Freedom is an idea that has, historically, been incarnated in many forms. The incarnations—forms of government—can be classified, but the idea remains a challenge.[68]

Politics, aimed at the establishment, consolidation, and preservation of freedom, takes its bearings from power. Power was defined by Jaspers as a "unity of wills" among men with respect to "the organization of their condition and their self-maintenance in the world."[69] It is power in this sense in which every man has a share, though he may not know it.

Jaspers distinguished purposive political action from two other types of purposive action—technological and cultivational or educational. Each type corresponds to a "sphere of mundane reality." Technological action is the making or shaping of things from a given material, from unorganic nature. "By consciously relating physical nature to my needs and purposes, I act against it; my natural world becomes a utilitarian world."[70] Both cultivational and educational action are concerned with objects of "independent essence," from which the actors "await some original aims, methods and tools."[71] We cultivate organic life and educate soul and mind.[72] Neither technological nor educational action can bring about "unity of wills," but both are related to power and political action in varying ways and to varying degrees in different historical situations.

"Life, the soul and the mind cannot be technologically made but [only] conditionally influenced."[73] Technological action influences the conditions under which political action takes place:

> For our every aim today is subject to the prior necessity of adapting ourselves to the technological world. Technology has determined our manner of work, our economy, our social structures, our bureaucracy. . . . Only the fundamental, final traits of man remain the same; the *conditions* of life are so transformed that history at large acquires a new character.[74]

Hypothetically constructed, the limiting case in which political action would effectively disappear would be "the world as totally made."[75] In this case, the individual would be "a tiny cog in a vast machinery." "He no longer knows his product as his own" (the alienation of labor, in Marx's terms) "and does not really know his needs either, but all of these will be satisfied by the work of others who work as he does, and whose work serves him as his serves them." All men live similarly, in the "same worldless satisfaction of needs by identically replaceable things and materials." Each man lives in dependence on others, but there is little or no personal contact. "The only freedom left men by the calculable course of this endless machinery would be the freedom to watch"—that is, there would be no freedom to make one's judgment and will felt, the freedom made possible by democracy. There would be, at best, spectating. Without personal contact there is no shaping and arousing of wills; the wills of men become "like motors" (like part of the machinery).[76]

Short of this limiting case in which political action would effectively disappear, the political task, given the conditions of advanced technology, is to ensure that there is justice introduced into the material order—"this is an unending task in the struggle for right"—and to ensure that this introduction takes place peacefully, in the broad context of world political order. What is done and made by individuals and groups "can be controlled by the community of men."[77]

Again, political action to accomplish this task of introducing justice into material conditions implies an unconditional element beyond calculation: "Justice prevails in current rational objectifications; the argument for it is always presented in such objectifications; but justice as a whole lives encompassingly by the origins that guide the rational form and lend it weight."[78] Justice, like freedom, is an ideal; it can be incarnated in many forms.[79]

Technological action influences political action—to such a degree that we are able to construct the influence hypothetically as overwhelming—but it cannot substitute for political action. Politics in the sense of "control by the community of men" must have space within society's "life-apparatus"; and politics itself must be permeated by the "suprapolitical element."

Life, soul, and mind cannot be made by technological action; but they can, in a sense, be made by educational action. They are not just "conditionally influenced" but directly aroused and shaped. The body can be trained, the soul which "experiences life" can develop (psychophysical coordination improves, perception becomes more discriminatory, particularly in an educative relationship of authority and obedience). The mind is educated through communication: "the unhistorical soul exists in the individual even if we think of him in isolation, the mind exists only in the individual who becomes a social and historical being."[80] That is, body and soul *can* develop without education, but the mind "comes from tradition."[81] The soul can be conceived as a matter of heredity, but the mind cannot: "man is not what he is solely in virtue of biological inheritance, but also, and much more, thanks to what tradition makes him. . . . he acquires that which, elaborated by the activity of his own being, is known as his culture."[82] This becomes for him, so to speak, his second nature.

The educator does not arouse and shape the will for mundane purposes. He shapes the "will to know," and in this shaping "no limitations are established by any tacit purpose known to only one side"[83] (educator or educated). Culture is that out of which experience, work, and action proceed: each successive generation is absorbed into the ongoing whole which the educator serves ("without making experiments"),[84] and from which all get their bearings in the world. Education fits an individual into the world, prepares him for political action. This is quite different from preparing him to fulfill a function, teaching him what will be practically applicable in life, "socializing" him in a Deweyan sense.

Education transmits a tradition. "The objectivity of tradition is a premise of freedom."[85] But "freedom itself cannot be propagated as a tradition . . . ; handed down it is not freedom any more, employed without a struggle it is lost."[86] The tradition of political freedom in the West is the premise for the establishment, consolidation, and preservation of freedom—for the task of the heirs of the tradition. There is no set relation between the individual and the world, or between the individual and the collective; with each successive generation, the configuration shifts.

> . . . the basic fact of being human, which distinguishes us from animals, is that there can be no perfect relationship of individual and collective. This is why man has a history. By his works, by his divisions of jointly performed labor, he produces structures—unlike biological inheritance—which are invariably brittle and easily upset.[87]

Education prepares the individual, on the grounds of adopted history, to repair or rebuild the worldly structures through joint action, to create a second world.

## The Inapplicability of Educational and Technological Relations to Politics

The teacher-student relation does not, in Jaspers's thinking, carry over into politics: "unity of wills" among those who act together, arising from their joint understanding, is ideally unity among equals. What Jaspers wrote of Kant in the following quotation is true of Jaspers himself:

> [He] did not give up the Platonic idea of philosopher-kings, but he transformed its appearance. Philosophy, i.e., reason, shall rule. But this reason can rule only if it materializes in nations. Effective leadership can be provided, not by individual philosopher-kings or supermen, but by the truth which comes to light in public discourse and intellectual contention. The state of the world is shaped by a moral-intellectual process of growth of nations, not by the insight of individuals. The inexorable challenge to us all as human beings is to renounce the superman-leader. The wisest of men is to turn to all others, knowing that he is one of their kind—a human being, no more. The advice in principle which comes out of public thinking can persuade because it is given to *a community in which all control and correct each other, enhancing each other's reason.* The philosopher-

kings are no longer individual men; they are the spirit of a public that comes to see reason.[88]

Philosophy is for Everyman. The authority of teacher over student, or expert over layman, differs from the authority of reason itself, in which all share or can share. The categories of educational action are not appropriate to political action.

And neither are the categories of technological action. Along with the challenge to renounce the superman leader goes the challenge to renounce the technocrat, the superman planner or the superman manufacturer.[89] Technological action results in something "mechanically intelligible and indifferent in itself, because it consists simply in alien matter."[90] If mechanical intelligibility is taken as an ideal in the realm of human affairs—if efficient machines are the model for human organizations— then men are conceived as material-like, and human history as surveyable, knowable as a whole, like the pattern of a machine's operation. "All total planning in the human kingdom operates with man as though he were known, and with expectations based on knowledge of man."[91] Accompanying the vision of the totally planned world is the vision of the superman "whom one can simply obey and who promises to accomplish everything."[92] Such a man strives for a kind of godlikeness:

. . . he loses his relationship to transcendence—he dons blinkers through the operation of which he loses sight of the experience of the origin and fundament of things, in favor of a semblance: mere movement in the world—the establishment of the right organization of the world for all time—he loses the possibility of upsurge, because he succumbs to an apparatus of terror and despotism—he brings about a perversion of the apparently loftiest idealism of the goal of humanity, into the inhumanity of squandering human life, into the transformation of the circumstances of life into an unprecedented slavery—he annihilates the forces that carry man forward—when he fails, he gives way in despair to the urge to ever more loathsome acts of violence.[93]

The opposite of the image of an organization for all times guided by a superplanner is the image of a net of organizations, flexible and devoted to tangible tasks and pervaded by reason: "the non-contractual but actual community of reason needs to prevail *in all forms of human organization*—in states, parties, churches, schools, unions, bureaucracies."[94]

Political action has often been considered in categories drawn from cultivational or educational action and from technological action. Political relations among men have been construed on the models of shepherd and flock, teacher and student, expert and layman (all are common in Plato's dialogues), and of maker and made, planner and apparatus. The cultivational and educational models imply a distinction of rank and a distinction between philosophy (engaged in by the few) and politics. The technological models also imply a distinction of rank, as well as a distinction between, on the one hand, philosophy and politics and, on the other hand, the apparatus for supplying material needs, in the extreme case of a totalitarian regime. A totalitarian regime leaves no room, no public space, for political action: "Germany could not free herself from National Socialism, but had to be liberated from outside. . . . no totalitarianism can be conquered from within. . . . the end of true politics terminates the interest in politics."[95] Thus the possibility of worldwide totalitarianism is the most awesome—there is no outside. And also "it is no accident that both National Socialism and Bolshevism would regard philosophy as their deadly spiritual foe."[96]

Jaspers's political thinking is concerned with how thinking can become an element of politics and how politics can be related to thinking's fundamental operation, transcending, and to the unconditionality of the transcending thinker's reentry into the world in action. It is concerned with the bond of communication, the "all control and correct each other"—with politics of and among equals, which takes its bearings from power as "unity of wills." "The germ of all public good lies in the meeting of rational men."[97]

The existential concept of unconditionality signals the existential dimension of Jaspers's political thinking; it marks the point at which the purposive categories, means and ends, are transcended.

> We possess an abundance of knowledge and prescriptions telling us what needs to be done if certain ends are to be reached. But such ends must themselves already be determined and finally must be something opposed to us; and the further and decisive question, which end we ought to seek, still remains. All thought and communication concerning what we ought to do abides in the antechamber of ethos. For nowhere does objective thinking meet with an ultimate and unconditional principle. It is therefore easily possible to doubt every pronounced and determined "ought," for an "ought" is determined by ends, and ends are not unconditionally established. . . .[98]

It is the rational community (*die Gemeinschaft der Vernünftigen*) which keeps open the possibility of thought and communication, which reaches beyond the antechamber of ethos, which keeps the space of action and thought open to be unconditional. It is "our only hope." And yet this community is hidden, nothing organizational can rest on it: how, then, is the germ of public good to grow?

## 3. REASON AND INTELLECT

### Preliminary Distinction

If intellect, without the "suprapolitical element" of reason, dominates the political realm, the result is (short of the limiting case of the world as totally made) the situation Jaspers described in *The Future of Mankind:*

> Intellectual thought is the inventor and the maker. Its percepts can be carried out and can multiply the making by infinite repetition. The result is a world in which a few minds devise the mechanics, creating, as it were, a second world in which the masses can then assume the operative function.

The contrasting situation is this:

> Rational thought . . . does not provide for the carrying out of
> mass directives, but requires each individual to do his own
> thinking. Here, truth is not found by a machine reproducible
> at will, but by decision, resolve and action whose self-willing
> performance, by each on his own, is what creates a common
> spirit.[99]

In a made world, willing is operating, functioning; in a world
where there is thinking space, willing is self-originated, self-
directed. To understand this distinction, we need to explore
Jaspers's contribution to philosophical analysis of the will.

### Volition and Grand Volition

The will is empowered either by the reservoir of
"psychophysical nature," "finite psychological impulses" and
"involuntary forces," or by "the font of . . . substantial
forces," the "supporting base" of ideas and Existenz.[100] In the
first case, Jaspers spoke of "formal volition": the channeling
and coordinating of psychophysical nature—which results in
the direct translation of will into physical motion—is a phenomenon "as familiar to us as it is miraculous upon reflection."[101] These miraculous translations are taken for granted
until they do not occur and we are "unable to bring the will to
bear." This situation may be remediable medically or
psychiatrically. However, more than a physical or psychological problem may be involved; there may be a "cleavage between will and decision."[102]

Volition does not exist without discriminating thought. That
is, volition is more than simple instinctive action, simple
striving and reactivity. Intellectual deliberating becomes "ac-
tivating" when means and ends are considered and when they
are brought into question; when I ask what I ought to do and
how I ought to do it, when volition is performed in a self-
elucidating manner.

> . . . there is in [this volition] something mobile which en-
> ables me to confront and examine all ends because I am not

tied to a fixed standpoint; there is no choice without a sense of this rational mobility.[103]

This drafting of possibilities for mundane action and testing them inwardly is the process of inner action: "I am able to think the possibilities through to make room for knowing my own will." The broader the range of intellect, guided and regulated by ideas of reason, the freer the choice: "the more the totality, without forgetting a thing, determines my visions and actions, my feelings and decisions, the freer I know I am."[104] But an ideal totality will bring forth freedom only if "everything will not just factually tie in with everything else, but will do so for my consciousness as the eye of possible Existenz."[105]

Discrimination is guided, in its rational mobility, by ideas, and it is dependent upon the inner action of Existenz. That is, at the bounds of formal volition there is a will, psychologically incomprehensible, which "in uniting purposive and existential clarity"[106] can move a man originally, because in it he is himself. Jaspers called this will the grand will (*grosse Wille*).

When the will cannot coordinate and channel impulses, psychological forces, its failure can be explored phenomenologically. The causation process can to a certain extent be isolated, but the exploration has a limit because the problem "is at the same time the phenomenon of a break in Existenz."[107] That is, the coordinating of impulses and forces is only the phenomenal aspect of willing; willing can also be elucidated (not known) as "the encompassing, as man's intrinsic power in his Existenz."[108] The sign for this elucidation is the "grand will" or "volition by ideas on the ground of Existenz."[109]

The cleavage between will and decision is a cleavage not between will and psychophysical nature but between the will and its ground, the source of resolution, Existenz. In Augustine's words: "Whence this monstrous thing? and why is it? The mind commands the body, and is forthwith obeyed; the mind commands itself, and is resisted."[110] Augustine spoke of an "infirmity of the mind," of a "war with myself" which was healed and stilled by God's grace. "It was I who willed, and I who was unwilling. . . . I neither willed entirely, nor was I entirely unwilling."[111] Augustine's conversion came in a leap, what Jaspers called the leap to resolution. "Resolution is unconditional. . . . irresolution as such is a lack of self-being; irresolution at a particular moment indicates only that I have not found myself as yet."[112]

Jaspers's discussion of resolution differs from Augustine's first in that resolution is not given, not the result of God's grace (*quid habes, quid non accepisti*). However, "in the hold I freely took of my own self I took hold of my transcendence whose evanescent phenomenon am I myself in my freedom."[113] Resolution implies a sense of one's own phenomenality, but it does not imply direct intervention by God. Second, freedom in resolution is not hidden completely away in the inner world—and attached to the will with the phrase "free will." Rather, "resolution in choice is *originally communicative*."[114] This is what Jaspers referred to when he said that truth in a rational world is found by decision, resolve and action whose self-willed performance, by each on his own, is what creates a common spirit. Freedom in resolution underlies the unity of wills for the accomplishment of mundane purposes, that is, the unitary power from which politics takes its bearings. And furthermore, if conditions in the world are not such that resolution can be communicated and unconditionality can permeate purposive action, freedom is curtailed (and this is not the case for freedom conceived as self-mastery alone).

Jaspers's adoption of Augustine's distinction of *velle* and *posse* is summarized in the following passage:

> The words "I can" or "I cannot," whether right or wrong in a particular case, refer initially to the physical and psychological energies of the empirical individual and to his domain in a situation, not to Existenz. I identify myself with empirical existence, turn myself into an object, and give up on my Existenz. But then it is possible to say, in the sense of transcendental freedom, "I can because I ought to," and in

the sense of existential freedom, "I can because I must." This "can" no longer refers to the factual realization of a mundane goal; it refers to my inner and outer action, even though empirically I should fail in it. In the sense of original freedom there are no bounds to what I unconditionally can.[115]

In short: "Existenz is not a state of being, but of *being able*. . . ."[116]

## Society and State

A man who, in a made world, assumes an operative function is a man whose psychological impulses are used by others "as a motor."[117] The impulse to obey, for example, is so used. That is, not only discriminating thought but "grand volition"— volition by ideas on the ground of Existenz—is foreclosed.

In extreme circumstances—and certainly under a totalitarian regime—most people have already surrendered to a blind political will, accepted a substitute for true authority. As he considered the state of Europe in 1931, Jaspers claimed that Bolshevism and fascism come into being "at the cost of renouncing, on the part of almost all of us, the right to be ourselves."[118] He understood that an independent political stance was becoming a rarity:

In his impotence . . . it is harder for the individual to apprehend his freedom to act, and to realize it, when, as today, the reason for it is regarded as purely secular; it is harder to be actuated by a simple sense of mundane responsibility in matters which, heretofore, were left to the divine authority of the State.[119]

Jaspers held that in such circumstances, a goal other than the sheer satisfaction of needs by means of a "life-order . . . will be disclosed to him alone who, despite everything, can fix his gaze upon Transcendence."[120] This gaze is necessary for "unceasing clarification of knowledge of the possible" by which a man becomes "ripe to collaborate in the shaping of the situation." There is an unceasing tension between mass order for the supply of necessities and "the decision that is based on power," that is, that arises in collaboration. It is "the tension between society and the State."[121]

After 1933, Jaspers would not have used a phrase like "fix his gaze upon Transcendence"—its weight was too unworldly, too apolitical. Instead he focused on the conditions of "grand volition" in which our relation to transcendence is felt. In this volition, man makes demands which "say in the world what must be done so that in struggling for existence man will in every social possibility achieve the form of existence most worthy of him, the form that can make him aware of his innate, transcendently related being."[122] Grand volition, by ideas on the ground of Existenz, calls for elucidating the ideas which make us aware of the substance contained in the social objectivity and that substance's subjective realization, without which all types of purposive action would be useless.

> Ideas are the substance and the guidance of all intellectual calculation in institutions such as universities, schools, productive enterprises; without ideas everything becomes a hopeless, monotonous, senselessly jeopardizing bustle. The idea is also the historic substance of a state, the source from which it derives a destiny and a continuous will.[123]

Ideas are either objectified as elucidations, "designs for action and indirectly communicated appeals," or are subjective as "forces of real existence."[124] Ideas are the *pathos* of grand volition, in distinction from "the power" of psychophysical nature. Demands based on ideas are meaningful: "at this historic place and in this occupation [they] are unconditional and therefore true."[125] But ideas are never objects possessed or incarnated in the world definitively.

The implementation of ideologies by force and the incarnation of an idea through joint action are as distinct as rule by decree and rule by law open to amendment.

> The essence of freedom is struggle; it does not want to appease but to intensify the contest, does not want to acquiesce but to enforce open demonstration. But the nameless enmity

to liberty transforms the spiritual struggle into the perverted spirituality of the Inquisition.[126]

This nameless enmity springs from "the will to a freedom from trouble and effort, the will to continue an extant life in unchanged forms," from the "hidden poison of dissatisfaction with one's own life," from nihilism. When man's world has fallen into decay, "when his ideas seem to be dying,"[127] a man may feel hidden from himself. But "volition is a relation to oneself,"[128] an active self-awareness. "This 'I' does not exist outright; it is only as self-creation. As Kierkegaard put it: 'the more will, the more self.' There can be no adequate motivation for this will except in original choice—in the *choice which no longer lies between things but serves to manifest the self in existence.*"[129] The opposite of self-struggle and struggle with others—self-communication and communication with others—in which the self is manifest, is the hiddenness and obscurity of selflessness and incommunicativeness, sophistry and secrecy.

### Gesellschaft and Gemeinschaft

Behind Jaspers's distinction of the intellectual association and the rational community lies the distinction between *Gesellschaft* and *Gemeinschaft* with which German sociology was preoccupied at the beginning of the century.[130] Jaspers agreed with Weber:

It is the fate of our times, with their characteristic rationalization and intellectualization, and in particular their disenchantment with the world, that precisely the ultimate and most sublime values have receded from public life to take refuge in the brotherliness of immediate relations between individuals. It is no accident [that our highest art is intimate rather than monumental, and] that today, within the smallest groups, between man and man, *pianissimo*, a Something throbs, which has its counterpart in the prophetic pneuma which in other days passed like a raging fire through the great communities and welded them together.[131]

But while Weber thought of this modern pneuma in terms of charisma and associated it with "exemplary prophecy"[132] and mysticism of a Tolstoyan stamp, Jaspers thought of it in terms of reason and associated it with the exemplary great philosophers.

A central problem of Jaspers's political thinking is the relation of the rational community to the societal and political realms, or the relation of existential communication "between man and man" and communication among men. Or, more generally phrased, the relation of the loving struggle of individuals to the struggle of arousing and shaping wills in the plural political realm. And this problem arises from two angles: first from the definition of political action as arousing and shaping of wills for mundane purposes, and second from the hiddenness of the rational brotherhood.

Weber was clearly in the tradition of Schopenhauer, Nietzsche, and Burckhardt with his idea that man's striving to impose his will on others is a universal characteristic of human action. Jaspers's definition of political action reflects this tradition. Politics conceived as "the possibility of imposing one's will upon the behavior of another person" (in Weber's phrase)[133] is very nearly politics conceived as war; the similarity of Weber's definition of politics to Clausewitz's definition of war has often been pointed out.[134] Beginning from such a definition, notions of supremacy, sovereignty, *Herrschaft,* are difficult to avoid.

Jaspers's repeated injunctions against national sovereignty and individual will to power would seem to call for a redefinition of political action. His definition is, however, simply an elaboration of Weber's definition:

> Politics orients itself between two poles: potential force and free association. . . . Power politics and parliamentary politics are by nature opposed; how they join forces sums up the practice of politics until now and for an indefinite time to come.[135]

Jaspers clearly recognized that it is a fallacy to think that political power is nothing but power through force. He maintained that political acion is the arousing and shaping of wills, not the imposition of one's will. But arousing and shaping implies, if not force, persuasion and suggestion. These are inimical in his own terms to existential communication and may be inimical to the "all control and correct each other" of the political realm. Politics orients itself by force *and free association:* it is only the latter which, in the Greco-Roman tradition, as opposed to that from which Weber and Jaspers drew, is truly political. Jaspers understood that free association constitutes the realm of freedom as opposed to the realm of violent necessity. But he did not, until he wrote *The Future of Germany* in 1966, make a distinction between free associations and parliamentary politics. As Germany became a "party oligarchy" after the war, Jaspers feared that political participation would be possible only through the parties and only in cooperation with party bureaucrats. As alternatives to such a system, he admired the American voluntary organizations, "neither parties nor partisan," about which he had read in Hannah Arendt's *On Revolution*, and the Swiss "district clubs" or local party open forums for free discussion and criticism.[136] But these alternatives and his recognition of the limits of parliamentary politics did not lead Jaspers to amend his earlier definition of political action.

Jaspers's faith remained with the other element he had added to his definition of political action as arousing and shaping of wills for mundane purposes—that is, with his notion of "grand will." Unconditionality, or the suprapolitical element, stands at the boundary of mundane willing, so to speak, and it is interjected into the political realm, into the ends-means, will-to-power framework, where it keeps this realm and framework from becoming all-encompassing. But this brings us to the second angle of the problem: the hiddenness of the rational community.

Existenz enters the political arena as an "alien element," at great risk. (Weber's career is again exemplary: the very characteristics of Weber's greatness—his rigor and honesty—made political involvement nearly impossible for him.) The rational community with its existential communication is distinct

from the political community with its political intercourse: how
they are related, or may become related, is unclear. The problem is apparent in Jaspers's description of the rational statesman "playing the game" of winning popular support without
betraying himself:

> He can do this responsibly, maintaining his independence,
> only if he has the gift of an actor who is not playing but
> controlling his parts. He can be himself in every part, be-
> cause his decisions at crucial moments are his own, and be-
> cause he stays in character by being true to his own self.[137]

The rational statesman is guided by something more than
Machiavelli's statesman, who "trusts in the incalculable ability
that is born of his *virtù* and in his awareness of the destiny that
makes him feel befriended by *fortuna,* fickle though she be."[138]
The ideas which were essential to Machiavelli—ideas of foundation and maintenance of the state, of republican liberty—did
not, Jaspers held, ground his work: "we see their broad presence, but they are not made a principle by the great analyst of
the will to power as such, who neither indicts nor vindicates
what he regards as beyond good and evil. . . ."[139] Machiavelli
knew no grand volition on the basis of ideas and Existenz: the
norm for action is not derivable from the reality of the situation,
"the origin of the norm is a new question, not answerable by
*virtù* or *fortuna.*"[140] The statesman must be able to play the
game of winning popular support and yet not lose himself;
similarly, the rational community must be able to make general
appeals without ruining itself:

> In existential communication we disdain the use of in-
> strumentalities, power or guile, but political intercourse de-
> mands specific means of combat and deception. It requires
> means which threaten to overwhelm the realization of possi-
> ble Existenz at any time.[141]

Given this threat, Jaspers held that it is "all but impossible for
politically active individuals to come into existential contact
when they meet; for they are dealing with concrete concerns of

existence, not with Existenz. In politics one should not touch the human essence.''[142] But if the human essence is freedom, and political freedom is the condition without which existential freedom is impossible, or without which it cannot be manifest, then ''concrete concerns of existence'' *are* concerns that touch on the human essence. If the crux of politics is that ''all control and correct each other, enhancing each other's reason,'' then political intercourse must in some sense be existential.

Jaspers wrote about the threat of political intercourse to communication in the *Philosophy,* in 1931, before his own political involvement, an involvement which he said, as we noted above, made his thought ''fully conscious, down to its metaphysical roots.'' His postwar political involvement closed the gap between politics and philosophy in his own life, and showed him that it is possible to stand in the harsh light of the political arena without ruin. It showed him that politics and philosophy both concern questions essential to every man's existence and Existenz and that public exchange of opinions can enhance one's reason. ''Only political freedom can make authentic human beings of us.''[143] He concluded that what saves the rational community from complete hiddenness is its ability to speak popularly: though it may not found a political entity, it lays the spiritual foundations and maintains the ''thinking space'' where ''truth is found . . . by decision, re-solve and action whose self-willed performance, by each of his own, creates a common spirit.''[144] But Jaspers did not ever say how the common spirit is to influence political action except to express his hope for its influence upon ''rational statesmen.''

## The Example of Solon

Great statesmen like Solon and Pericles are capable of that dual orientation by force and by freedom, guided by non-violent reason. Self-assertion by force calls for cunning and lies; reason calls for candor, sincerity, and reliable treaties. Self-assertion implies taking responsibility for the conse-quences of political acts in the interests of national power; reason demands moral character, which assents to success, force and power only when they serve the suprapolitical ends of man.[145]

Even more than Pericles, Solon was Jaspers's exemplar for the portrait of the rational statesman. In an essay called "Solon," Jaspers described this man whose "faith in all-conquering reason" allowed him to put his trust "in the right and thus in other's insights, born of their own conviction."[146] As a statesman Solon was an educator who allowed "all to share in his deliberations—which were completely sincere, not a means to an end."[147] "Wherever democracy has since been tried in the West, we find Solon's spirit of measure, his community feeling, his denial of the individual will to power . . . , his sense of law and justice that permits constant improvement of the laws."[148] This portrait of the rational statesman was Jaspers's answer to the fundamental flaw he perceived in Germany under the Kaiser—a flaw which the Weimar Republic, even though it was a republic, never really corrected. "Political thinkers such as Max Weber saw the fatal weakness of an empire whose policy-makers were appointed officials rather than statesmen with the gift of leadership—for leaders emerge only from the political struggle, which was non-existent under the Kaiser."[149]

Jaspers emphasized Solon's orientation toward freedom, his concern for free association. But Jaspers's own apprehensions about orientation by force are clearly superimposed upon his portrait, to address it to our times. Jaspers calls Solon a naive figure, lacking tragic consciousness or "consciousness of boundary situations." "Alive in him was the good spirit of realizing freedom in existence—without, from the frontiers, experiencing the mental enhancing and simultaneously destructive impulses."[150] The statesman in our time is confronted with force as an ineluctable boundary situation. Solon could rely upon the "authority of legality," as opposed to the "authority of faith" or the "authority of reason" (both of which will be discussed below), because for him, "the suprapolitical ends of man" could be served by politics. For Solon life itself was political.

Jaspers felt that the conditions of political life had changed so drastically during and after the Second World War that maxims once acceptable to statesmen and laws designed to further them would no longer do. For example, "Men used to say: *Si vis pacem, para bellum,* if you want peace, prepare for war. And they were not just being insincere. Today, that advice is sincere but almost impossible to take."[151] The present world situation is, in itself, a boundary situation. At the boundary is what Jaspers called "the question of evil," and we will turn to this question before we make our way back to Jaspers's concepts of authority.

## 4. THE QUESTION OF FREE WILL AND THE QUESTION OF EVIL

### Determinism and Indeterminism

Jaspers pointed out that those who argue for freedom of the will are usually motivated by a fear that responsible action will cease on the day that all men become determinists. And those who argue against it may be motivated by truthfulness; that is, they acknowledge that they cannot find freedom anywhere in the world, on the grounds that there is *nihil sine causa*. Or they may be motivated by the desire to take comfort or refuge in the consequent of a conditional; for example, if all is written out in advance, then no man is guilty. Jaspers himself argued that both sides mistake the problem (besides laboring under the illusion that a theoretical discussion constitutes a decision). He did not, however, try to dissolve the problem or clear up a linguistic muddle; he moved to a level beyond the antithetical positions and appealed to the freedom of Existenz, which is "revealed only to our volition" and is thus nonobjective and undemonstrable.

> In any event, determinism and indeterminism put the matter on the wrong plane. They reduce the existential origin to a state of dependence. One side asserts the existence of freedom while falsely objectifying and thus voiding it in fact; a defender of freedoms that do not really amount to freedom

thus turns his very success into an unconscious denial. The other side denies freedom but applies the word to an objective phantom.[152]

First, what are the "freedoms that do not really amount to freedom?" Jaspers thought the so-called *liberum arbitrium indifferentiae*[153] an "empty thought that proves nothing. . . . [it shows] freedom as coincidence and license, not freedom proper."[154] Second, freedom of action or choice without external disturbance or coercion is freedom psychologically defined: the freedom of the will itself is not in question; and questions concerning whether one's motives or character or constitution are determined, whether one is free to choose the standards by which choices are made, and so forth, are not raised. The third kind of freedom which does not really amount to freedom "concerns human power relationships in society and in the state." "Sociologically, we can distinguish personal, civil and political liberty. Their existence in general cannot be doubted, but it does not answer our question about the freedom which is Existenz itself, for this may be in doubt despite those other freedoms."[155] In summary:

> The psychological and sociological freedoms are never freedom itself. They are not, however, irrelevant to it. I want them to be real. I must want this if I know I am originally free, for *they are conditions of the appearance of freedom in existence if I want realization in the world, not merely possibility and internality.* Original freedom lends substance to the objective ones; deprived of this fulfillment, they become delusive. I have lost myself precisely where I want objective freedom and believe that its achievement has already made me free. This shows in the ambiguity of all libertarian phrases.[156]

Jaspers indicated two types of pseudoindependence which correspond to taking, on the one hand, psychological freedom and, on the other hand, sociological freedom, as definitive. These are, in effect, two concepts of sovereignty. The first is the ataraxic ideal already discussed above: "If I withdraw into

myself, if I grow indifferent to what does not under all circumstances rest with me alone, my independence comes to be the
pride which an empty self-being takes in being unshakeable."[157] The price of self-sovereignty is immobility, solitude;
the limits of self-sovereignty are the existence of the body,
bodily needs, and the need for some kind of communication or,
at least, appreciation of one's independence ("somewhere it
will prove to be actual dependence on the mirror of somebody
else's view").[158] Retreat from disturbance and coercion leaves
only the happiness of living in a Phalleric Bull, at whatever
temperature current circumstances dictate. On the opposite
side is the ideal of ruling over the most extensive realm: "I set
out to secure and expand my existence by calculation,
foresight, and prudence."[159] In the extreme, this implies sovereignty over things and men: "I silence my fears of existence
by making sure of my power to dispose; I satisfy my pride in
existence by feeling the effects of my power."[160] The attempt
to determine the conditions of one's existence is limited by the
impermanence of property and the resistance of men to rule,
the very condition of plurality.

   To equate freedom with a stance in an objective situation is
"to reduce the existential roots to a state of dependence." The
independence of Existenz itself is limited by external situations
and by the "toughness of self-being," but as "the true historic
realization of self-being in communication it is unlimited."[161]

## Freedom and Nature

In these reflections, Jaspers built on Kant's insight that objective thinking makes freedom disappear. On the one hand, there
is an internal causal chain, or network; on the other hand,
there is such a chain, or network, in the world.

   The categories as principles (e.g., the causal necessity of all
   happening) have objective significance throughout the realm
   of possible experience. Apart from them I can have no objective knowledge. But my awareness that all objects of my
   knowledge are appearance is rooted in a limiting concept

which itself relates to no object—the thing in itself, the noumenon, the intelligible. And this thing that cannot be known is present in our freedom. . . .[162]

Thus Kant saved freedom from the phenomenal by a theory of two causalities: "freedom begins a chain of causality in the phenomenon, but in the sense that the phenomenon which results from former states through natural causality is produced from the intelligible by the causality of freedom."[163] The intelligible character is the cause of my actions as phenomena; it determines the will itself.

Ethical action *presupposes* freedom; "the presence of an ethical 'ought' teaches us that freedom does exist," but it cannot be proved.[164] Practical reason discloses the intelligible world through the ethical law, the categorical imperative, though freedom is transcendent for theoretical reason. The theory of two causalities is "a rationally simple solution, but at the cost of involving a second objective world."[165] Only the *intellectus archetypus* could conceive phenomenal necessity and intelligible freedom as one; but in action and through recognizing the ethical law, there is nonconceptual certainty of freedom for self-being.

For Kant, and for Jaspers, the very limit of theoretical reason, the inability to conceive the noumenal, is the key to man's freedom. In Jaspers's words:

> I must will because I do *not* know. The being which is inaccessible to knowledge can be revealed only to my volition. Not knowing is the root of having to will. . . . This is the passion of Existenz: that its not knowing is not an absolute agony because it wills in freedom. The thought of an inescapable unfreedom would plunge me into despair at the fact of not knowing. . . . The roots of freedom exclude it from the existence I explore; what rests on freedom is the being which I myself can be in existence.[166]

Man cannot know Being, and thus cannot know what plan or pattern the world may be following as emanated from Being, created by Being, or identical with Being; but this not-knowing is the root of having to will.

The problem that remains is that man does act into the world; there may be freedom with respect to actions as phenomena, but these actions take place in a world governed by causality, in a world whose course is unknown, a world which is other, alien. "What merely happens is not free. Each happening in what I comprehend as *nature* is determined by necessity. It is *caused,* and thus no longer random. Its existence is necessarily the way it is, due to something else."[167] Man, freed from Providence or Fate, seems all the more cast down by the sheer givenness of the world. Jaspers, instead of either reinstituting a kind of providence or taking a stance of revolt against this necessity, claimed that Existenz "as the true historic realization of self-being in communication . . . is unlimited" in its independence. Although freedom is based upon an absolute, it is relative in the world; "whatever freedom an individual has must be antithetical, must unfold in process and struggle, and thus must always be restricted."[168] But it is in the loving struggle, communication, that freedom is unlimited; man is most at home with other men, even in a world that is less than ever man's home both because of what men have done and because of what they are capable of doing.

## Between Two Necessities

Jaspers did not adopt the view that man is nature, identifying all being with the mode of natural necessity and affirming it as such (the view which underlies "naturalistic ethics"). Nor did he adopt the view that sets man heroically over against nature, claiming "reality is dubious in itself. . . . [It is] either indifferent, neither good nor bad, or [it is] radically corrupt in essence."[169] The latter view is held either in an attitude of endurance amidst absurdity or in an attitude of nausea toward existence. In either view, some part of the Kantian notion of freedom is sacrificed. But on the other hand, Jaspers saw that moral law (in the Kantian sense) also represents a form of necessity. "In existential freedom I see myself between two necessities, the irremovable resistance of reality, and the moral law, the rigid form of a rule."[170] To see how this tension is maintained, we will turn to Jaspers's concept of evil and its relation to Kant's "radical evil," and to Kant's moral law.

## Evil Will and Formalistic Ethics

Jaspers defined evil as the conscious will to exclude Existenz, as the free abdication of freedom, as a "nameless enmity" toward freedom itself. Evil is an "affirmative absolutizing of pure existence."

> The will does not choose between good and evil; it is its choice, rather, that makes it good or evil. The act of choosing either liberates it, as good will, or enchains it as ill will. . . . Good will is the way of freedom, the way that lets self-being soar in existence; ill will is my way to enchain myself in the confusion of self-being and existence.[171]

Evil is not substantial, there are not good and bad works. Evil comes to appear in the world as "hatred of any show of truth by possible Existenz, or unconditional historicity, of the mobility of being."[172] For Jaspers, the conscious and unlimited lying of totalitarian regimes, the suppression of individual initiative, the blocking of communication by censorship or curtailment of the right to assemble, the attempt to prevent men from distinguishing themselves, making independent decisions, taking risks—these are all manifestations of evil will.

For example, unity of wills becomes evil when the unity is coerced. The power which derives from joint action comes to rest in the hands of a few and is turned against those who originally produced it. The opposite is power resting with governments "instituted among men, deriving their just powers from the consent of the governed." Jaspers cited de Tocqueville's remarks about the leaders of the French Revolution: "true and respectful subjection to the will of the majority was as foreign to them as subjection to the will of God," and "never has anyone shown less trust in the wisdom of the community than did these men.''[173] Expressed dialectically:

> We may well say there is a deficiency in the spirit that does not become power, and a deficiency in the power that does not combine with the profundity of humanity; the spirit becomes impotent, the power evil.[174]

For the will knowingly to turn against itself, it must "shroud itself somewhere, by curbing its will to know, by breaking off communication."[175] (This implies an abandonment of the Socratic-Platonic idea that no man knowingly does evil—unless this not-knowing is interpreted as lack not of cognition but of inner action, "which makes evil evaporate.")[176] Jaspers considered the mutiny of empirical existence against possible Existenz to be initially a matter of impulse; evil is active accord with this impulse. The possibility of evil is opened if inner action becomes action "with instantaneous violence, upsetting my development and creating a hodgepodge of moods and ineffectual volitive impulses."[177] Evil comes about if this condition of random self-effectation is accepted. Or, to put the matter another way, the possibility of evil is present with lack of unconditionality: "I do not struggle any more, I do not make things clear any more. . . . Unknowingly, yet with a bad conscience I have only drowned out, I rotate endlessly in a circle of trivia."[178] Evil comes about if this condition is accepted. In these senses, evil is a possibility for every man: it is not something pathological or demonic but something made possible by any relaxation of the tension of communicative self-concern. Jaspers claimed that "pure unexistential existence is not evil but nugatory."[179] A man who has given up himself, given up any possibility, is not evil but like a nonbeing (as Jaspers said of the ataraxic man). "Only a dull, indifferently continuing life without questions and without despair makes every possibility trickle away."[180] A man whose life was sheer operative functioning in a made world would not be evil, but he might be the tool of an evil will, as armaments are.

These descriptions of indifference and nugatoriness are part of the existential elucidation in Jaspers's 1931 *Philosophy*. But even though he had long thought in this way about the existential conditions of evildoers, Jaspers was reluctant to accept the notion of his friend Hannah Arendt, set forth in her 1963 *Eichmann in Jerusalem*, that Adolf Eichmann was a banal, thoughtless man. Jaspers felt that something more than thoughtlessness must have moved this man, some brutality in his nature. But Arendt persuaded Jaspers—to the point where he planned to write a book about her *Eichmann in Jerusalem* to introduce her book in its German translation. The controversy that arose over Arendt's work warned Jaspers that many Germans had not accepted the lesson he took as fundamental: "The guilt was not Hitler's; it was that of the Germans who followed him."[181] Jaspers did not have the strength in the last years of his life to write his book about Arendt's work, but he did make this point about the Germans' responsibility again and again in *The Future of Germany*.

However, even though he found Arendt's notion of the banality of evil appropriate for Eichmann, Jaspers retained the notion that hers was intended to question—that is, Kant's "radical evil." By this notion, Jaspers meant no Gnostic doctrine of innate evil or inborn malicious reason, for he, like Kant, did not think of men as devils. Following Kant, Jaspers held that:

> The question is in what sense we subordinate our sensual motivations [impulses] to our moral ones. Which of the two mainsprings will qualify the other? . . . This is the evil: that in fitting the mainsprings into his will he reverses the qualifying relationship. "He makes the mainspring of self-love and its leanings a condition for complying with the moral law, whereas the latter, as the supreme condition for satisfying the former, should be fitted as sole mainspring into the general maxim of the arbitrary will."[182]

The will which reigns in impulses—the will to happiness—must be subordinated to an ethical principle like the categorical imperative. If it is not, radical evil ensues.

Jaspers accepted the Kantian notion of radical evil, but he viewed the categorical imperative, the moral law, not as a law but as a guideline. That is, he criricized Kant's "formalistic ethics" insofar as it divorces the principles of actions from the consequences of action.[183] "Ethical action cannot be considered separately from our material life in the world. Every concrete act has its consequences. The categorical imperative does not derive its unconditional validity from experience but can fulfill it only by experience. The law can only be applied in view of the world. The consequences are part of the material world in which the categorical imperative helps men to find their way."[184] Commandments and prohibitions represent a necessity like natural necessity, and it is between the two types of necessity that existential freedom is for men.[185]

A case in point is the commandment "thou shalt not lie." Kant maintained that it is impermissible to lie under any circumstances. Jaspers agreed that as a general law, "thou shalt not lie" is inescapable; there is no justifying a lie. "The only question is whether there can be existential action whose truth is *not* comprehensible on grounds of a general law, action whose essence cannot be stated, therefore, and which sets no example."[186] In a circumstance in which "a man's unspoken, half-conscious attitude toward me is *homo homini lupus,* I am lost with him as with an animal unless I protect myself and prepare to do battle."[187] This situation is different in principle from one in which a man "meets me as possible Existenz . . . he as himself approaches me as myself,"[188] that is, from communication. When a precept like "thou shalt not lie" is laid down, it is "not purely ethical any more"; it is like a legal tenet, without connection to "freely transforming subjectivity."[189]

Jaspers opposed to the objective universal the exception: "the essence of an exception is that we find no reasons for it; it is precisely on its objective side that an exception is not only uncertain but absolutely dubious because it runs counter to objectivity. The exception must take a chance. It involves both the experience of self-being as truth and the experience of guilt, of the objectively unjustifiable."[190] The opposition of the universal and the exception was first formulated by Kierkegaard (though the protest of Schelling against all universals lies behind it). Kierkegaard "loved the universal, the human in men, but as something other, denied to him. Nietzsche [also] knew himself to be an exception, and spoke 'in favor of the exception, so long as it never becomes the rule. . . .' Nietzsche turned away those who would follow him: 'Follow not me, but you!'"[191] Jaspers did not call for the exceptional as such; but rather for room for the exception in ethics and action, for recognition that generally valid laws are, in certain circumstances, an obstacle to Existenz. "A deeper ought may turn against one that has solidified into a general formula."[192]

"Laws may be broken with the positivity of Existenz to be; but in most cases they will be broken by those lost in negativity."[193] Objectively, either kind of lawbreaking appears as evil self-will. But only negative lawbreaking is "blind submission"—not to the law, but to the temptation to break it. Breaking the law cannot be justified in either case; but in unconditional action

> . . . it is communication that must take the place of vindication. Unconditional acts grow lucid in the communication that transcends all mere community of interests and all deceptive kinship of character, in the communication that allows men to be unreservedly truthful in searching their historicity for the current law as the phenomenon of the ever-obscure law at large.[194]

This brings us back to the proposition that the independence of Existenz is "as the true historic realization of self-being in communication . . . , unlimited."

Jaspers added to the Kantian ethics of principle (*Gesinnungsethik*) an ethics of responsibility (*Verantwortungsethik*), following Max Weber. However, the two are by no means exclusive:

> It is an infinitely affecting experience when a mature person—no matter whether young or old in years—senses

[his] responsibility for the consequences really and with his entire being and, acting from ethical responsibility, says at a given point: 'Here I stand, I can do not other'. . . . Any one of us who is not inwardly dead may someday find himself in this position. In this sense the ethics of principle and the ethics of responsibility are not absolute opposites, but complementary; together they make the real man.[195]

As Jaspers appealed to statesmen not just for the Solonic authority of legality but also for authority of faith, that is, an existential as well as an objective authority, so he appealed to all people not just for formalistic ethics but ethics of responsibility. In both cases, it is exceptional, or boundary, situations which mark the inadequacy of laws or moral maxims. No institutionalization—legal, political, or moral—can withstand a protracted conflict or crisis of faith in the individuals who have produced it.

There are two sides to any political structure: on the one hand the institutions and laws, and on the other the way they actually work, owing to the human intentions behind them or to conflicting purposes for which the institutions are misused.[196]

In Jaspers's terms, the large-scale and institutional equivalent of Kantian radical evil is the inversion of the proper relation of society and state.

## 5. SOCIETY AND THE STATE

### Life Order and Political Order

In his 1931 *Philosophy,* Jaspers wrote:

Existence in time is the structure of human society. Our concern with temporal existence makes us want things to endure. It makes us seek the order that will assure our existence and expand our living space and our opportunities for life. In all concerns with existence, no matter what the form of the safeguards and opportunities, the liberties and compulsions, the state will be the sovereign and final authority; the condensed power of society that makes it possible to take decisive action regarding the whole. What men want in the state is to use power to realize institutions they consider lasting and just, as the foundations of a future humanity. The state is the objectivity that lets me participate in the real fate of mankind. . . .[197]

Society's concern for existence, for self-maintenance, is, in the modern age, bound to the order for supply of mass needs "by rationalized production with the aid of technical advances."[198] The state is of a deeper and more lasting importance.

In terms of Jaspers's schema of "the modes of encompassing that we are," society is structured existence in time, the objectivity of Dasein. At the boundaries of this structure are "state, mind (Geist), and humanity itself—as the origins which do not enter into any life-order, although they are essential to making this order possible."[199] The state is "the supreme authority for decisions in life" which, if it becomes subservient to the mass order, "has lost all relationship to true destiny."[200] The state "has its weight as the crystallizing core of volition";[201] it is the "condensed power" of society, the "unity of wills" in objective form.

There is a basic tension between the life order for the supply of necessities and "decision that is based on power"[202] and that concerns "the historical concreteness of life in the whole,"[203] between society and state. The state makes the life order possible by letting it function without consuming the space for human thought and action, letting it sustain life without eliminating what makes life worth living.

For the state-will,[204] the life-order is not merely the object of rational planning on behalf of all human beings, for [as such] it becomes the object of exclusive decisions through encroachment upon its powers. The state-will does indeed incorporate the idea of promoting the general welfare by means of the economic order, but over and above this, it is directed toward man himself.[205]

The state must control the life order. But more importantly, the state "is directed toward man himself"; its fundamental purpose is the "highest possible development of man"; its ultimate goal is "to promote the higher development of mankind."[206]

Jaspers's 1931 distinction of society and state may become clear by contrast with Wilhelm von Humboldt's reflections during the French Revolution (*Ideen zu einem Versuch die Grenzen der Wirksamkeit des Staats zu bestimmen*, 1792). Von Humboldt suggested that

> there is one vast difference between ancient and modern governments. The ancients sought to develop the energy . . . of men as men; the moderns are concerned with their welfare, their property and their ability to earn a living. The ancients sought virtue; the moderns seek happiness. . . . the ancients sought for happiness in virtue; we moderns have sought all along to develop virtue out of happiness. . . .[207]

Von Humboldt also acknowledged that the ancients maintained their independence in the state from the life order by the institution of slavery: "their philanthropic philosophers . . . approved of slavery, while at the same time recognizing it as an unjust and barbaric means for assuring to one part of humanity, by sacrificing another, the highest degree of power and beauty."[208] Von Humboldt called for government to "abstain from all solicitude for the positive welfare of its citizens, and . . . not to proceed a step further than is absolutely necessary for its internal and external security; let it limit the freedom of its citizens for no other purpose whatsoever. . . ."[209] That is, von Humboldt located freedom in the private realm and advocated a classical laissez-faire doctrine of the state—one that J. S. Mill adopted and developed.[210]

The crux of such a position is that the maximum development of individuals requires freedom from government: "The more a man acts on his own, the more he develops himself." This is clearly different from Jaspers's idea that the state aims at promoting the development of mankind, that such development requires the possibility of participation in the state, joint action. Von Humboldt bases his principles for limiting the state on the conditions of monarchy:

> It is not uncommon to appeal to the history of Greece and Rome . . . , [but] those states were essentially republics; such institutions . . . as we find in them were pillars of the free constitution, and were regarded by the citizens with an enthusiasm which made their harmful restrictions on private freedom less deeply felt, and their active character less pernicious. They enjoyed, moreover, a much wider range of freedom than ourselves, and anything that was sacrificed was sacrificed only to another form of activity: participation in the affairs of government. Now in our states, which are in general monarchical, all this is utterly different; and whatever moral means the ancients might employ such as national education, religion, moral laws, would with us be less fruitful, and productive of far greater harm.[211]

Von Humboldt held that the freest development of human nature would be directed as little as possible to citizenship. Thus not so much energy should be sacrificed to the state and the role of citizen, "since the State is regarded merely as a means."[212] The great fear of von Humboldt (and Mill) was such one-sidedness, *Einseitigkeit.*

This concept of freedom is merely negative, as Jaspers pointed out in *The Origin and Goal of History* (1949):

> *Legally,* scope is left to the individual for the play of his arbitrary will (negative liberty), through which he also can shut himself off from others. *Ethically,* however, liberty consists precisely in the openness of life in being together that can unfold without compulsion, out of love and reason (positive liberty).
>
> Only when positive liberty has been realized on the basis of the legal safeguarding of negative liberty, does the proposition apply: Man is free in the measure in which he sees freedom around him, that is, in the measure in which all men are free.

The individual has a dual claim: That he shall be protected against force, and that his judgment and his will shall have the opportunity to make themselves felt. Protection is guaranteed by the *constitutional State,* expression of his judgment and his will is made possible by *democracy.*[213]

The state provides internal and external security; but an individual is not free, and his development is not possible, without the space to express judgment and will. "To the inviolability of the rights of the individual personality is added the right to participate in the life of the whole."[214] There is, to use von Humboldt's terms, happiness in virtue, in enthusiasm for the institutions which provide for participation in human affairs.

## Planning and Regulating

Jaspers differed from von Humboldt not only in advocating a republic rather than a monarchy but also in conceiving of human development and politics as related rather than distinct. On the other hand, they shared the distinction of society and state and the idea that the state must be limited in its involvement with economic interests.[215] The main shift in Jaspers's position—the direct result of his experiences under Nazi rule—was his abandonment of the notion that the state is the "supreme authority for decisions in life." This shift forced him to elaborate his distinction between society and state in the light of postwar conditions.

Today, the life order requires planning. The state can either confine itself to the "ordering of free initiative by means of laws," or it can itself embark upon "undertakings that bear a monopoly character *apriori.*" "In the latter case, the limit is reached when the state, in principle, assumes control of everything in total planning."[216] There is either a free market economy or a totally planned economy. Total planning presupposes total knowledge, the possibility of which Jaspers denied in every sphere.

No one can oversee the entanglement of economic realities. Our knowledge never extends beyond simplifying aspects.

We are already living in an unintentionally created world. If we pursue within it our finite purposes, on the basis of our finite knowledge, we bring about with these purposes results that we cannot see. No will can create this world in its entirety, no cognition can know it. Just as we cultivate organic life but destroy it by total intervention without being able to reconstitute it, so we do the same to the world of historical existence created by man.[217]

The whole is always beyond our grasp, and every action within it modifies it, producing unintended, unforeseen consequences. Planning is, under certain conditions, possible in the realm of the mechanical, the technological, but there are always limits.

The state's assumption of control in total planning is marked by the rise of a bureaucracy; total planning rests "upon the uncontrolled arbitrariness of bureaucracy and those to whom authority is delegated, and can be altered at will. . . . It is not the origin [in an electoral procedure] but the limitation of government power that preserves it from complete arbitrariness."[218] The rise of a bureaucracy marks the decline of the state as a "unity of wills." It marks the beginning of the exclusion of worthy leaders from government. It marks the beginning of a one-sidedness more dangerous than that envisioned by von Humboldt and of a disrespect for truth and reason.

The thinking of total planning begins with reason, with the aim of elevating it to absolute sovereignty; but it ends by annihilating reason. For it has not grasped the process upon which the growth of reason is dependent: the interplay of individuals with various knowledge and various opinions.[219]

In short, total planning "has to destroy everything that threatens it: truth, i.e., free science and the free world of the writer—just legal verdicts, i.e., the independent judiciary— public discussion, i.e., the freedom of the press."[220]

The absorption of the state into the social sphere is accompanied by the withering away of the other original modes that stand at the border of the life order: mind, culture, and man's humanity. "Just as the State as man's ally may be paralysed, so also can the mind be paralysed, when it ceases to function sincerely in virtue of its own origin and is falsified through subservience to the masses and by working in subordination to the finite purposes of these."[221] Man's humanity, which is "not, properly speaking, real, but exists only under certain conditions,"[222] disappears under rule by force, under conditions of meaningless warfare.

## Total Planning and Violence

In 1931, Jaspers wrote:

> Today war seems to have undergone a change of meaning, in so far as it is not a war of religion but a war of interests, not a war of conflicting cultures or civilizations but a war of national areas, not a war of human beings but a technical struggle of machines one against another and all against the noncombatant population. It no longer appears as if in war human nobility were fighting on behalf of its future. . . . An unconditional venture of one's life is only possible when a true human existence is at stake, that is to say on behalf of a genuinely historical destiny, and not where the matter concerns nothing more than the interests of national areas and economic corporations.[223]

Total planning grew out of the situation after World War I. After the Second World War, there was an intensified situation "of disaster, in which the work process and the whole enterprise were in danger."[224] In this latter situation wartime planning and modes of production became firmly established:

> In the want attendant upon war . . . total planning is clearly the only means of providing and distributing the necessities of life so that the shortage falls equitably upon all and everyone receives a small but equal share. What is in this case done meaningfully and for limited purposes under abnormal conditions, is transferred into the totality of the economy, work, production and supply and above and beyond this into the whole existence of man.[225]

In a situation in which war has become meaningless, we live with a war-oriented, war-based life order. War is no longer viewed as a last resort after political means fail; politics is viewed, on the contrary, as a last resort after war has failed, as the prosecution of war by other means, as "cold war."

Violence, in its potential for physical and spiritual destruction, is a boundary situation for men. It is the ultimate obstacle to the establishment, consolidation, and preservation of freedom, the very point of politics. Force may bring about a new situation, open a space, but it cannot bring about "unity of wills": "unity by force does not avail; in adversity it fades as an illusion." [226] Force founds nothing. The space opened by force cannot long be maintained by force. Force is the opposite of communication, alien to the contention of minds, destructive of humanity in every sense. Force demands "cunning, deception, surprise." "Where force rules there is fear, silence, concealment, coercion, unrest . . . . in the state based on force there is universal mistrust."[227]

Force is, like the life order itself, a means. If the instruments for supplying material necessities and the instruments of violence control the political realm, there can be no freedom. "Man seems to be undergoing absorption into that which is nothing more than a means to an end, into that which is devoid of purpose and significance."[228] In our times, Jaspers saw two alternatives for the absorption process to come to completion: totalitarian domination or the atom bomb.

The only possible means to eliminate force or restrict it to local police activities is the establishment of a world order of states which have renounced absolute sovereignty for the common weal: "where sovereignty remains which is not that of mankind as a whole, there also remains a source of unfreedom. . . ."[229] This was Jaspers's postwar cosmopolitan vision; it embraces and extends his 1931 view:

A new world order cannot arise out of the crisis [of our time] through the work of the rational life-order as such. What is needful is that the human being shall achieve something more than he brings to pass in the life-order, shall achieve it by way of the state as expressive of the will towards the whole, but the state to which the life-order has become nothing but a means—and also through mental creation, whereby he grows aware of his own being.[230]

## 6. FREEDOM AND THE AUTHORITY OF THE STATE

### Types of Authority

Jaspers distinguished four types of authority: the manufactured authority of the organization of technological labor, or societal authority; the authority of legality; the authority of faith; and the authority of reason.[231] These types correspond to the "modes of the encompassing which we are": Dasein, Bewusstsein überhaupt, Geist, Existenz. "One man alone cannot live. But if men live together there is always some cohesive authority which the individual heeds without feeling unfree. There are standards, acknowledged in fact without being clearly thought out. A feeling of substance, a common ground, establishes affinity and an order of existence."[232] Among the Romans, this authority at large was manifest in the private sphere (in the person of *pater familias* or *matrona*) and in the political sphere (in the institution of the Roman senate), and in "religious acts, cults, and concepts adopted and formed, each in its historic way, by churches."

> Both the word and the concept of authority come from Roman thinking. The *auctor* is he who originates, fosters, augments; *auctoritas* is [that] which brings forth, aids, intensifies. Each term has a double meaning. It is not only to "bring forth" but to "keep in being," not only to "be active" but to "prevail," not only to "lend support" but to "pose a challenge."[233]

Authority refers to a common ground, to the ground laid in the beginning; it is, for those who live by it, the present manifestation of the historic past, "guidance from the depths of his-

tory."[234] Authority also refers to transcedence, to the divine,
however this is conceived. These two factors—the reference
to beginnings and the reference to transcendence—"make me
conscious of an order into which I fit. An *unpurposive shel-*
*teredness* preceding any act lies at the bottom of authority; it is
followed only later by the guidance for whatever I do in the
world, by the direction of my purposes, *which can never be*
*ends in themselves.*"[235]

It is just this sense of an order into which I fit that has disappeared in the modern world; the loss distinguishes the present
situation.

> It was the age of technology, and this alone, which breached
> the world of authority. Not since the beginning of humanity
> in the "Promethean age" can we image so incisive a
> breach as the one we are involved in. Round about us, as all
> around the globe, remnants of the old authoritarian worlds
> still stand, strong but steadily weakening and of small mo-
> ment in the course of events. . . .[236]

Both of the factors which "make me conscious of an order into
which I fit"—immemorial history and the divine presence—are
missing in what Jaspers called "the authority of our time . . . ,
the organization of technological labor." In the *Apparat* for the
supply of mass needs there is no "unpurposive sheltered-
ness."

> The world of technological labor knows nothing but the obli-
> gation to perform. Fulfilling the norm is both living condition
> and honor—if this word still has meaning. It is limited to the
> realm of work and to the living conditions that promote
> work. It fragments the entirety of life into disciplined work-
> ing hours and more or less bewildered leisure hours gov-
> erned, in analogy to the joint authority of the past, by a living
> practice of wishing to act, to talk, to live, to show and ex-
> press oneself like everybody else. . . .[237]

This is not an authority which the individual heeds without
feeling unfree. The activities in which men have felt their free-

dom, acting, talking, showing themselves, are transformed into activities in which men sacrifice their freedom to a deadening conformity.

Jaspers did not try to replace lost traditions and lost beliefs: "the reconstitution of authority lost is a process as artificial as the erection of stage props."[238] He tried to find ways to make the past accessible without the tradition that has heretofore made it accessible, ways permitting faith to reach out to the divine presence without the institutions and particular beliefs that have heretofore been said to represent it. Jaspers's development of the idea of the Axial Period of human history is the opening of a new access to the past. Or rather, it is a formulation of what might be called a tradition of access.

> In each new upward flight mankind returns in recollection to this period, and is fired anew by it. Ever since then it has been the case that recollections and reawakenings of the potentialities of the Axial Period—renaissances—afford a spiritual impetus. Return to this beginning is the ever-recurrent event in China, India, and the West.[239]

Each return, each recollection, gives impetus to a rebirth. The rebirth is not a repetition of the past as handed down, but an adoption, an assimilation: "the function of assimilation is to enable me, by keeping my gaze fixed upon past altitudes, to find my way to the summit of a reality that is possible of achievement today."[240] In conjunction with this access to the past, Jaspers elucidated an access to the divine presence independent of religious institutions, particularly of the Christian church.

> There are authorities, binding powers, without faith in revelation. From those, the claim staked out by ecclesiastic authority differs in principle. The revelation administered by the Church is not an authority like others, one added to others—it is the only authority. . . . The Church claims divine authority as interpreted by itself.[241]

The church's claim has been advanced by excommunication, inquisition, war, and persecution, as well as by preaching, teaching, and persuasion. None of these methods characterizes authority freely obeyed and unfixed in form. An institution claiming to be the sole vehicle of truth is claiming uncommunicatively that the deity speaks unequivocally: "yet where communication is broken off, the end result is force and war."[242] "There is no talking to religious warriors," as Max Weber said. For Jaspers, access to transcendence is of a different sort: "it is philosophical consciousness of transcendent reality opposing the material reality of transcendence."[243] It is consciousness of the hidden God (in Kierkegaard's phrase) through ciphers, not of the revealed God. It is philosophical faith, and cipher-reading, not faith in revelation, prophecy, expounding Scripture, or apostolic witness.

Historically we may view Jaspers's rethinking of our ways of access to the past and to transcendence as an adoption of the Roman concept of foundation and the Platonic-Christian concept of transcendent guidance. Rather than the act of founding Rome, eternal Rome, by heroes (founding fathers) to whom all subsequent generations were tied, there is the founding of makind's spiritual being in the Axial Period. Rather than a realm of ideas or of revealed standards and laws or commandments—requiring the interpretative wisdom of philosopher-kings or priests—there is existential communication among men of philosophical faith.[244]

## The Authorities of Legality and Faith

Both the authority of technological labor and the authority of the church, in their different ways, threaten (or threatened) total control by determining the state. (Hence the many variations on the two-sword theory, in which the pope retained the spiritual sword and relinquished the material sword to the king, who was to wield it *ad nutum*, at the pope's bidding.)[245] But the Apparat for the supply of mass needs threatens to absorb the state. In both cases, however, there is no political authority per se.

In our times, political authority is primarily a problem of the relation of society and state—not of church and state. But the relation of politics and faith is still critical:

> The characteristic political requirement of our time—a requirement of which we have been made aware by totalitarianism—seems to me to be the separation of politics from faith.[246]

But Jaspers did not mean by this that politics should henceforth have nothing to do with faith; on the contrary, he wished to distinguish faith from both needs and ideologies. "The separation of politics and faith can itself be achieved only by faith—by that relation to Transcendence which is inherent in every historic religion and makes all of them allies on the field of existence against radical nihilism.[247] He meant that authority and freedom can be saved for our time only if different faiths and ways of life are left free to compete communicatively.[248] That is, if there is authority in the political realm to guarantee freedom for ways of life and faiths, then these can permeate the political realm in all their diversity. Such a guarantee is completely lacking in a totalitarian regime. Authority and freedom can be saved for our time only if the authority of legality maintains an order which allows men of different faiths to live together:

> The legality of existential order is a greatly reduced authority, insufficient for life as a whole. Yet it is authority. For once we tie ourselves to legal methods, we assume a basic attitude of trust, of bowing even though we may oppose. . . .[249]

The authority of legality is of smaller scope than the authority of faith; but if the authority of legality is established, the scope of faith, in communication, is unlimited.

> Rational politics deals with questions of existence, not of faith. It does not want to link the two, for the philosophical faith that unfolds in the movement of reason is not faith in

the sense of a creed; rather, it means liberation of whatever does not claim totality by force. Questions of existence, having to do with material interests, are always open to negotiation, to compromise, to agreement. Only the faith that claims totality and the will to power that is not satisfied short of world rule make a joint settlement of existence questions, a politics of particular "interests," impossible.[250]

What is made impossible under total rule is not just a politics of particular "interests," a politics for the regulation of the apparatus for the supply of mass needs, but political activity as such—that is, acting, talking, appearing in public, distinguishing oneself, electing leaders, sharing power.

The assumption that men cannot bear freedom or find truth by themselves—the assumption of Dostoyevsky's Grand Inquisitor—justifies "liberating" men from freedom, from doubt, from thought. Only when this liberation is accomplished will men be happy. The liberators themselves rule in the name of God or of necessity—natural or historic—with self-denying, and ultimately faithless, concern. They set themselves up as the earthly authority. But "the demand that a rule in the world be obeyed as the rule of God, or of history, is not made by God or by history. It is made by men."[251]

If neither God nor history is to be appealed to as the root of authority, then one might turn to the sovereign will of the people. But Jaspers, in elucidating the idea of democracy, warned against this: "democracy is not the fiction of the sovereign people as a personal ruler—an authority whose supreme wisdom is charged with the sole responsibility by all individuals, who then feel free of responsibility themselves. Democracy is every individual."[252] The "deified sovereign people that no one wants to be"[253] is as easily a source of unfreedom as the deity which no one is but which someone must represent or as the course of events which no one can alter but which requires a vanguard or a group of midwives to deliver it of freedom. As the fiction of a general will—revealed through another fiction, that of public opinion—absolves the individual of responsibility and disguises the multiple relations involved in plural political action, so the fiction of a general interest disguises or denies the interplay of particular interests. There is no social or political person with a voice and an interest except in the minds of those who would like to have it so.

> The democratic idea . . . knows no reigning and governing sovereign, but it knows a will that must constantly evolve anew in a process of self-education, in institutions which, for all their firmness and despite all checks and safeguards, remain modifiable. It requires solidarity of the most diverse members of the rationally oriented and directed community. . . . The way of the democratic idea is an incessant common struggle for truth. Everything is subject to unlimited public debate. . . . Complying loyally with what in given situations are common decisions, the minority in turn enjoys the protection of the laws and of a solidarity founded upon the common democratic idea. . . .[254]

## Authority and Power

The authority of legality is distinct from both the authority of faith and the "manufactured" authority of the Apparat. It appeals neither to God nor to history, yet it is permeated by the faith of a rational community that feels its ties with the foundational or axial period of human history and with transcendence. But politics takes its bearings from power, from the "unity of wills." What then is the relation of the authority of legality to power?

> The union of authority and power is the vital problem of nations. They derive their rank from the content of authority, their permanence from power. . . . If authority and power part company, both will be lost.[255]

A case in point is the history of the "rights of man." The rights of man have been proclaimed since the eighteenth century without ever having been adopted by a state power or by a federation of states and having thereby been given historical reality. Burke's assessment has proved correct: "each individual can rely only on the rights he possesses by virtue of his nationality—in other words, by virtue of a power that commands force." "The law is morally based, but real owing to force."[256] And yet:

> Today the unity of mankind is an idea imposed upon us by reality itself. It can be wrought only by unanimity about the rights of man. . . . They antedate the rationality which puts them into words but does not invent them. They face man with a challenge of encompassing authority. . . .[257]

The authority of legality in its most encompassing form should be embodied in the rights of man. When historical ties are broken, when there are masses of uprooted men unprotected by rights possessed by virtue of nationality, stateless, this is particularly urgent. Jaspers had learned this urgency painfully:

> The basic experience [of the years 1933–45] was the loss of legal guarantees in our own country. . . . How I longed for an authority above nations, a law above all states, capable of giving legal aid to an individual abused and rendered without rights by his state.[258]

And a case in point of the misalliance of authority and power is the United Nations. The member states endow the United Nations "with authority for their political manipulations, but it has no genuine authority."[259] The United Nations has no executive power; all the members retain their sovereignty; and in the Security Council the five permanent members have the power of veto:

> Politics is, on the one hand, to become a legal process that eliminates force from its arsenal; on the other hand, it cannot become such a process, since sovereignty and the veto stand in the way.[260]

On the "great politics" scale, Jaspers envisioned the rights of man as the authority of legality for a federation of states. Such a federation is to be clearly distinguished from world government with control of all force. "Whatever combines all force in one hand will soon crush freedom. Political freedom can be preserved only by the separation of powers, by the system of checks and balances that has been conceived and variously realized in modified form ever since Antiquity."[261]

But this possibility on the largest scale presupposes the existence of separation of powers, checks and balances, on the smallest scale:

> . . . free and responsible local government is indispensable to the genesis of a democratic ethos. Only that which is practiced on such a scale in their immediate surroundings at every moment of their lives is capable of rendering men sufficiently mature for the tasks which they must realize on an increasingly large and finally vast scale.[262]

The democratic ethos is an ethos of community life "that has come to be regarded as axiomatic: the feeling for forms and laws, natural modes of human intercourse, consideration and readiness to help, constant respect for the rights of others, unfailing readiness to compromise in matters of mere existence, no oppression of minorities."[263]

On both a world scale and a local scale, the authority of legality depends upon an independent judiciary. A court must be connected to a power with means to enforce its decisions—as the International Court of Justice is not. The relation of the suprapolitical element, reason, to the political realm is embodied in the relation of the judiciary or constitutional tribunal to the executive and the legislative branches of government: "a 'politicized' judiciary is not only destructive of the suprapolitical element but ruinous of politics as well."[264] The people participate in the executive and legislative branches by periodically electing representatives and executives; they participate in the judiciary by bringing matters before it and by serving on juries. The judiciary is the embodiment in the political realm of the principle that "all control and correct each other," which enhances each man's reason. Judge and jury must be able to assess the facts of a matter, to empathize—to look at the matter from many points of view—and (in Jaspers's terms) to read the cipher "man," for which the rights of man are a guide, as a reflection in the political realm of the concepts of Existenz.

# THREE
# THE FREEDOM OF PHILOSOPHY

## 1. PHENOMENA, EXISTENTIAL SIGNS, CIPHERS

### The Two-World Theory and Nietzsche's Critique

Nietzsche offered the following history, "How the 'True World' Ultimately Became a Fable," in his *Götzendämmerung*:

> 1. The true world, attainable to the sage, the pious man and the man of virtue,—he lives in it, *he is it.* . . .
> 2. The true world which is unattainable for the moment is promised to the sage, to the pious man and to the man of virtue ("to the sinner who repents"). . . .
> 3. The true world is unattainable; it cannot be proved, it cannot promise anything; but even as a thought, alone, it is a comfort, an obligation, a command. . . .
> 4. The true world—is it attainable? At all events, it is unattained. And as unattained it is also *unknown.* Consequently it no longer comforts, nor saves, nor constrains; what could something unknown constrain us to? . . .
> 5. The "true world"—an idea that no longer serves any purpose, that no longer constrains one to anything,—a useless idea that has become quite superfluous, consequently, an exploded idea: let us abolish it! . . .
> 6. We have suppressed the true world: what world survives? the apparent world perhaps? . . . Certainly not! In abolishing the true world we have also abolished the world of appearance! . . .[1]

Nietzsche thought of himself as the exploder and the man able to illuminate the aftermath of the explosion, "the end of

98

the longest error; mankind's zenith; Incipit Zarathustra.''[2] He repudiated the distinction of the true world and the apparent world as an "exegetical principle." But then he later offered a "new exegesis" of the will to power, a transvaluation of all values. Becoming, life, nature, formerly the world of appearances, became the true world in the new exegesis.

Jaspers's comment on Nietzsche's explosion of the two-world theory will provide us with an introduction to his own attitude about the theory as well as to his adoptive metaphysics.

In criticizing the two-world theory, Nietzsche only dealt with its formulation as a crude rationalistic dualism that does indeed end in an empty beyond or in nothingness. In thinking in this fashion, he had to dispense with all those ways of using the categories "reality and appearance," "truth and illusion," "being and existence," which permit them—apart from any assumption about the world outside of the present one—to express such existential tenets as the transparency of things and the cipher-nature (*Chiffresein*) of the world. During these periods of his thinking, he took no cognizance of all those interpretations of world-being, gained in meditative probing, in which (in accordance with his own demands) no concession is made to what does not show itself to be present here and now and which yet avoid a narrowing of world-being to particular categories or to that which can be grasped in determinate knowledge: in them, no "other world" reflects a deceptive dream, and their relation to transcendence (God) supports, within this world, the self-being of those who entertain them in their thoughts.[3]

Jaspers's own threefold distinction of phenomena, existential signs, and ciphers is the basis for an approach to the two-world problem that meets Nietzsche's demands and also Nietzsche's dilemma: given our perspectival worldliness, how shall we make sense of things after the conceptual explosion without somehow reverting to the two-world framework (for example, by turning it upside-down)?

## The World and the World as Phenomenal

Jaspers spoke of a "cognitive object" as detached from subjective existence. But as we have seen, there is a limit to this detachment. The world of objective reality, the world without an I, "remains accessible only as it can be visualized, experienced and conceived by a really, and thus specifically, existing I."[4] The word "world" has two inseparable meanings: the world is "the entirety of everything else," objective reality; and the world is my world, my subjective existence in the world, in what is not-I.[5] When we think beyond our immediate subjective worlds to an objective, general world and become aware anew of ourselves in our situations, of our irreplaceable and singular worlds as "measured . . . by the objective world at large,"[6] a new possibility arises from another source: "I become certain that the entirety of my existence rests upon Existenz as my proper being."[7] Existence is the objectivity of possible Existenz.

> Yet it is precisely then, when this entirety of existence has been existentially pervaded, that it will not be sufficient unto itself. It is then that I come to understand my phenomenality and begin to look toward a transcendence which never becomes mundane, whose every mundanization will obliterate it as mundanity—a transcendence that has no existence on its own but lends a cipher character to all things of the world.[3]

The factual encounter of the empirical subject Dasein with its environment leads to the subject's world orientation as consciousness at large and then to the subject's renewed self-awareness, the subject's awareness of being-in-situations, of its particularity in the light of generally valid truths of world orientation. These back-and-forth movements provide the momentum for a leap beyond existence analysis to existential elucidation.

At this point the two meanings of "world" give way to another: the world, in its twofold existence, is set against the world-as-appearance. "Either the world remains worldly, as a blind and opaque existence, or it becomes phenomenal, as the place where an Existenz related to transcendence chooses whether to be or not to be. Its ambiguity lies in the fact that it can always be both."[9]

Jaspers has not, in this thinking operation, revised the two-world theory. There is objective cognition, and there is existential reflection on objectivity; the one world's ambiguity is that Dasein and Symbolsein are like two dimensions of it.[10] Jaspers accepted Kant's distinction of two kinds of being, that of the phenomenon and that of thing-in-itself, but "we may disclaim the phrasing insofar as it implies an objectification into two worlds—for there is only one world of objects. . . ."[11] Jaspers spoke not of two worlds but of two experiences: transcending and not-transcending. "Man does not only exist; he can transcend, or he can refrain from transcending."[12] Even for the man who does not transcend, transcending is a possibility. Jaspers spoke of objectivity and metaphysical objectivity (cipher): they differ only in the mode of experiencing.

In the fourth, post-Kantian, stage of Nietzsche's "history of an error," it is suggested that what is unknown cannot constrain us: "what could something unknown constrain us to?" Jaspers turned this question around by asking, in effect: what can not-knowing constrain us for? Not-knowing constrains us for openness, both in existence and in the mind.[13] "A thought which, quarter'd, hath but one part wisdom" has, as Hamlet knew well, "ever three parts coward" for the truth-seeking man. In Jaspers's terms, resolution in action comes from a source other than knowing, a source past quartering, past speaking. This notion is as old as the word "philo-sophy," which means love of wisdom, not wisdom. What cannot be cognitively possessed draws us, gives us no rest. For example:

It can indeed only be shown, not proven, that the world is not self-sustaining but perishing in time. This aspect will be as self-evident and ever-present to one man as the statement will seem senseless to another—too senseless for him to know what to make of the words, he will say. The source of transcending is an otherwise irremediable disquiet about the permanence of all existence.[14]

Man is aware of his own being in time (*Zeitdasein*), his own situatedness and finitude, and he comes to realize that he does not know about the world's being in time (the former is an awareness of the empirical subject, the latter of the subject as consciousness at large and Geist). This is the beginning of Jaspers's reconsideration of the Kantian insight that time is the phenomenal form under which a timeless reality appears to the subject which is of this world but also "in itself." Time is, for Jaspers, the phenomenality of Existenz.[15]

To explore Jaspers's distinction of "phenomena of reality" and "existential signs" (the "concepts of Existenz") in terms of the distinction of objective time and existential time, we must first see what characteristics Jaspers attributed to objectivity.

## Characteristics of Objectivity

We may isolate three general characteristics of objectivity, which Jaspers discussed in Kantian terms: otherness, unity, and form.[16]

The object is, first of all, *other,* not-I, either as the "alien being of matter" or the "kindred being of another I." [17] Consciousness is intentional: "What is not I may be without me, but for me its being is *as I make it appear to myself.*" [18] (As we shall see below, Jaspers also spoke of "metaphysical intentionality" vis-à-vis metaphysical objects, ciphers.)

The object is a unity. Jaspers, following Kant, speaks of unity as subjectivity conferred; the subjective unity is categorical and transcendental. The unity of the categories themselves (including the category "unity") rests on the "transcendental unity of apperception." But to this ground objective thinking cannot take us; the origin is a mystery. Furthermore, "the mystery of the origin recurs in a new form when [Kant] speaks of the imagination which mediates between the understanding and sensibility and makes the former applicable to the latter." [19]

The mystery of imagination is of particular importance to Jaspers because he held that imagination (not the random one of consciousness, but an imagination "playing with the existential roots") "emerges as the organ that lets Existenz make sure of being."[20] This belief moves in the terminology of the third Kantian *Critique,* where contemplating the beautiful is a link between nature and freedom (analogous, but on a different level, to the role of the schematism of imagination between sensibility and the categories). But there is a third role for imagination: besides its relation to consciousness at large and Existenz, imagination is related to the mode of the encompassing that is called Geist.

> . . . as objective, [imagination] conquers the reality of our existence, the endlessness of thought, and its own profusion. It does so by transforming everything into a temporarily closed system. Its encompassing reality understands, adopts, incorporates everything, eliminating what is alien at the moment. . . . The whole is called idea. Self-contained, it is the Hegelian idea of the spirit; open, it is the Kantian idea of reason. . . .[21]

(This is the imagination that, Kant said, accompanies reason on pleasure trips.)

That which is *Gegen-stand* is "other" and is standing (*es besteht*) as a unit, determinate. Finally, the object is most broadly characterized by its being-formed. "We can analyze the object itself according to matter and form without thinking of its relation to the subject through which alone its object-character is possible . . . [but] form exists through the spontaneity of the subject's thinking; matter exists through the receptivity of the subject's sensibility."[22] The object is constituted in respect of its general form—not its existence—by the subject. (The terminology is borrowed, of course, from the formation of works, the plastic arts.) "We have, on the one hand, subject, form, a priori, pure, and on the other hand, object, matter, a posteriori, empirical."[23] Jaspers emphasized again and again that to take either side of this dualism as the more fundamental or real is a distortion. Both positivism and idealism, for example, emphasize entirety and universality: "to a positivist, the crux is the lawfulness of nature. . . . to an idealist the crux is the entirety of the one world."[24] But for positivists, "being and objective being are one," and for the idealist, "being is identified with the being of the mind."[25]

The generality which characterizes objectivity does not characterize Existenz.[26] The categories individual and general are inappropriate, as are the categories essence and reality. We go wrong "if we regard the general and the essence as primary, as lasting, as the proper being, and the individual as an infinitesimal case" (as with both positivism and idealism). But we as surely go wrong "if we call Existenz primary, preceding the general and the essence . . . , since the individual needs the general to be himself"[27] (as with Sartre's existentialism). Jaspers suggested that these (and other) categories have to be extended: they must become "objectifying guidelines,"[28] or signs of Existenz. The characteristics of objectivity are the negative guide to considering Existenz in its relation to transendence.

## Concepts of Existenz

To the category type "quantity" in Kant's table of categories, Jaspers contrasted "the level or rank of Existenz." This concept is Jaspers's adoptive reflection of Nietzsche's concept of a "state" (*Zustand*). "Psychologically we can designate it as mood, ethically as attitude; but it is the encompassing and as such more than any psychologically investigable state or any attitude that, on this basis, can be construed in an ethical sense."[29] The states are "the transcending and pervading essence, the source of life-governing impulses; within them and through their movement Existenz becomes conscious of itself and of being."[30] Such states were nobility, heroism, Dionysiac "genius of the heart," "boundless contemplating," and so forth. The level or rank of Existenz is (for Jaspers) visible in both Existenz's wordly manifestation and the "existential relations to transcendence."

To the category type "quality" (objective reality or sensuous affectedness as such; negation; limitation), Jaspers contrasted "unconditionality at the decisive moment . . . *Empirical reality* confronts the *content* of decision."[31] An object is constituted in time; it can (while remaining the same) "fill out one and the same time, i.e., occupy inner sense more or less completely, down to its cessation in nothingness."[32] Time can be filled and empty ("appearances may, one and all, vanish");[33] it is the always underlying medium of appearances. Jaspers contrasted the "unexistential continuity of the flow of time" to historic time:

> . . . the fulfilled time whose appearance rounds out and brings to the present what has intrinsic being by its relation to transcendence. If the moment is existential as a link in a continuity, this continuity must be the realization of what exists irreplaceably at each moment of its temporally limited course: continuity must be conceived as the moment that has become *encompassing*. . . .[34]

This paradox, this historic sense of present eternity, "has found its expression in speculative thinking about eternal recurrence."[35]

To the categories of the type "relation" (inheritance and substance; causality and dependence; community), Jaspers contrasted the beginning and vanishing of Existenz in time, the self-origination of Existenz as it appears to itself in time, and communication between self-beings. (In abbreviated terms: historicity, freedom, communication.)

To the categories of the type "modality" (which concern the relation of representations to time in general, possibility; to some determinate time, actuality; and to all time, necessity), Jaspers contrasted "the unsettled future that creates the possibility of choice—which is my Existenz," the realization of Existenz in time, and "the unsettled future that creates the possibility of choice—which is my Existenz," the realization of Existenz in time, and "the fulfilled time of the moment."[36] "Existenz has *its* time, not time pure and simple."[37] (For Kierkegaard, man is the "disciple of possibility"; for Nietzsche, man is "the as yet undetermined animal.")[38]

The concepts of Existenz are pure signs. That is, they "lack

the power to define new objects";[39] they point to Existenz
without objectifying it. The signs are reciprocally defined: each
illuminates the others. But all express freedom.

By the signs of existential elucidation we express what for
possible Existenz is true being—not as an established objectivity, but as the *being I cannot grasp without willing it
because it is potentially my own.* Existential signs are the
general terms for freedom as the activity of a being which
depends upon itself.[40]

Existential elucidation is not an ontology, for an ontology "ties
us to an objectified being and voids our freedom."[41]

## Cipher-Reading

Existential elucidation is not an ontology, and neither is the
cipher-script. In traditional ontologies, the facets of philosophizing (elucidation of existence, categorical definition,
material world orientation, an appealing elucidation of Existenz, a reading of ciphers; in short, knowledge, volition, and
vision) were fused in one train of thought. Jaspers maintained
that these facets must be distinguished and delimited: "our
force is distinction; we have lost the naive approach."[42]

Ontology originated as the fusion of all modes of thought
into one encompassing thought aglow with being; sub-
sequently it became the doctrine that the *one being can be
known.* Reading ciphers, on the other hand, reserves the true
*unity for acts* of existential reality, because thinking in
ciphers does not veil the disjointedness for knowledge.[43]

Existenz and transcendence are bound, but they are not identical, as thought and being are in ontologies: "in the cipher I
confront, as being, what has to do with the rest of my own
being, and *yet will not become one with me.*"[44]

The culmination of Jaspers's concept of communication is
the relation of Existenz to transcendence: the cipher "language" is the means by which transcendence communicates
with Existenz, appeals to Existenz. "The magnetism of tran-

scendence for Existenz is voiced in ciphers."[45] In analogy with communication between men, the language of transcendence appeals without definitiveness, without pronouncement or revelation; transcendence draws Existenz to actualization.

The point of my existential imagination is to grasp all being as saturated with freedom. To read ciphers means to know about being in a sense that makes existent being and free being identical, so that in the deepest view of my imagination there will be, so to speak, neither the one nor the other, but the ground of both.[46]

Kant's mediation between nature and freedom, contemplation of the beautiful, is here transformed into an *active* mediation—communication through the cipher, "active contemplation."[47]

The signs of Existenz indicate the appearance of free Existenz; the ciphers are the appearance of transcendence. Speaking analogically, in both cases: "as neither the freedom of Existenz nor transcendence has a specific phenomenality, we might speak of analogues to phenomena."[48] "To our imagination, being is visibly present in the cipher."[49] The ciphers are metaphysical objectivities, but their objectivity is ambiguous, evanescent, suspended. They are not other, unitary, and formed in the same sense as the objectivities present in consciousness at large. Of the ciphers there is no knowledge. What the ciphers "tell" Existenz is the possibility of freedom: "Transcendence made me possible Existenz—in other words, it made me free in temporal existence."[50]

## 2. THE CHARACTERISTICS OF MODERN SCIENCE

### Modern Science and the Aspiration to Total Knowledge

Kant claimed that, with his own work, philosophy had entered upon the "sure path of science."[51] The three *Critiques* were to be the prologue, the propaedeutic, for the doctrinal (as Kant said in the preface to the third *Critique*). The *Metaphysics of Nature* and the *Metaphysics of Morals* were intended as elaborations of concrete and definite a priori knowledge of nature and morality. With Hegel, Kant's distinction between critique and doctrine disappeared: "In Hegel's philosophy, one might say, an initial critique of being unfolds by absorbing the matter of the world."[52]

Kant and Hegel represent the climax of thinking under the aegis of what Jaspers referred to as the "totalist conception of science." But even after Hegel both scientists and philosophers continued to aspire to total knowledge. "This identification of modern science and modern philosophy with . . . the old aspiration to total knowledge was catastrophic for both of them."[53]

Modern science dates from the period of Galileo and Kepler. But Jaspers emphasized again and again that Descartes failed to understand the new science. Typical of Descartes's misunderstanding was his criticism of Galileo's work on the velocity of bodies falling in a vacuum. Descartes claimed this work was built up without a foundation, for Galileo "should first have determined what gravity is; if he had known the truth about that, he would know that it is nonexistent in a vacuum."[54] In this and similar criticisms, Jaspers marked "the scholastic attitude which we find also in Bacon, whereas the new science, which was to prove so fruitful, set aside the question of essences as unanswerable and concentrated on investigating empirical laws."[55]

Jaspers criticized the identification of science and philosophy, and the idea that total philosophical knowledge is scientific knowledge. He sought both a pure science and a pure philosophy. Both are necessary "for the sake of the sciences themselves,"[56] as "science left to itself . . . becomes homeless,"[57] directionless, ultimately meaningless.

## A Composite of Main Characteristics

In many of his books and essays Jaspers presented lists of the main characteristics of modern science. The list below is a composite:[58]

1. Universality. Nothing in the world—in existence, in the

mind—is indifferent to modern science; everything is subject to investigation. Jaspers distinguished the ideal of a universal science, a universal method, from the universality of science's concerns.

2. Incompleteness. Modern science is interested in all particulars rather than in a knowable whole; its advance is cumulative and unlimited. Modern science does not engage in Cartesian attempts to derive particular truths from eternal principles, to proceed deductively. Implicit in it is an awareness of hypotheses and a refusal to leave hypotheses untested (Newton's *hypothesem non fingo* applies to nonmethodic hypotheses like those of Descartes). "The modern sciences attach little value to *possibilities* of thought; they recognize the idea in definite and concrete knowledge, after it has proved its worth as an instrument of discovery and been subjected to infinite modifications in the process of investigation."[59] In short, there is no knowledge without knowledge of limitations, and no certainty without uncertainty.[60]

3. Plurality of Method. The conviction that "there are as many methods as there are subject matters to be dealt with" (Vico) led to the ideal of a cosmos of the sciences (as opposed to the ideal of *a* science for *the* cosmos). In contrast to classifications of sciences from antiquity (e.g., dialectics, physics, and theology) and the medieval university disciplines, the modern groupings (from Bacon to Comte) were intended to make all positive knowledge surveyable and to provide a framework for integrating all new knowledge.[61] (The encyclopedias of German idealism also aimed at a rounded whole—but at the expense of ignoring empirical science proper.)[62] Jaspers held that systematics are necessary "if knowledge is not to be scattered into disconnected and indifferent parts,"[63] but temporary; for "we do not know the ultimate reason why all knowledge belongs together, although this reason alone will make us seek knowledge as such."[64] The unity of knowledge is an idea, an "infinite challenge," of imaginative reason, never an accomplishment.

4. Radicality of Inquiry. "Thought that contradicts visible

appearances . . . precisely for the purpose of comprehending visible appearances in a better and unexpected fashion, dares everything." This kind of thinking is particularly prevalent in modern physics with its use of nonperceptual mathematics.[65] Daring everything and its corollary, freedom of experiment, are in the tradition of what Jaspers referred to as the "passion for novelty" (which Descartes certainly shared, but which he transferred to philosophy, where it does not belong).[66]

5. Plurality of Categories. In addition to developing methods appropriate to various subject matters, the modern sciences have "an unclosed theory of categories."[67] In certain sciences, certain categories may predominate: causal or genetic analysis, for example, was of particular importance to Leibniz, Hobbes, and Vico and to the mathematical and historical sciences they influenced. "The problem becomes the suitability of categories and methods, and not the superiority of any one of them."[68]

6. Practical Consequences. Modern science has been characterized since the seventeenth century by an enthusiasm for technical inventions and technological visions of the future. The exact sciences began to inspire technical invention to a great extent only in the nineteenth century; prior to that time science was largely the consequence of technological development. Jaspers emphasized that technology is a means "in itself . . . , neither good nor evil"[69] and that science is distorted if technical production becomes its end.[70]

7. Scientific Attitude. This attitude is fundamentally a methodological attitude; it consists (in Nietzsche's words) of an "instinctive distrust of the aberrations of thought," and "the most extreme circumspection."[71] Science has the double function of advancing knowledge and impugning absolute knowledge. Scientists have the double responsibility of communication, free exchange of information, and avoidance of cults or creeds and blind assertions in the service of extra-scientific interests. The scientist heeds the Enlightenment's challenge, Dare to Know:

Mundane reality has to be conquered for knowledge; I never have it directly. I am not sure of it until thought takes me to a discovery or an invention. . . .[72] Questioning awakens me from merely living in the world to the cognitive existence of seeking an imaginary point outside the world, a point from which all there is might be faced as a world that can be known in a generally valid fashion. The danger that I and the world might be unfathomable will not deter me from this quest. What spurs me on is the passionate knowledge that there is but one way to truth: objective cognition, no matter where it may lead, no matter if it does not lead to real truth as yet. Instead of merely living in my world, I begin to explore it. This critical turn to original curiosity is a fountainhead of philosophizing.[73]

The disenchantment (as Max Weber put it) of existence by science is, so to speak, repeated: by the scientist in the disenchantment of science itself by unceasing, undogmatic effort and by the philosopher in the disenchantment of science's knowledge by self-awareness, existential elucidation.[74]

The modern preoccupation with the question of certainty has its roots in Descartes's thought. The Cartesian *cogito* divorced from the world of extended things, the Cartesian method of universal doubt, and the Cartesian identification of science and philosophy provide the roots of modern radical subjectivism, modern doubt concerning the conditions and even the possibility of knowlege, and the modern "crisis of science" and "crisis of philosophy" (or metaphysics). In the first section of this part, we considered Jaspers's attempt to reexamine the concept of objectivity and to rescue the subject from confinement within the limits of the mode consciousness at large (*cogito*). We turn now to what Jaspers referred to as the "relativity of cogency" and to Jaspers's distinctions of levels of truth—pragmatic truth, cogent truth, conviction, and communication. In the following section, we will return to the relation of science and philosophy and to methodical doubt, methodical delimitation, as the premise for the method of transcending.

Modern science is characterized by its cogent insights. But these are particular insights, tied to methods and categories. It is characterized by its incompleteness or endlessness. And this endlessness remains "unconquered." Modern science is characterized by the universality of its concerns and the radicality with which it pursues them. But it does not attain a universal theory or a unitary world image.

## The Relativity of Cogency

> I acquire cogent insight, but the cogency does not become absolute. I prevail over endlessness, but it also remains unconquered. I attain unities, but not the unity of the world.[75]

Jaspers distinguished three kinds of cogency. The first, "the compelling thought of mathematics and formal logic,"[76] has become of paramount importance in the modern reduction of science to mathematics; mathematical and logical forms seem to be preeminently knowable, since they are the products of the human mind, without sensory apprehension. Jaspers did not question that in mathematics and logic "a valid world constitutes and defines itself. . . . it sustains itself by means of its necessary axioms, which bring it about; and it depends upon them, [whether they] are arbitrary or evident."[77] He distinguished, however, universal mathematics and a *mathesis universalis,* claiming to embrace all knowledge and to comprehend being.

> The universal method is directed toward everything that can be known; consequently it must first free itself from all content, and is afterward unable to recapture it.[78]

Jaspers considered the idea of a productive intellect, "which has nothing but itself to work on," a source of error, "for the intellect can produce only by taking in material that is not intellect."[79] Jaspers asserted, in Kantian terms, the material of intuition and, in Kierkegaardian terms, the existence of the thinker himself.[80]

The second type of cogency is "the compelling reality of objective experience in the natural and intellectual sciences." What is cogent for these sciences is the fact, "yet facts need to be determined."

> What makes facts accessible is not pure sense perception but reflective apperception. *Consciousness of the method in which we bring them to mind is the critical test of whether and in what sense they are factual.* The distinction of real sense perceptions and delusions, the accuracy of measurements, the meaning of testimony and documentation, the changes caused in an observed object by observation itself[81]—all these are not critically ascertained by watching, but by theoretical and exegetical means; and they are never free of a remnant of uncertainty that has led to the saying "any fact is theory."[82]

The cogency of facts depends upon their critical ascertainment; the cogency of theories depends upon their being borne out by the facts: "cogency in empirical sciences is tied to theory, and in regard to theory, to facts."[83]

The third type of cogency is the "compelling visuality of categories, essences, and possibilities of objective being."[84] Categorical views and views of essence (the phenomenologist's *Wesensschau*) have a cogency which exists "quite as itself," not limited from within, for such a view "claims to be neither real nor logically compelling, only to be lucid within and about itself."[85] The limit lies in detail: "qualitative infinity is both unattainable and rationally unpredictable in temporal existence."[86] This distinction can be illustrated by the difference between a printing press designed to deal with all the possible combinations of a twenty-six letter alphabet, and a written book, a meaningful book; the press, set working, combining, might indeed print out a meaningful work eventually—but it would take a human mind to recognize it.[87]

(Jaspers's example is similar to the one of the monkeys seated before typewriters producing the works of Shakespeare.)

> . . . infinite productivity is unintelligible. It is not a mechanical endlessness in calculable variation; it is an infinity that *combines possibility with choice*. It does not produce first and select later; its choice among unrealized possibilities will be made even before its emergence, and there are no limits to the depth and enhancement of its creative action. . . . It is infinity in reality as the process of surmounting endlessness.[88]

Qualitative endlessness is conquerable by research, which makes things finite only to use them as steps; and it is conquerable in reality by creative production.

Creative productions are also the loci of the appearance of ideas in reality. Ideas as "the modes of infinity in the reality of the mind"[89] are nonobjective: "we elucidate ideas by the cognitive echo invoked within use by their objectivity," that is, by their appearance in creations or forms.[90]

> Never objectified as themselves, ideas incarnate themselves in the objective world as unities revealed in infinite progress and never quite given. They are not the elements of knowledge in world orientation, but they provide the impulse of it and set its limits. In the thought of ideas I transcend world orientation.[91]

Such ideas as those expressed by "the beginning," "the end," "the largest," "the smallest," involve us in contradictions when we try to objectify them. This is, of course, the basis of Kant's doctrine of the antinomies.

Jaspers used the word *Denken* as a generic term: *Erkennen* and *Wissen* are species of thinking. A cognitive experience is "the current outcome of methodically developed inductive-deductive research"; whereas thinking is "the consequence, for my consciousness, of the execution of thought-movements."[92] Thought-movements leave traces, so to speak, in consciousness—which are manifest as forms and creations. We know indirectly, in created works, the process of surmounting endlessness, the process of choosing and concentrating. We have what Jaspers called "secondary comprehension," or "comprehension of the comprehended,"[93] which implies both a certain distance from primary comprehension—as given to us, for example, in a work of art—and a certain participation in it (since one's *own* primary comprehension is only suspended, not eliminated, in dealing with another's work). In the words of the Belgian literary critic Georges Poulet:

> My thought is a space in which my thoughts take place, in which they take their place. . . . My thought is not made up solely of my thoughts; it is made up also, even more perhaps, of all the interior distance which separates me from, or draws me closer to, that which I am able to think. For all that I think is in myself who think it. The distance is not merely an interval; it is an ambient milieu, a field of union. Thus there is revealed another aspect of literature, a hidden aspect, the invisible face of the moon. Objectively, literature is made up of formal works, the contours of which stand out with greater or lesser clarity. . . . Subjectively, literature is not at all formal. It is the reality of a thought that is always particular, always anterior and posterior to any objectification; one which, across and beyond all object, ceaselessly reveals the strange and natural impossibility in which it finds itself, of ever having an objective existence.[94]

This thought that is always particular is, in Jaspers's terms, a concentration, the trace of a thought-movement, a fragment—a mode of infinity in the reality of the mind. The subjective side of the work is the phenomenality of Existenz—the movement which makes the mind, as the living space of Existenz, ambient, "a field of union."

The surmounting of endlessness in creative production is an endless process in itself; no work marks its success. "I am one thing, my writings are another,"[95] as Nietzsche said; the failure of our conquest of endlessness "shows that our being has another source."[96] Theoretical conquest of quantitative or qualitative endlessness and conquest in creative work become, in their failures, "springboards of transcending, though the substance of transcending comes from the freedom of possible Existenz."[97]

The third experience of the limits of world orientation is that the unity of the world is impossible. Science attains unities within the spheres of mundane reality—unorganic nature, organic life, soul and mind—but not the unity of the spheres. Each sphere is original, irreducible; there is no common denominator, no single principle, no single method appropriate to all; and a false picture arises from taking any one of the spheres as fundamental and the model of the others. No analogy—living organisms as machines, human society as a living organism—can hold the spheres together; no single image—the universe as a clock, the universe as an ensouled being—can be adequate to the facts.

The *idea* of unity is a spur to the sciences. But systems and world theories are absolutizations of the forms in which the idea makes its appearance. Closed, self-rounding worlds have been given "their most impressive philosophical forms" by Aristotle and Hegel; but they "leave us only the freedom of knowledge, not of Existenz," that is, not "true freedom and the vista of an open world of uncertainty, risk, possibility and creativity."[98]

## The Crisis of Science

The limits of cogency, the limits of the conquest of endlessness, and the limits of the attainable unities are limits for consciousness at large. Vis-à-vis these limits, the freedom which we exercise in knowledge as "self-awareness" (the object is never completely pure, detached from the subject) and in taking part in ideas (the idea is never objectifiable without contradiction) is "the premise and medium of existential freedom."[99] The only freedom science itself understands "is that of conscious knowledge and ideal legality,"[100] and this understanding is necessary for approaching the freedom of Existenz;

the limits of objectivity point to the nonobjective, and every "idea points to its foundation in some Existenz."[101]

Jaspers saw a positive side to what is often called the "crisis of science." For example, he noted one development:

> Physical reality has become more and more alien. First it was conceived in terms of bodies arranged in non-perspectival space, without relation to a perceiver; then it was reduced to the underlying spatial being of particles differing from each other only quantitatively in size and motion; and finally now nature cannot even be imagined, but can be described only in mathematical formulae. The same thing happens to our knowledge of human existence. . . .[102]

The positive side of this development is that it forecloses total conceptions and the totalist conception of science.

> The radical undermining of the modern mind . . . is not an undermining of modern science. Insofar as its methods are above-board, modern science has not been shaken at all, but has become progressively more trustworthy, lucid and assured—*within its limits*. What has been shattered for many people is the meaning of science.[103]

The "crisis of science" relates not so much to the limits of scientific capacity as to our sense of the significance of science in general.[104] Science itself does not, cannot, consider its own meaning and significance; this is the task of philosophy. Science must look to its own freedom—the freedom of knowledge.

We will look at the issue over which this freedom has been brought into question—the issue of "value-freedom—and then turn to the relation of science and philosophy as Jaspers conceived it.

## Value-Freedom

A confusion of terms has complicated the question of value-freedom. The term "value" has a specific meaning in the context of political economy; in Mill's definition, for example, "value, when used without an adjunct, always means, in political economy, value in exchange."[105] Furthermore, "political economy has nothing to do with the comparative estimate of different uses in the judgment of a philosopher or a moralist. The use of a thing, in political economy, means its capacity to satisfy a desire or serve a purpose."[106] Thus the adjunct "intrinsic," which is used in judging the value of an object outside of its relation to the exchange market and other objects in that market, is not part of the political economist's terminology.

If ideas and moral ideals are drawn into the social realm or the life order—that is, if the standards of philosophers and moralists which Mill set outside the exchange are drawn into it—under conditions in which their relativity is emphasized, they are viewed as functional "values," of no intrinsic significance. For example, Nietzsche held that "truth is the kind of error without which a definite species of living beings cannot live." Life-promoting error can not properly be called either truth or error: "the concept of truth is non-sensical. The whole realm of the 'true-false' has to do only with relations between living beings, not with the self-existent. There is no self-existent living being."[107] A "truth" is a "value" in terms of relations between living beings. This drawing of ideas into the social realm—which is a refutation of their status as transcendent entities as well as of the identity of thought and being[108]—leads, finally, to the idea that values must be created: "change of values—that is the change of creators," proclaimed Nietzsche. "As yet no one knows what is good and bad—except the creator!—He is the one who creates the goal for mankind and gives the earth its meaning and future. . . ."[109] Thus Nietzsche replaced the old values with new values, but the new values—the creator's values—were no less subject to relativity than the old ones, the remnants of a tradition which noncreators are loath to call passé.

On the face of it, then, value-free science would seem to be an invitation to chaos—an admission that since there are no sure standards for making judgments, then the unsure standards should be abandoned as well.

Jaspers maintained that

the natural sciences can be value-free in principle and on the whole. They can be confined to cogent knowledge of facts, and to methodological knowledge of their current premises and theories, without thereby being reduced to mountains of factual rubble; for their significant scientific ideas are objectified in theories and systematics that serve to question the facts or put them in their place of the moment. . . . The questions to be asked of any natural-scientific research are the following: What are the established facts? Which theoretical idea constitutes the horizon? What is its rational construction as a theory? How about its fruitfulness, that is to say, its capacity for discovering and connecting facts—a capacity for which success is the sole criterion?[110]

Pure, scientific world orientation has two main consequences, in Jaspers's view. First, "the totality of a world image has dissolved. . . . there is no longer a whole in which all things have their place." It refuses the ontological whole of scholasticism; the absolutized whole of mechanistic, organological, and other categories and methods; the dialectical whole of Hegel. And second, "all that remains true, instead of a *system* of the whole, is the *systematics* of relative categorical and methodological orders . . . , [and] the two most encompassing [systematics]—the system of the sciences and the system of spheres of the mind—are themselves the most uncertain and relative."[111] But Jaspers went on to say that "*philosophically* this purified world orientation as the point of science remains based upon the metaphysical impulse. . . . Insofar as science is meant philosophically, as knowledge in the unity of knowledge, it is not self-fulfilling; it finds its fulfillment when Existenz, in the process of world orientation, is cast back upon itself by that orientation and is thus opened to transcendence."[112] Thus Jaspers could state both that "metaphysics has no place in science" and that "metaphysics makes for meaningful science" (providing the impulse and goal—the "leap to possible Existenz")[113] Finally:

> . . . while the ideal of a pure science does make sense if viewed as an ideal umpire with the authority of cogency, it becomes senseless when it is held to consist in itself, by its own authority. It can neither create substance nor provide impulses; all there is to it, without metaphysics, is random accuracy. . . .[114]

At which point the question arises: what is the difference between the "factual rubble" which value-free natural science avoids and merely "random accuracy," which natural science without metaphysics cannot avoid?

For Jaspers, a science derives its *reality* from method, "from the specific craftsmanship that starts the flow of knowables in proximity to the topic." It derives its *articulation* from categorical thinking, "which enables it to make distinctions in its own realm and between this and other science." And its *motivation* "comes by way of the idea from an existential interest that makes cognition serve to touch the being of transcendence."[115] The flow of knowables is factual rubble without articulation, systemization; but systemization results in only random accuracy. Value comes from existential interest, and existential interest constitutes the value of science.

> In the world, by world orientation, we find no peg to which science might be fixed so as to be sure of its meaning. It is the existential relevance of world orientation that knowledge will cease, that Existenz, confronting the abyss of nothingness, will get its chance at transcending. Knowledge does not give us the ultimate satisfaction, but it is the way for Existenz to find itself. Driven to know in world orientation, Existenz will forge its own world transcending faculty from other material. And thereby hangs the ultimate meaning of science.[116]

From these passages, it is clear that Jaspers did not try to redeem science from the loss of absolute standards, total images,

systems, by eliminating even relative standards, guiding images, systemizations. He did not attempt the legerdemain of
creating meaning or substance out of nothing. He accepted the
limits of science: on the one hand, that matter is "alien . . . ,
impervious to the logos"[117] and, on the other hand, that the
mind is more than any of its products or objectifications, as the
carrier of Existenz.[118] And he saw at these very limits room for
freedom. That thought is unable to fit the world to itself without a remainder implies not that the world is meaningless for
men but that meaning comes from another source. Thinking is
a preparation; thought founders, but the thinking man does
not; he experiences, as possible Existenz, in the foundering of
thought, the cipher of transcendence.

For Jaspers, in short, value-freedom was not an end in itself.
Confusion might have been avoided by speaking of value-
suspension or simply freedom from system, dogmatism—to
avoid the confusion that surrounds the word "value."[119] It was
precisely against a situation in which ideas are nothing more
than commodities with exchange value that Jaspers spoke,
calling for communication:

> Insofar as everything has been made dependent upon the ren-
> dering of the life-order absolute; insofar as the economic
> forces and situations, the possible powers, strive toward this
> end—so likewise is mental activity similarly directed, as if
> this were the one thing that mattered. The mind has ceased
> to believe in itself, as self-arising, and becomes a means to
> an end. Having thus grown fully mobile as a mere instrument
> of sophistry, it can serve any master. It discovers justifica-
> tion for any state of affairs, either extant or regarded as de-
> sirable by the powers that be.[120]

When the mind is drawn into the realm of production and supply, into the exchange market, it is a means for socialized men
to accomplish the everything which is permitted. ("Science,"
said Lenin, "is a whore.")

On the other hand, the freedom of the mind does not mean
that there is freedom to restore the lost standards and

measures—that is, to restore transcendent entities, or to reassert the unity of thought and being. Verification, in world orientation, is accomplished (within limits) by making something perceptible or logically compelling, by producing or achieving something.[121] But this type of verification does not characterize existential elucidation or metaphysics.

> In existential elucidation I verify by my way of dealing with myself and with another, of being assured of myself by the unconditionality of my actions; I verify by the motions I experience inwardly as I am uplifted, as I love and hate, as I seclude myself and as I fail. . . . I verify by my self-being, *without having another yardstick than this very self-being,* which I recognize by the transcendence of the cipher.[122]

That which makes science meaningful is not a transcendent value; it is self-being.


## 3. SCIENCE AND PHILOSOPHY

### Relations between Science and Philosophy Rejected by Jaspers

> . . . It is impossible to prove scientifically that there should be such a thing as science. . . . The choice of an object of science that is made from an infinite number of existing objects on the basis of this object itself, is a choice that cannot be justified scientifically. . . . The ideas that guide us are tested in the systematic process of investigation, but they themselves do not become an object of direct investigation. . . .[123]

The relation between science and philosophy is analogous to that which Kant postulated between intuition and concepts: science without philosophy is blind, philosophy without science is empty.

The claim that science is an end in itself is usually an endorsement of "the intrinsic value of any factual discovery whatsoever, of each and every correct application of method, extension of knowledge and scientific occupation."[124] This type of endorsement is a direct outcome of mistaking the characteristic of universality for a purpose. The endorsement's result is twofold; on the one hand, scientific dilettantism on the part of those who would rather know very little about many things than make a judgment about what is significant and, on the other hand, what Nietzsche called spiritual overconscientiousness on the part of those who would rather know everything about something of no significance than very little about many things. In general, there arises a superstitious faith in the results of science for their own sakes, in limitless know-how.[125]

If the superstitious faith in science wanes when know-how proves inadequate or generates new difficulties, then antiscientific superstition waxes. Help is anticipated from "powers which negate science," but the search for this help is disguised as science. In 1931, Jaspers spoke of astrology, Christian Science, theosophy, spiritualism, clairvoyance, and occultism as examples of so-called true sciences which were "clouding the mentality of our generation."[126]

The incompleteness which characterizes modern science can be taken as a temporary condition. Comte, for example, posited three stages on human thought's way—the theological, the philosophical, and the positivistic—and laid out a program for the completion of the third stage in principle (that is, he devised a framework into which newly discovered details could be set). The completion of science implies the overcoming of philosophy. In a quite different manner, Marx expected that philosophy would be *aufgehoben*. Philosophy may be conceived as that mode which is overcome in science's completion, or it may be conceived as the agency of science's completion—as the synthesizer of the knowledge obtained by the special sciences. Fechner, Lotze, E. von Hartman, and Wundt each in his own way held that the task of philosophy was synthesis.

The plurality of methods and categories which characterizes modern science can be taken as the topic of philosophy. Philosophy's task, then, is the formulation of a general methodol-

ogy of the sciences (e.g., Scheler sought *one* method), or it is
the handmaiden of the sciences as epistemology or logic or
phenomenology (philosophy, in Husserl's phrase, is a strict
science). Cohen, Windelband, and Rickert, each in his own
way, held that philosophy's task was to explore and explicate
the principles of science. (Jaspers characterized Rickert as a
man who "practiced philosophy like a physicist" with the difference that unlike a physicist, he did not subject his
constructions—value-systems—to realistic tests.)[127]

Science is "in the nature of a public secret." "It is public
because it is accessible to everyone; it is secret because it is far
from being understood by everyone."[128] As science's inquiries
have become more and more "radical," the secret has become
less and less public; this is obvious when the results of scientific investigation and theorizing are expressed in mathematical formulas which cannot be translated into the general
medium of language. If science were (as Scheler held) an expression of the will to power, this situation would be extremely
dangerous; or to the extent that science is such an expression
(and is, thereby, inauthentic in Jaspers's terms), it is dangerous. If science is a public secret, the need for guidance from
philosophy is obvious; and so is the need for philosophy to be
public, without secrets, communicative. Science is not for
Everyman, but philosophy must be.[129]

Another way in which science can be conceived as a means
results from confusion of the "spirit of research" and the
"pragmatic spirit of invention." "Knowledge reduced to
pragmatic terms is not the whole of knowledge." If philosophy
is thought of as a kind of science inspired by the "pragmatic
spirit of invention," the result is, for example, a calculus for
the computation of the greatest good for the greatest
number—in the manner of the British utilitarians.

The preceding examples illustrate ways in which the conception of science influences the conception of philosophy.
Science as an end in itself is science divorced from philosophy.
Science as the culmination of human endeavor is science
standing on the shoulders of philosophy, or science which has

left philosophy behind. Science in need of a general methodology is science in need of philosophy's service (and, implicitly, subservience). Science as a transposer of ends into means, motivated by the will to power, has no need of philosophy at all, nor does science as a means in the pragmatic sense. But in either of these last two cases, philosophy may be swept into the ends-means categories as a kind of science.

## Levels of Truth

For Jaspers, the dialectical relation of philosophy and science is an expression of the conviction that the premise that all truth is in the form of cogent knowledge—from which it is concluded that all knowledge is uncertain—is false. The despair or skepticism or nihilism that this conclusion evokes blinds men to the multiplicity of truth itself; the value of truth is questioned, while the limits of the definition of truth as cogent knowledge are ignored. The premise that knowledge has an absolute character can lead to the conclusion that knowledge is responsible for the joylessness or the hopelessness of life, the disenchantment of existence; whereas the realization that cogency is relative can leave the way open for transcending. The premise that analysis of life, of experience, or motivations, is essentially conclusive or definitive can lead to the conclusion that analysis voids its object, or more generally, that rationality is unnatural; whereas the realization that analysis cannot exhaust reality and cannot touch Existenz (either to create it or destroy it) can enable men to respect analysis for its capacity to void what is insubstantial or delusive.[130]

Jaspers offered a schema of types of truth, each type being corollary to a mode of the encompassing which we are (Dasein, Bewusstsein überhaupt, Geist, Existenz). Generally, it can be said that the criteria of truth in science lie entirely in the object, in the content of thought, in judgment, while in philosophy they lie in inner and outer action, in the state of the soul, in decision. In the sciences, proof depends on objective research, inquiries, tests, while in philosophy proof depends upon existential reality—what cannot be caught in concepts, but what can be appealed to. The truths of science are universally valid but relative to a determinate sphere of objectivity (or sphere of mundane reality—unorganic nature, organic life, soul, mind); the truths of philosophy are absolute in origin though historic ("because we as possible Existenz are historic")[131] and relative to their objective expression, their appearance in the medium of language. These general claims follow from the particular analyses of types of truth.

1. "Existence is always particular, and it wills to preserve and extend itself; truth is what furthers life, what works; falsity is what harms, limits, paralyzes it."[132] Truth, as a function of the preservation and extension of life, is proved by usefulness in practice. Or to put the matter another way, truth is the satisfaction of existence resulting from its interaction with its environment. The environs of the empirically existing being provoke sympathy or antipathy accordingly as they enhance or threaten it; self-interestedness is purposeful (if not always, or even usually, far-sighted) and unlimited; the two fundamental modes of relation are conflict of interest and identity of interest.[133]

2. "Existence, as consciousness or soul, manifests and expresses itself. Truth is the adequacy with which the inwardness of existence is manifested, and the adequacy of the expression and of consciousness to the unconscious."[134] When consciousness is "an interchangeable point of mere thought" its expressed truth has validity as compelling correctness: "it proves itself by evidence."[135] Both ordinary language and rational argument depend upon adequation of word or sentence and thing,[136] but in the former case, the thing is not the detached and pure object of consciousness at large, or to put the matter differently, perception of the thing is not accompanied by methodical apperception which "detaches us from what we think, do and are."[137]

3. "Truth at the level of spirit is conviction. It proves itself in actuality through existence and thought, to the extent which it submits to the wholeness of ideas, thereby confirming their truth."[138] Ideas are (in Kantian terms) not only regulative principles, checking dangerous pretensions of the understanding;

they lead the understanding to the consideration of nature according to a principle of completeness.[139] Ideas bring coherence to thought; for the spirit, "truth is what produces wholeness."[140] "Truth of the spirit exists by virtue of membership in a self-elucidating, self-contained whole. This whole does not become objectively knowable; it can be grasped only in the action of the membership which endows it with existence and knowability."[141]

4. Existenz appears to itself as existence, as consciousness at large, as spirit, and it can contrast itself with each of these modes and with immanence in general. "Existenz experiences truth in faith. Where I am no longer sheltered by a certifying effectiveness of pragmatic truth, by a demonstrable certainty of the understanding, or by a protective totality of spirit, there I have come upon a truth in which I break out of all worldly immanence. Only from this experience of transcendence do I return to the world, now living both in it and beyond it, and only now for the first time myself. The truth of Existenz proves itself as authentic consciousness of reality."[142] This truth is in communication. It cannot be defined with reference to anything else—to purposes, to perceivable and thinkable objects, to ideas or systems.[143] Transcending aims at the source (*Ursprung*) from which all objects, all frameworks of objectivity, all horizons, derive the possibility of their particular existences.

## Philosophy in Our Times

> The differentiation of truth—of the truth I know as *cogent* from the truth I *share* (as an idea) and the truth I *am myself*—is what enables Existenz to become reality. . . . My truth—which as Existenz I am simply in my freedom—comes up against other existential truth. By and with this, it comes to be itself. It is not unique and alone, but unique and uninterchangeable in its relation to others.[144]

The distinction between science and philosophy is, in relation to truth, clear-cut for Jaspers: truth is either cogent and thus not chosen, or it is made unconditional by a communicative

choice.[145] Philosophy is the way toward choice, the preparation for choice, and the reflection upon choice: philosophy is
the "form of *Existenz reaching out for others.*"[146] Philosophy
is the form of philosophizing activity.

The distinction frames the paradox of existential truth: absolute validity and relativity do not exclude each other. Relativity always applies to the objective appearance, the form of
what has been thought and said, the *capita mortua,* as Jaspers
often phrased it, of conceptions, the traces of philosophizing.
Validity is always absolute in Existenz alone, in unconditional
choosing. The formulation of existential truth is always relative, the origin of it is absolute.

There is one general world of philosophy and of philosophical possibilities; but knowing this is still world-orientation
about the philosophy that occurs in history as a sum of
thought-structures. It remains possible to unite and to know
all objective world views and formulas in one brain. But all
this is always only a means, not truth itself. I remain this
historic creature which *cannot skip its own origin* by way of
knowledge. As I enter into the objectivities of a general
being, into its intelligibilities and techniques of thought,
what I rediscover in the contents of these media is the possibility of my self-being. . . .[147]

The historical philosophies of our time—from Dilthey's
studies of *Weltanschauungen* through Cassirer's *Philosophy of
Symbolic Forms*—are, in Jaspers's terms, means. They enable
men to meet in the most encompassing of common rooms.

Existential truth, existential elucidation, is distinct from
knowing the sum of historically manifest thought-structures
and also from any thought-structure which claims to be all-
embracing with respect to Existenz, that is, from any ontology.
Jaspers presented a schema of ontologizing possibilities: on the
one hand, ontology takes its start with a concept of "the All"
from which subjective and objective multiplicity arise; on the
other hand, it takes its start with a concept of "the Many."

As a doctrine of the All, an object-oriented ontology became a metaphysical realism; a subject-oriented one became an idealism that dissolved all being in self-consciousness. As a doctrine of the individual, an object-oriented ontology turned into pluralism, and a subject-oriented one into monadology—both approaches to an inquiry into Existenz.[148]

Jaspers's *Grundwissen*, basic knowledge, is an illumination of the modes or realms, the origins, of our experience· in the world, of what we find in ourselves; it is the illumination, furthermore, of the *possibilities* of another kind of basic knowledge, "of the varied designs of Being, the ontologies and cosmic images that go today with the great ciphers."[149] However, the modes of the encompassing do not, themselves, become ciphers: "while showing what ciphers can be and that they can be transcended, the basic knowledge commits us to no particular way of life and leaves us as open to order as to chaos."[150] If the modes were "an organism of Being, they would make just another ontology"; they would be a multilayered fundamental ontology. Jaspers called his breakthrough from the ontological way of thinking "the step from ontology to periechontology."[151]

The first step on this way—one lacking in methodological self-consciousness—was taken in the early (1919) *Psychologie der Weltanschauungen*.


## 4. WELTANSCHAUUNGEN AND EXISTENTIAL RELATIONS TO TRANSCENDENCE

### The Scandal of Philosophy

Kant wrote, in 1787, that "it still remains a scandal to philosophy and to human reason in general that the existence of things outside . . . must be accepted merely on faith, and that if anyone thinks . . . to doubt their existence, we are unable to encounter his doubts by any satisfactory proof."[152] Any attempt to describe the external world presupposes a distinction between described and describer; *that* there is something to describe is presupposed. When a description is actually given, a view about *what* is described is assumed.

It is possible to question both the existence of the distinct *that* and possible views of *what* that is (or the feasibility of evaluating various possible views of what that is). And it is also possible to ignore both questions.

The first question was ignored, for example, by Husserl. The question of the reality of things can be "bracketed" while we go on to consider objects as they are for consciousness and consciousness itself, the "noetic-noematic correlation." This is comparable to the position of the ataraxic man who eliminates from his little world all that is not subject to his rule, who establishes self-sovereignty or pointlike autonomy.

The second question can be ignored by positing a definitive conceptual scheme. Kant's demonstration of the necessity of his conceptual scheme rested on the assumption that Aristotelian logic, Euclidean geometry, and Newtonian mechanics were definitive, final. Contemporary developments of propositional logic, non-Euclidean geometry, and quantum mechanics have opened that assumption to question. But the definitiveness of the categorical scheme is questionable even on Kant's own grounds, these particular (and also not definitive) developments aside. As Jaspers pointed out:

Kant himself says: We discern the *a priori* forms not in experience, but on the occasion of experience. From this we may infer, as Kant did not, that future experience may provide the occasion on which new *a priori* forms will become known. Where the occasion of experience has not yet occurred, the *a priori* can in fact not be known. . . . Conversely, in rising to the first categories and principles, we never attain to the absolutely "pure" *a priori* . . . in the first category of the "I think" there is also an *a posteriori*. The first steps from the "I think" to the concrete and particular are not known solely through the self-elucidation of reason, but are occasioned by experience, and then elaborated as pure *a priori* forms.[153]

A closed conceptual scheme or a total world image (its objective correlate) denies the plurality of possible views of the *what* of the world; it is the "perpetual peace" after the combative history of philosophy.[154]

The grandest version of such an answer, Hegel's system, allowed each previous view its day in the sun and each historical period its visit from Geist. Hegel's system also addressed itself to the first question—concerning the existence of the external world—by reasserting the identity of thought and being: what is real is rational, and what is rational is real. From Hegel's system, the modern materialisms and idealisms derive.

Jaspers's philosophy ignored neither question. The weight of the sheer *that* which no proof can reach redounds upon the man who faces the world without the protection of these proofs. It is in boundary situations that this weight makes itself felt; "to experience boundary situations is the same as Existenz."[155] And furthermore the force of the *what* that Kant so circumscribed returns in existential elucidation. Namely, discontinuity and intermittence in space and time, hazard, novelty, fate. "Indeed, all these things do not exist in the objective world and do not exist as objects of knowledge. But when an explanation of Existenz is attempted, all these words come back."[156]

The plurality of descriptions and views of the *what* was crucial to Jaspers's endeavor from *Psychologie der Weltanschauungen* on. It is to this work, and its implications for the character of modern philosophy, that we turn now.

## Jaspers's Psychology of World Views

In his *General Psychopathology* (first published in 1913), Jaspers distinguished explanation, "the recognition of objective causal relationships," or the psychologist's view of the mind from the outside, and *Verstehen,* the "perception of mental phenomenon from within."[157] The psychologist explains causally, constructing patterns from repeatedly observed elements; but he understands genetically, empathetically "seeing" how one mental process evolves from another. The two procedures are interrelated. The psychologist who understands:

> . . . starts from an intuitive overall conception. This he dissects, clarifying successively: expression, contents and phenomena on the one hand, non-conscious mechanisms on the other hand; there is an awareness of Existenz, the fundamental factor that cannot be empirically explored. Finally, an enriched understanding of the whole is reconstructed, based on the facts and possible meanings displayed thus. In every concrete case, whatever concrete result has been achieved is questioned; the procedure is repeated and intensified through the collection of objective data, new conceptions of the whole alternating with renewed dissection.[158]

(One might say that Verstehen without explanation is empty, and explanation without Verstehen is blind.)

Jaspers's Verstehen psychology made apparent the presence of the psychologist himself; it "introduced the psychologist into psychology."[159] The limits apparent in the natural sciences due to the presence of the scientist (as formulated in, e.g., Heisenberg's uncertainty principle) thus became apparent in the intellectual sciences. Jaspers's early work was an attempt to make explicit the frameworks which the psychologist brings to his work, the entire range of his methods. The *Psychologie der Weltanschauungen* is the application of Verstehen, an empathetic tour of human possibilities; however, it is a description not of the psychologist's frameworks but of the frameworks in which an individual's life of the mind moves.

By the time Jaspers had spent ten years as a professor of philosophy and had written his *Philosophy,* he was critical of his last work of psychology: "A doctrine of world-views drafts images by esthetic empathy or logical constructions; it cannot take us to the point of any real world-view."[160] A doctrine of world views is the product of world orientation; it is the prelude to taking a stance, to "personal performance."

> Today contemplation has advanced so far that we have grown conscious of it as a universal relativism. Everything is valid from a specific, definable standpoint which I can take, abandon and change. I need only to be understandingly at home in every standpoint, without standing on any. Freedom is the random interchangeability of standpoints.[161]

But the result of such freedom may be "that I am no longer myself." "I can defend everything and refute everything."[162] This is the opposite of the condition that Jaspers dealt with in the *Psychologie der Weltanschauungen*: the world view can become a shell (*Gehäuse*) into which a man retreats. Unfreedom in stasis and unfreedom in random movement, fanaticism and amorphousness or sophistry—these extremes undercut the possibility of philosophizing and of commitment without inflexibility, without uncommunicativeness.[163]

The *Psychologie der Weltanschauungen* was the work in which Jaspers broke with traditional philosophy. The possibility of "universal relativism" is initially freeing; it is comparable to the "unmasking psychologies" of Nietzsche and Kierkegaard.[164] For Jaspers, it was a step that emphasized the sign that became central to his philosophizing—communication. "There is a radical abyss between the dogmatic and the communicative modes of knowing the truth."[165]

> Philosophically, to become conscious of communicative truth comes to this: so to think through all the modes of the Encompassing that potential Existenz has the largest space in the world. Existenz, as irremediably as movement in time, should hold itself open before the whole range of possibilities and actualities. Only then can that radical will-to-communicate which springs out of reason and Existenz work; whereas the possession of truth as though it were conclusively asserted in fact breaks communication off.[166]

Universal relativism is not an end in itself; it opens the way for thinking of philosophy not as result-producing but as genuinely liberating. "The reality of philosophizing . . . does not lie in objective results, it is a posture of consciousness."[167]

## Communication and Positive Philosophy

Communication is the sign of Jaspers's positive philosophy. Schelling's distinction of negative and positive philosophy rested upon an insight which Jaspers adopted thus:

> The rationally conceived universal as such is critical and negative; that is to say, the understanding [*Verstand*] by itself is dissective. Only the historical reality [*Geschichtlichkeit*] of the irreplaceable being that is not universal, that stands on its own and is one with its source, is positive. Such a being remains not merely concealed but even insubstantial until it gains illumination through the mediation of the understanding.[168]

This implies that denial and assertion, dissolution and creation, annihilation and generation (these opposite tendencies permeate Nietzsche's work), are not on the same level; they differ as do intellect and reason.

In modern Existenz philosophy two types of positive philosophy other than Jaspers's own can be distinguished: the ultimately self-defeating and the ultimately self-destructive.

Positive philosophy—concerned with man in his historicity—is self-defeating if it becomes "rational universal," if it becomes doctrinal and is expressed in direct statements rather than appeals. Thus Schelling's positive philosophy ended in an attempt to seize upon "an objectification that he thought would take him beyond the bounds of objectification." Jaspers's characterized this as a "speculative identification with the personality of God."[169] And Nietzsche's positive philosophy brought him to the doctrines of eternal recurrence and the will to power, both of which tend in the same direction of elevating and ennobling man (hence the superman).

Positive philosophy is self-destructive if it slips into the place of assertion, creation or generation, a disguised negation: for example, if Being is said to be nothing. Heidegger's doctrine—fundamental ontology—is a reinterpretation of man's relation to the world in terms of a fall. It claims that man has fallen from a godlike status (his existence and essence are identical) into the world and into the company of others.[170] Death then stands as the emblem of return and restoration, of freedom from both worldliness and the guilt that decline entails.

Jaspers attempted to go the way of positive philosophy without ending in doctrine, self-defeated, and without setting a new negative at the center. The *Psychologie der Weltanschauungen* contains Jaspers's preliminary criticism of negative philosophy; on the ground it cleared grew the *Philosophy* as the appeal of positive philosophy.

## Existential Relations to Transcendence

Jaspers avoided any attempt to state a "new image of man." An image of man would take away man's freedom.[171] Even if it is stated that "man as possible Existenz is a philosopher," this implies no definition, for the philosopher

cannot definitively be anything that might be generalized— not merely contemplative, not merely active, not any kind of type—and neither is there a final result in existence. His ceaseless impulse to become entire drives him on and allows him no permanent rest at any point. . . . However, since man as a philosopher finds no definitive form of his existence and understands that in temporality he cannot find it, he needs *poise* to protect him from getting lost in the tumult of his emotions; he obtains the psychological reality of *humanitas* that makes him ready and open to the other; and he sees the threat of a *passion* that shows him the boundary of a possible darkness underneath. . . . Poise, *humanitas* and passion must be borne by Existenz if they are to be possible truths. . . .[172]

With this threefold character to his search Jaspers elucidated the "existential relations to transcendence" that are the later development (in the *Philosophy*) of the doctrine of world views.

In the *Psychologie der Weltanschauungen,* the spirit types were delineated as responses to boundary situations. In the *Philosophie* the starting point is similar: "Our discussion . . . will proceed, in view of boundary situations, to visualize the existential relations in which the transcendence we experience is considered—the relations in which it is conceived, and thus objectified, only to fade away again."[173] Jaspers presented four antinomical relations in which Existenz can move; if any one side of any of the relations is hypostatized, so that it becomes permanent "either as a psychological experience or as a mythical object,"[174] then a fixed world view results. In this presentation, there is not random movement through possible world views but patterns of movement, tensions, and "only the tension in the antinomies is the true phenomenon of Existenz in its relation to transcendence."[175] To sustain the tension requires poise, *humanitas,* and passion.

The four relations are presented schematically ("elucidative schemata") as: (1) defiance and surrender; (2) rising and falling; (3) diurnal law and order and nocturnal passion; (4) the One and diversity.

1. The boundary situation in which defiance (*Trotz*) arises is that of revolt, radical renunciation of an existence that seems pointless, arbitrary, eminently perishable. Defiance is "cognitive existence," ceaseless questioning of the very judgments that inspired the initial revolt; "the relentless consistency of truthfulness itself becomes my relation to transcendence."[176] (In a tragic situation this is the life of Oedipus, who recoils from the truth and then pursues it to the end—"I cannot leave the truth unknown"[177]—and of Hamlet.) Defiance may give rise to its own reversal, to surrender, "the readiness to live, no matter how, to accept life whatever happens."[178] ("Watching the tragic hero, man recognizes his own potentiality: he can stand fast no matter what happens.")[179] Answers to the defiant

question "how could it be so?" are theodicies; theodicies legitimate surrender. But defiance can rise again when "we try in vain to make a formula generally valid," when we try to validate such doctrines as the Indian karma cycle, Zoroastrian, Manichean or Gnostic dualisms, predestination. For such doctrines, even as they fail to satisfy, "appeal to the activity of our freedom. . . ."[180] The isolation and hypostatization of either defiance or surrender is a decline: it results in either hatred of life and vindictiveness, the "license of determined subjectivity"; or sheer passivity and consequent submission to authorities.

2. Rise and fall ("coming to myself or losing myself;" ascending from "existent nonbeing" or declining from "my intrinsic self") are possibilities for "becoming the way I judge." Men are guided either by definable normative concepts or by an "indistinct, noncompelling, but evident sight of rank in the physiognomic character of all things."[181] Definable normative concepts, like theodicies, entail fixation, formalization, or mechanization; and "sight of rank" may also become fixed, formal, mechanical, there may be "transcendently set" goals rather than "transcendently related" goals. Of the latter, Jaspers claimed:

> I can name such goals: purity of soul; historic appearance of the substance of my being; responsible action based on the historic determinacy of the entire circle of existence that I can fulfill. But all of these trickle away when I mean them as such rather than as signs. . . . There is no objective form in which the transcendent goal of my life will become visible. It cannot be conceived for all time, nor identically for all men.[182]

Wholeness, achievement of transcendent goals, is impossible in time: "to live in temporal existence without entirety, to live philosophically at his own peril, is the fate of one who knows that he ought to be free."

Jaspers alludes to the Romantic idea that this peril, this unshelteredness (*Ungeborgenheit*) is overcome through genius, with the *mythical* concepts of genius and daemon. In interior communication "genius and daemon are like the forms of my intrinsic self." Genius and daemon are mythical objectifications, indicators of the unattainable entirety of the self. The sign "immortality" is similar. Though there is no way to either prove or disprove immortality, "an uplifted self-being is assured of immortality by its uplift."[183] Complementary to these uninvestigable subjective clues of entirety are objective clues to the entirety of the world:

> It is in its own rise and fall that possible Existenz comes to see a whole in which its existence is entwined. I treat this whole as though it were rising and falling itself. Once it is clear to me that all things are subject to evaluation, I look on the possible rise and fall of existence from the viewpoint of my own being.[184]

Thus arise images of world cycles, of the world as split off from the deity in a kind of apostasy, of the world systole and diastole, and so forth. And thus arise philosophical readings of history in which process and human action are entwined; images of the end of time; and eschatological myths of perfection or annihilation, Golden Ages lost or to come.

3. The negativity of defiance and fall, the poles of surrender and rise, the sources of tension, may become "an annihilation that is positivity itself: what previously seemed sheer negation turns into truth, comes bewilderingly to be not just a temptation but a claim."[185]

Jaspers called this positive negativity "nocturnal passion" and opposed it to "diurnal law." The mythical objectifications of these two powers take many forms. In a polytheistic world, chthonian gods of intoxication and destruction oppose celestial gods of measure, light (Dionysos and Apollo, in Nietzsche's schema). In a dualistic world, anti-God opposes God. In a monotheistic world, the one God is both loving, merciful, and wrathful, avenging.

In an individual's life, day is always bounded by night; even a man acting with goodwill, for all his goodwill, "cannot act without transgressing."[186] Man is "prey to the boundary situation of unavoidable guilt."[187]

It is not only in the course of the world in time that nothing can last; it is like a will that nothing intrinsic should be permanent. Foundering is what we call our experience—one we can no more anticipate than we can avoid—that perfection is also disappearance.[188]

That men's actions never have a definable or definitive end and that even men's creations, apparently more permanent, pass away, have in the past turned men from the realm of action to the realm of fabrication and from the realm of fabrication to that of good works eternally recorded in God's book. But Jaspers's dialectical schema of diurnal order and nocturnal passion opens a way for accepting both, for living in the tension of both. Possible Existenz is never realized unless it chooses among diurnal and nocturnal possibilities—even though this inevitably entails guilt, the guilt of rejecting the other possibilities. If possible Existenz does not choose, if it seeks to remain pure possibility, to avoid all delimitations and bonds (Kierkegaard is an example of one who lived by such denials), it suffers from the guilt of avoiding reality.

The tension between diurnal order and nocturnal passion is central to Jaspers's philosophizing. It is reflected in the presence of both Enlightenment exemplars (Lessing, Goethe) and modern-day victims, the exceptions (Kierkegaard, Nietzsche) in Jaspers's philosophizing. Jaspers himself loved the light—but without avoiding the night, without refusing to "look down into the abyss." And without confusing the deeper night with its phenomena, instinct, lust, the blind will to exist. Jaspers's ideal is the man who lives in a "lucid realm."

In the very throes of passion he is marked by clarity and circumspection. The I that speaks out of him will never be impossible to communicate with. There is dependability in him. . . . He shows the tension of constant self-disentanglement in the peril of rising and falling; but his is also the calm serenity of well-founded self-assurance. He listens to questions and arguments and recognizes in their medium an unconditional law, albeit one that eludes all definitive substantial phrasing. He seems unbreakable and yet infinitely flexible. There is no point in him that must not be touched, but there is readiness without reserve. To him the diurnal law grows lucid, and he understands the possibility of truth in another's night.[189]

4. The delimitations that Existenz accepts—with concomitant guilt—bring about a unity, historical definition, as opposed to dispersal. Decision by choice is the "unity of existential origin," as opposed to indecisiveness. Unity as an idea is opposed to "accidental multiplicity."[190] These unities, in which and through which Existenz relates to transcendence, Jaspers referred to as the One, in tension with the schematically opposite wealth of diversity.

If we look . . . upon the forms of unity accessible to us, we see in each a possible relation to transcendence. Our metaphysical grasp on the One itself is rooted in the *existential* One. Our relation to transcendence has room to exist in the *mundane and historical* One. And the logical forms of the One are the means of expression, which make rational sense even without transcendence.[191]

The logical forms referred to here are numerical unity, the unity of form or of a whole, and the "unity that we can be." The latter is the unity of consciousness, self-consciousness, and personality—each of which can be a way of approaching transcendence, conceiving of transcendence speculatively as numerically One, as the One form of all things or as the one person.

The distinction between many and One is reflected in the difference between polytheism and monotheism (although the concept of the deity as One often stands behind polytheism, even if the One is not worshiped as a deity, as in "the mythical All-Father of the primitives" or "the Greek *theion,* the divine-at-large'').[192] Jaspers considered the historical progression from polytheism to monotheism as stages on the way to "the liberation of man."

> The liberation of man proceeds from dark, savage forces to personal gods, from gods beyond good and evil to moral gods, from gods to the one God, and on to the ultimate freedom of recognizing the one personal God as a cipher. We may call this last liberation the ascent from God to the Godhead [*Deus* to *Deitas*], from the ciphers to what makes them speak. It is our liberation from the hobbles with which our own conceptions and thoughts prevent us from reaching the truth that halts all thinking.[193]

When Jaspers elaborated his fourfold scheme of the existential relations to transcendence, he was seeking the ground on which he later wrote his *Philosophical Faith and Revelation*—to which we will turn in the next sections. In 1931, Jaspers wrote out of his experience as a psychiatrist, but he had not tested his schematism on a particular exemplary life—nor had he had the existential relations profoundly tested in his own life. After the Second World War, in an effort to help the Germans free themselves from blind submission to the authority of their tradition, Jaspers turned to their greatest poet, Goethe. In a lecture called "Goethe and Our Future," the fourfold scheme informs—from behind the scenes—the popular, loose style of presentation.

Jaspers described Goethe's defiance and surrender, his rise and fall, his diurnal order and nocturnal passion, as well as his pantheism as a scientist, his polytheism as a poet, and his after-a-fashion monotheism ("if my personality as a moral being should require a God," wrote Goethe, "that too has been taken care of"). The center of this remarkable essay, which caused a storm of controversy among those admirers of Goethe in Germany who felt that Jaspers had maligned the German national greatness, is the pair diurnal order and nocturnal passion. It seems that this pair rose to prominence in Jaspers's mind during the war.

Jaspers admired Goethe's lucid self-understanding but was disappointed by his self-limitation, evident in truths he uttered about himself such as this: "I find injustice easier to bear than disorder." Jaspers, so close to the injustices and the disorders of the Nazi era, during which he had turned for support not to Goethe but to Aeschylus, Shakespeare, and the Bible, commented that Goethe "knew about the abyss, but he himself did not want to fail. . . ."[194] At the crucial moments of nocturnal passion, Goethe had withdrawn, refused his feelings, and yearned for order. Jaspers wrote sympathetically about Goethe—in terms that he might have used of his own youth, his life and work prior to 1933—but he felt compelled to warn that such a retreat entails grave limitations on what one is able to see and understand.

Jaspers's own effort to face the "abyss" of our times—in the political world and in the mind—yielded an extension and elaboration of the "existential relations to transcendence." And we turn to this now.

## 5. THINKING AND SPECULATING

### Characteristics of Thinking as Opposed to Knowing

Objectivity is characterized, in its relation to the *knowing* subject, by otherness, unity, and form, as we noted above. The three characteristics can be used as guidelines to characterize the self-relation of *thinking* and the thinking being, "master of thoughts."

1. Thinking is not essentially an always relative, uncertain acquisition of something other, but a "soaring of one's own being." "Transcending of one's own nature . . . , guided by whatever is revealed in thought" is "the basic trait of philosophical reflection from Plato down to Kant's formulation of enlightenment as man's 'exodus from the state of tutelage for which he has been to blame.'"[195] Thinking guides the thinker's transcending and ascertains the experience.

2. Thinking reaches beyond the unity of objects toward the

unity of the world, the unity of all men as the "goal" of
history—never attainable to it—and opens the way for the One
that is Existenz in its historicity, the One that is "unconditionally grasped,"[196] as it seeks the One that is transcendence.

3. Thinking is reflective; only a thinking being has a natural
relation to itself and is, in Socrates' terms, capable of self-
harmony. "Only one who is consistent with himself can agree
with others. To achieve harmony in oneself is to make friends
with oneself and gain others as friends."[197] Thinking guides the
thinker in his self-formation; as inner action, thinking is the
*self*-formative process. The thinker's self-formation is without
end, as is communication itself,[198] and there is thus no form
objectively graspable.

The crux of Jaspers's thinking about thinking is reached with
the statement that "the ultimate point of all philosophical
thought is philosophical life"[199] (not the contemplative life).
Thinking is preparatory and guiding; the ultimate point of it is
"being as I now become in thought."[200] Thinking guides the
thinker to what is other than his empirical existence, to the
unity that is in decision, to the form that is the philosophical
life.

Existenz is "suspended" between intramundane and extramundane being, a border, a boundary, reality at the limit of
empirical reality; thinking leads toward this boundary reality
through "concepts of Existenz." The thinking which goes beyond, toward transcendence, is speculation. We will first dis-
cuss Jaspers's characterization of speculation and then the operation called "formal transcending." This will bring us to
three paradoxical characterizations of transcendence based on
the guidelines set out here (otherness, unity, form): transcendence as immanence, the sole universal, reality without
possibility.

## The Three Languages of Transcendence

Jaspers spoke of three "languages" in which transcendence
speaks—to possible Existenz, not to consciousness at large.

First, in a singular historic moment, transcendence may speak directly to the absolute consciousness of Existenz, in what Jaspers called a metaphysical experience.

The original, present reading of the cipher script is without method, not to be produced according to plan. It is like a gift from the source of being. As a mundane ascertainment of transcendence it seeks out the light from the root of possible Existenz, and its content is not an advancement of knowledge but the historic truth of transparent existence.[201]

This first language is echoed in languages created by men, intended to convey the first language. "The objectifications of language with a metaphysical content appear in three palpable forms: as "discrete myths," as "revelations of a beyond," and as "mythical realities."[202] As an example of the first: "the real sea is to us the cipher of something unfathomable; in the form of sea gods as speaking symbols it becomes a discrete myth."[203] As to the second, a revelation from a beyond "devalues empirical reality into mere sensory contents, into essential nonbeing . . . but the beyond appears in the myth, gives signs, and works wonders."[204] The beyond is in some sense a duplication of this world; the divine character of this world is bypassed, and "an Existenz . . . enters into another world of being proper. . . ."[205] In the third mode of objectification, "reality itself is simultaneously mythical, it is neither devalued nor complemented by a discrete objectivity. . . . it is seen as such, and at the same time it is seen in the significance conferred on it by transcendence."[206]

With these three types of the second language, in which trnscendence and the experience of it are conveyed in generalized form, Jaspers delineated types of which the Greeks, the Christians, and modernists like Van Gogh are exemplars.[207] These types are the contexts of various world views, like historical parameters for the psychological types. But the types do not constitute a history of error: "truth would be lost if its transformation into something universal and identical for all were to deprive it of its indirect language,''[208] but it is not lost in its general, historical communications, ''manifest to an Existenz that hears what is truly at issue.''[209]

The first language is a cipher language, the second is a symbol language (symbols refer beyond themselves, that is, back to the original experience, to the first language). A third language can be written or spoken in response to the original cipher language; the thinker "conceives transcendence *in analogy* to his palpably and logically present mundane existence.''[210] But this speculative thought is itself a cipher: "speculation is a thinking that drives us to think the unthinkable.''[211] In Kantian terms, an intuition can be supplied to a concept either directly (schematically) or indirectly (symbolically): if our "knowledge" of God is thought of as schematical, the result is anthropomorphism; if all intuitive elements are abandoned, the result is deism; but if our knowledge is thought of as symbolic, there is both nearness and distance.[212] Jaspers formulated these possibilities as follows: "The intellect at large . . . can see two possibilities: either the world is everything, the world is God, or there is a world and transcendence. . . . To a transcending Existenz the intellectual alternative is a decline, whether to a pantheistic immanence without transcendence or to the worldless transcendence of a beyond. What happens in genuine transcending is the deepest possible affirmation of the world, performed toward mundane existence as a cipher language because that language transfigures the world, and what we secretly hear in it is the voice of transcendence.'' [213]

The writing of a cipher-script or the transmitting of a cipher-script through a generalizing form represents "the deepest possible affirmation of the world." Jaspers's metaphysics is like Nietzsche's "experimental philosophy," in that it wants to get to the opposite of nihilism, "to a Dionysian saying Yes to the world as it is, without subtraction, exception, and selection''[214]—but with the all-important difference that this world-as-it-is is also and essentially the language of transcendence.

## Formal Transcending

Speculation proceeds by reaching toward what Kant called the "X-*ignotum*" through the "general forms of thinkability," the categories. A category, or several, are absolutized, thrust, so to speak, beyond the bounds of thinkability. One category may be absolutized in a tautology: "truth is truth." Or two opposites may be absolutized as identical: "nothingness is being" (the procedure is that of *coincidentia oppositorum*). Or one or more categories may be absolutized in the form of becoming, as in Spinoza's *causa sui* or, in quite a different manner, Nietzsche's eternal return of the same.[215]

These three procedures begin from categories of three different types, which Jaspers labeled: categories of objectivity at large (e.g., being and nothingness, unity and duality, form and material, possibility, reality, necessity, chance, cause, universal and individual, meaning), categories of reality (e.g., time, space, substance, life, soul), and categories of freedom (e.g., freedom in the intellect, in the idea, and in Existenz).[216] The transcendence which arises from the absolutization of the categories of objectivity at large is a logicized transcendence— God is the light of cognition, bestower of the clear articulation of insight, God is truth as cognition, He is knowledge, *logos*, wisdom. The transcendence which arises from the absolutization of the categories of reality is a naturalized transcendence: God is the ground of reality, the cause of existence; God is truth as being, nature, omnipotence. And the transcendence which arises from the absolutization of the categories of freedom is an anthropomorphized transcendence: God is the highest good, source of the right order of life; God is truth in action, love, personality, goodness.[217]

These procedures, this "wealth of approaches," does not make transcendence thinkable; the unthinkability remains. But they allow the thinker to "find the intrinsic unthinkability and to make sure of it in all its modes";[218] they keep the thinker from setting an arbitrary limit past which he cannot go, at which questions cease; they prevent a passive acceptance of a limit, passing over in silence.

The transcendence that comes to appear in this fashion remains indefinite, incognizable, and unthinkable, and yet it is present in my thinking in the sense *that* it is, not *what* it is. ... Transcendence becomes visible in its traces, not as itself, and always ambiguously. It does not become extant in the world. But to Existenz it may mean the perfect peace of being, a superabundant being that has nothing definite about it any more.[219]

Plotinus's "it is what it is," or the Old Testament thinker's attribution to God of the "I am that I am" are "formal tautological propositions whose possible fulfillment is unfathomable." But even these tautological propositions require categories of objective being ("it") or free being ("I").[220]

Jaspers attempted to transform the limits of thought into living limits—not what Camus called "closed doors," but signs of an incomprehensible *that*. His attempt is an appeal to others to rest neither unbegun nor in defeat nor with an uncritically accepted image or state (doctrine or mystical communion). As Existenz remains an uncomprehended *that,* so does the *that* which draws it. Transcendence "brings forth our questioning and permits it no rest."[221] Jaspers's concern was with the impact of ciphers and speculative cipher-scripts on thinking, on the thinker, with the preservation of motion—that is, of freedom.

We should like to get in touch with the truth of ciphers. We are not asking for the immense realm of facts from mythological or religious or psychological history, nor do we follow psychological or sociological lines of questioning. What concerns us is the question of truth as such—more specifically, the question of the truth of ciphers that cannot be known, that can only be experienced existentially. In the historic forms of ciphers we look for their appeal as possible truth. Thus we are not acting objectively—that is to say, not scientifically, not historically, not psychologically or sociologically—but neither are we following subjective tastes or inclinations. Instead, *we yield to the impacts that turn thinking into inner action wherever we are engaged.*[222]

Inner action in this sense is similar to the free play of the cognitive faculties that Kant described as our relation to the
beautiful: "the freedom of aesthetic play is the most perfect,
because it is unconfined by interest and reality."[223] Jaspers
related metaphysical speculation to art explicitly but drew the
following distinction:

> . . . art is granted fulfillment, whereas long practice in
> speculation only makes us feel less articulate. In meta-
> physics more than anywhere else, conclusiveness would
> doom philosophizing. Speculation is a thing in process;
> instead of turning into art, metaphysical philosophy re-
> veals to those who philosophize how truth can be seen in
> the forms of art. . . . Adoption in philosophical conscious-
> ness leaves even perfect art not quite untouched. The non-
> committal [disinterested] delight will be disrupted; the de-
> liverance will be seen as mere anticipation and put in doubt
> again; the music that goes beyond all we can say will finally
> drive us back to words; and the sight of art, to thoughts.
> . . .[224]

Objects in the world are other than the subject as consciousness at large. Jaspers rejected the alternatives of identifying
world and God—pantheism—and of locating transcendence in
a beyond completely other than the world, as intellectualistic.
Going deeper than these alternatives, he offered a paradoxical
formulation: immanent transcendence. This formulation, in
addition to going more deeply than objectifying formulas, is
distinguished from the existential experience of becoming
other through inner action, or becoming what you are.

> Immanent (precisely as distinct from transcendent) is that
> which can be concurrently experienced by everyone in con-
> sciousness at large. In other words: the world is immanent.
> Also immanent is the existential certainty of being oneself (a
> certainty not accessible in any consciousness at large but
> present in the respective self-being, as distinct from tran-
> scendent being—in other words, from that which Existenz
> in its essence relates to). When transcendent being comes

into the presence of an Existenz, however, it does not do so as itself, for there is no identity of Existenz and transcendence. It comes to mind as a *cipher*, and even then not as an object that is this object, but *athwart all objectivity*, so to speak. Immanent transcendence is an immanence that has instantly vanished again, and it is a transcendence that has come to exist as, the language of a cipher.[225]

The object is a unity as subjectively constituted. The unity that characterizes transcendence is, again, paradoxically expressed: transcendence is the "inconceivable unity of the general and the particular." This is contrasted to the unity of Existenz in its historicity.

> The paradox of transcendence lies in the fact that we can *grasp it only historically,* but cannot *conceive it as being historic itself.* . . . It is not itself either in generality for a consciousness-at-large, like objects, or in historicity, like Existenz. For Existenz the reality of transcendence is the *sole universal*, that of which there is no particular case any more; it is the inconceivable unity of the general and the particular that has nothing distinguishable without or within. Where it is conceived in distinction or seen as an image, transcendence is already a historic phenomenon and not universal.[126]

In objective terms, the universal is that form under which the particular is subsumed as a case. (Kant called this determinate judgment.) Second, it is the objectivity fulfilled by the present Existenz that grasps transcendence in it. (This is similar to what Kant called reflective judgment: seeing through the particular toward the universal, guided by ideas, as in writing a cipher-script, speculating.) Third, the universal is the "ineffable and unimaginable singularity that is encountered as the only reality." (This encounter is a metaphysical experience.)

A third guideline to transcendence is the notion of possibility. In objective terms, whatever appears in one form can be thought of as appearing in another, or as not being. In existential elucidation, possibility is an appeal to the freedom of the self; it is an index of the ceaselessness of self-formation. Jaspers defined possibility in metaphysics as "the game of trying, recollecting, anticipating in objective form what can be present only in a historically concrete sense of being: the transcendent *reality that has no possibility*."[227] This reality, in Schelling's phrase, "strikes down whatever comes from thought," that is, it is not an "*addendum* to what is possible" (a true world in Nietzsche's terms). It is that which is unthinkable because it is without possibility; it cannot appear as itself in any form, and it cannot be thought of as not being.

These paradoxical formulations mark the point at which all thought founders.[228] Existenz cannot think the *what* of transcendence; it can only, in a metaphysical experience, experience the *that* of "the Encompassing." Speculatively, *Deus* can be pictured; but *Deitas*, the Godhead, cannot.

Knowing is our way of relating to the other, of unifying, of forming. Thinking is both objectively oriented, tied to knowing, and inwardly oriented, indirectly effective because it prepares for inner action and ascertains it. Knowing achieves results, though they are always relative, (cogency is always relative); thinking is a performance continually renewed, objectively resultless. Speculation is that kind of thinking which is most easily mistaken for knowing because it achieves a picture, a formulation, a script, and it can be embodied in a thought-system or a work of art. But for Jaspers, speculation must remain a thing in process.

Existenz is suspended between the objective world in which freedom is not yet and the transcendence in which freedom is no longer, the end of motion—certainly a peace which passes all understanding.

## 6. PHILOSOPHICAL FAITH AND REVELATION

### Reason and Faith

Through the twelfth century, philosophy and Christian theology remained unified in concept: "To Anselm as to Augustine, thought as such aimed at the deity, which in turn led the way.

A distinction would have stripped philosophy of content, and theology of reason.''[229] For Aquinas, philosophy, the work of human reason, was subordinate to theology, which was supra-rationally rooted—the natural realm was distinct from the realm of grace. Augustine's concept of cognition as due to divine illumination was abandoned: ''Aquinas considered it a natural activity of the mind. . . . thought lost its supernal splendor and became a creative realm of its own as man's proper, healthy, natural common sense . . . , mere intellectual labor.''[230] Theology became ecclesiastical science rooted in revelation; philosophy became human science based on perception and intellectual thought.

The clear, harmonious Thomistic order in which revelation and reason were distinct and of different rank but not completely divorced and irreconcilable was split apart in Protestantism. ''The world was deemed free and autonomous as the realm of sin; for eternity, there was vindication by faith alone''[231]—and this faith was completely detached from the world. ''Reason itself was corrupt, and the only truth lay in worldless isolation or in common prayer, both related to God's eternity.''[232]

This ''irresponsibility toward the world'' was intolerable to many; even among Protestants there was opposition to Luther's *pecca fortiter,* and the appeal of Aquinas's order and Greek encompassing principles like Aristotle's *Nous* and the Stoic *Logos* persisted. ''The greatest harmonizing endeavors were those of Leibniz and Hegel, with Hegel's the more impressive for his vision and interpretive acceptance of all negativities and horrors.''[233]

The relations that have obtained between reason and revelation, philosophy and theology, range from identity to complementarity to antipathy. Jaspers claimed that ''none can satisfy'' and asked: ''can we come to a better insight?''[234]

Such an insight would demand clear distinctions, on the one hand between intellect and reason[235] and, on the other hand, between reason and revelation or philosophical faith and religious faith in the Christian tradition.

Philosophy in our time cannot ignore the characteristics of modern science and return to a union with theology without falling into superstition.

> Augustine despised the sciences. . . . to his mind the superstition supported by the Bible was no superstition. And the crucial argument against superstition was not better, methodic insight into the realities of the world, but belief in God and the striving to save one's soul. Accordingly, we find nearly all the superstitions of his time strangely intermingled in his work.[236]

Philosophy today must take its guidelines from science, from world orientation, and this precludes the principle that unified philosophy and theology for Augustine—namely, that all insight comes from within where it has been deposited by God, through recollection similar to the Platonic.

If the Thomistic distinction of ecclesiastic and human science were adopted, it would render philosophy, as Jaspers put it, "not serious as philosophy" and, from the point of view of the believer, "*ersatz* religion."[237] Any conflict between philosophy and theology would be resolved in favor of the latter, entailing a *sacrificium intellectus,* a closing of the thinking space. Jaspers rejected a handmaiden status for philosophy, considering the task of rendering proofs and rational arguments in support of revelation an impossible one: "no general concept enables us to predict an act of God as possible, or to comprehend it afterwards. . . . the case for revelation lies solely in hearing it and accepting God's work."[238] The thinking which prepares the way for existential performance and reflects on that performance cannot do the same for God's performance.

Finally, philosophy cannot exist when it is believed that reason is corrupt—whether this is in Luther's terms or in the terms of the late nineteenth-century writers (like Klages) who considered man to be a diseased animal, the disease being reason. "Irresponsibility toward the world" is irresponsibility toward the very condition of Existenz.

Jaspers appealed for a faith—philosophical faith—independent of church, state, mass movement, or party, responsible only to an "authority that we establish for ourselves and find in four thousand years of philosophy"[239]—that is, the common authority of reason itself.

The possibility of such faith, as distinct from revealed faith, is evoked in the question: "could it be, we ask as we philosophize, that not just the content of a revelation but the reality which believers claim for it may become a cipher? . . . Can a cipher of Transcendence carry weight by being physically felt as a reality in the world and yet known to be no such reality?"[240] Jaspers found the following paradox to be "inescapable":

> . . . the contents of revelations would become more pure, more true, if their reality were discarded. The reality as such would turn into a cipher of the presence of God, lending an extraordinary weight to the contents.[241]

Jaspers's discarding of the reality of revelations as such is a form of "demythologizing," but the point of it is to retain the contents, not to "discard the entire world of myths"[242]—as he interpreted Bultmann's project.

## Between Mysticism and Authority

Jaspers described the limitations of two attitudes toward the political realm that deny it as a space for the manifestation of Existenz: retreat from it into the pointlike state of ataraxy and absolutization of it accompanied by a claim to total knowledge. Analogously, he found—for himself, as a philosopher—two religious attitudes toward the world objectionable: retreat from it into unworldliness, irresponsibility toward it in what Weber called inner worldly asceticism, and (attempted) control over it in Catholicism, uncommunicative and worldless. Jaspers rejected both unworldly union with the deity and objectification of the deity in worldly churches and cults, modes of worship and doctrines making exclusive claim to truth and redemptive power (*extra ecclesiam nulla salus*).

Analogous to the problematic relation of freedom and the authority of legality is the relation of freedom and the authority of faith. As we have seen, Jaspers separated the authority of legality and the authority of faith; this separation is particularly important with respect to Christian authority because unlike other religious authorities, "the exclusive revelation defined by the Church brought the new total authority," a claim to "jurisdiction over all men."[243]

> The Church rests upon sacred writings whose content will always offset the totalitarian trend and never allow human dignity, freedom and justice to vanish altogether. The ecclesiastic horrors happened in the atmosphere of superstition, replete with mysterious meanings; the modern horrors happen in an atmosphere ruled by the superstitions of intellectual enlightenment. The totalitarian Church lacked the means of limitless power which the technological age puts at the disposal of the state, and nowhere today does the state serve as an arm of the Church as in times past. . . . Yet even now the ecclesiastic faith, with characteristic totalitarian naiveté, regards itself as the sole, authorized infallible vessel of truth and inwardly denies the equal rights of the 'heathen,' the infidel, the heretic.[244]

Neither the atmosphere of superstition replete with mysterious meanings nor the atmosphere ruled by superstitions of intellectual enlightenment is compatible with the "atmosphere of reason" that leaves room for freedom of thought and action.

The "atmosphere of reason" reflected in Lessing's *Nathan the Wise* is an ideal, even though "historical reality shows us a different picture," a picture of "profound clash of substances with existential roots."[245] It shows us a picture of communities adhering to symbols which have for them "community-founding powers" and engaging in uncommunicative, often violent, struggles with other communities: "the tale of the three rings does not reflect our situation."[246] Nonetheless, Existenz must not adopt such a historical situation as definitive:

> To an existing Existenz transcendent truth is not a timeless extant one, to be comprehended like rational insights. This is why it must have historic form. Yet as long as that truth keeps a free existential community in motion, an Existenz that does not confuse the meaning of the universal will keep an open mind for other truth. The unconditionality with which it adheres to its own truth while recognizing it as historic—this very unconditionality would make it shun any exclusiveness and any claim to universality, and would prevent it from granting the character of timeless valid rational truths to its own form of historic truths. . . .[247]

True authority is founded in such an unconditional adherence to a truth recognized as historic; it opposes "the arbitrary plurality of intention and will"[248] while leaving room for the plurality of intentions and wills, the very condition of men.

Uncommunicative or uncommunicable unworldliness and religious authority claiming total jurisdiction are two extremes which leave no room for the communication that is truth. Jaspers elucidated two extremes in general form under the headings "the exception" and "authority." "Exception calls everything into question, is startling and fascinating. Authority is the supporting, protecting and reassuring fullness."[249] Both extremes seem to threaten not only "the validity and freedom of cogently valid rational knowledge" but all truth.[250]

> The man who is an exception is an exception first to universal existence, whether this appears in the form of the ethos, institutions and laws of the land, or the health of the body, or any other normalcy. Secondly, he is an exception to the universally valid, cogent and certain thinking of consciousness-in-general. Finally, he is an exception to spirit, in belonging to which I am a member of a whole. To be an exception is actually to break out of every kind of universality.[251]

The norms of Dasein, Bewusstsein überhaupt, and Geist are breached by the exception as he seeks a unique path of realization; "he can lose the world in the service of transcendence, and can virtually disappear in consequence of negative resolutions"[252] (like Kierkegaard). The exception is illuminative of possibilities for each Existenz, but he is never a model; he illuminates the universal from the situation of the nonuniversal.

Authority, on the contrary, does not break with the forms of truth that characterize Dasein, Bewusstsein überhaupt, and Geist. It binds them together; it is at once external command, universal knowledge (as expertness), and idea of the whole.

> The unconditional character of authority . . . consists in its being an *historic unity of truth* for the person living in it. On the foundation laid at the beginning, authority embraces the historic past speaking in the present, in images and symbols, in institutions, laws, and systems of thought—all this by historic assimilation of the unique present that is identical with myself.[253]

The historic nature of authority keeps it from fixation. It is in constant motion and in constant tension, both with its own tendencies toward stabilization and with the freedom of individuals.

> Authority becomes untrue when those individual modes of truth separate that belong together—whether existence, compelling certainty or spirit—and try to become autonomous, usurping authority for themselves; when it becomes a mere power in existence without enlivening all the sources of truth; when it claims validity merely by virtue of the position of single individuals who have no power in the world, who do not make the sacrifices and take the risks needed to win and to maintain authority; when I relinquish the freedom of selfhood and on the strength of supposed insight "freely surrender my freedom"; when I act in thoughtless obedience instead of yielding to the depths of authority.[254]

Both the exception and authority can be destructive of freedom—but both must be confronted and illuminated—and the illumination of the exception and authority is the task of reason.

. . . truth is not one, because the exception breaks out of it, and because authority realizes truth only in historical form. But as long as reason is present, the impulse to go beyond the multiplicity to the universal truth remains undiminished, despite the spectacle of the exception, and despite obedience to authority. . . . Reason is the total will to communication.[255]

Reason enables Existenz to confront the exception without succumbing to his fascination or being ruined in his explosions (the hammering, lightnings, and dynamitings of Nietzsche, for example) and to live with and in authority without sacrificing freedom.[256]

## The Question of Mediation

For most Christians, the reality of revelation lies in the reality of Jesus, "discoverable in the synoptic Gospels by means of historical criticism,"[257] and in the *kerygma,* the preaching of the apostles in which Jesus is conceived as the Christ. For Jaspers, however, Jesus was human, the last of a line of Hebrew prophets, "neither a self-appointed Messiah, nor a self-made sacrament—by instituting the Last Supper—nor the founder of a church."[258] For Jaspers, Jesus, as a man, is a cipher of being human: "It says that a man who lives and thinks as he did, a man who is true without any reservation, must die at the hands of men, because human reality is too untrustful to bear him."[259] In the course of time, however, the adoption of this cipher has evolved so that Jesus has been conceived as the Son of God sacrificed for men, as a model for martyrdom, as the source of redemption. Jaspers appealed for men to "make the human Jesus and his faith prevail"—which faith he called biblical faith rather than Christian faith ("a complex situation caused the biblical faith to be dressed up in the name Christianity").[260]

In making this appeal, Jaspers is following a tradition that goes back to Lessing. In his *Die Religion Christi,*[261] published in 1780, Lessing distinguished the religion of Christ—the religion which Christ "accepted and practices as a man" and

which "every man can have in common with him; which every
man must necessarily wish all the more to share with him the
more exalted and attractive the image he has of Christ as a
mere mortal"—from the Christian religion. The Christian religion accepts the idea of the apostles that Christ was "more
than man, and as such makes him an object of veneration."
The religion of Christ and the Christian religion are, Lessing
held, "utterly incompatible." As Lessing pointed out, the religion of Christ is clear in the Bible, but "the Christian religion is
so uncertain and ambiguous that there is scarcely a single passage which, in all the history of the world, has been interpreted
in the same way by two men."

The ambiguity of the Christian religion, the polarities with
which the Bible is replete, are the starting point for Jaspers's
"return to the original source." The polarities and contradictions in the Bible are "a prefiguration to all life's contradictions," and to explore them is "to be made free for all possibilities and for the unremitting struggle for the elevation of
man."[262] Jaspers gives examples of opposites:

> . . . the religion of the cult and the prophetic religion of the
> pure ethos; the religion of the law and the religion of love; . . .
> the religion of the priests and the free religion of prayer that
> is carried on by individuals; the national God and the univer-
> sal God; the covenant with the chosen people and the cov-
> enant with man as man; the balancing of guilt and retribu-
> tion in this life (happiness and unhappiness considered as
> measures of sin and virtue) and the attitude of faith of
> Jeremiah, of Job in the presence of divine mystery; the reli-
> gion of the congregation and the religion of the men of God,
> seers, prophets; magical religion and the ethical religion of
> the rational idea of creation. . . .[263]

Jaspers appealed for a biblical religion purified of nationalism,
legalism, and, most importantly, of the idea of the God-man. In
much the same terms as Lessing, Jaspers claimed that "no
man can be God," and "the spirit of Christ belongs to every
man."

Rather than linking the immanent and the transcendent, men

in the world and God, with the figure of the God-man, the doctrine of incarnation or, in Kierkegaard's terms, the paradox, Jaspers spoke of the world—all things and all men—as the speech of God, the cipher world. And revelation, viewed as a cipher, would have in the cipher world no higher rank, no higher claim. Revelation would be

> the cipher that allows man's boundless yearning for the real presence of God to be satisfied for an instant, so to speak— but only so as to thrust him back at once into the hard, great, free state he was created in, and in which God remains inexorably hidden.[264]

The transformation of revelation into cipher is the premise for the meeting, the communication, of philosophy and religion; Jaspers appealed for what is, in effect, a new Protestant Reformation. The abandonment by Protestantism of the principles of Catholic religion—God's incarnation in Jesus Christ and the presence of Christ in the *corpus mysticum* of the church—for its own principle of a past incarnation present only for individuals in words, witnesses' accounts, not in the church itself, is to be carried further: the incarnation is a cipher. In Jaspers's view, the Protestants really remained imprisoned by the Catholic principle:

> They clung to an inwardly disparate Catholicism and blocked the breakthrough that was their principle. Protestantism must be completed in earnest, or else it will sink into the trivial and dishonest mimicry of a Catholicism it can never equal.[265]

Faith must become in a new way "a personal responsibility of the individual."[266]

If the reality of revelation were relinquished, if revelation became a cipher, Jaspers held, the fears and unfreedoms that have bound men in their actions would be transformed: "resolution will no longer be due to fear of something, but to the very different fear of the free for their freedom and for eternity."[267] This would have consequences in every realm; for example, the threat of punishment in the afterlife, felt as a political necessity even among America's revolutionary Deist founding fathers, would be transformed.

> The eternal punishments of hell . . . used to have great terrifying and controlling power. Does the cipher retain its impact if at decisive moments we are not menaced with a future hell but impressed with the inconceivable eternity of our decision? Or will it then, perhaps, be even more manifest that human actions bear eternal weight—will the cipher reveal more clearly than the crushing fear of punishment that man's own self is his to win or lose? Instead of experiencing guilt and punishment as separated in time—the sin now, the hell in the future—will he perhaps come to feel them united in his act as a manifestation of instant eternity, of the irrevocability that we conceive in the cipher of infernal punishment?[268]

Such a cipher would be central to an ethics of responsibility in an era in which "embodiment cannot be maintained unchanged," in a world illuminated by scientific realism. Such a cipher would be part of the substance of an existential community in its political manifestation.

> Though embodiment may strengthen our psychophysical vital forces, it weakens veracity, and thus our existential forces. Embodiment is capable of holding even one who does not believe; but the disembodied ciphers cleanse the faith of free Existenz.[269]

This is one example of how "in its political appearance philosophy shows what it is." Cipher-reading, metaphysics, bears upon the actions of men in the world; in distinction from the way in which religious authority bears upon those actions, it works inwardly, shaping grand volition.

### Between Paradox Deified and Atheism

Philosophical faith is illuminated by comparison with authority, particularly with authority grounded in the reality of revelation. On the other hand, it is illuminated by comparison with the exception: for Jaspers, contemporary philosophizing must confront the exceptions Nietzsche and Kierkegaard, who "created the actual situation for philosophizing in this epoch."[270] "The problem for us is to philosophize without being exceptions, but with our eyes on the exception."[271]

"Kierkegaard points in the direction of an absurd Christianity before which the world sinks away. . . ."[272] With such a Christianity, the church was totally denied. Kierkegaard's "dexterous but not dishonest way to save the embodied God-Man"[273] is inseparable from his attack on the church; to take over the "dialectical theology" and yet affirm the church (to continue, in Kierkegaard's phrase, to "take part in playing God for a fool") is impossible. If the dialectical theology were right, "it would mean the end of Christianity in the world. . . . if the Christian faith is what he construed it to be, probably no one can believe it any more—and Kierkegaard, though passionately eager to believe, never claimed to be doing so in person."[274]

Nietzsche's philosophizing points to another kind of leap: to the doctrine of the eternal recurrence and the idea of the superman. But in these symbols "there is no longer any transcendent content."[275] The richness and ambiguity, the contradictoriness, the motion, of Nietzsche's philosophizing has been lost, and his ideas taken over piecemeal: "it seems as though every attitude, every world-view, every conviction claims him as authority."[276] As Nietzsche himself predicted, most of his readers have been "looting soldiers."

In both cases: "Nobody has accepted their answers; they are not ours. It is for us to see what will become of us through ourselves as we look upon them."[277]

> The philosophizing Existenz is found in its pure origins only insofar as it sees itself confronting another reality which is not true for itself, but only for that other: before revealed religion and atheism. This alternative to philosophy on both its sides—the obedient churchly belief of cults, and atheism—is a reality of world-dominating importance.[278]

Authority and exception orient philosophizing for the question: "what now?"

# CONCLUSION

In the 1920s, while Jaspers the psychiatrist was making what he called his "ascent to philosophy," most German academic philosophers were making an effort to revive German idealism. They were neo-Kantians (of two schools: Baden and Marburg) or neo-Hegelians. Even Husserl, concerned with going "back to the things themselves," ultimately arrived at an idealist transcendental consciousness. The disconcerting attacks upon philosophy produced by Nietzsche and Kierkegaard were either deflected or relegated to a realm outside philosophy proper. But the period of general reorientation brought philosophy itself into question. To delimit the proper subject of philosophy requires us to ask "what is philosophy?" as much as does an effort to say that philosophy should be all-encompassing, though in a very different way. For as Jaspers remarked, "There is nothing that is not philosophy's business."[1]

Jaspers and Heidegger were the two thinkers who saw most clearly that the fundamental concepts with which philosophy had been operating until Hegel's time needed a fundamental critique. They both learned deeply from Kierkegaard and then from Nietzsche. Heidegger saw in Jaspers's *Psychologie der Weltanschauungen* (1919) a new beginning, but a beginning inchoate, without methodological self-consciousness. *Being and Time* (1927) was Heidegger's effort to look back through the history of philosophizing in the West to its origins and to ask how the basis of all concepts, intertwined in the roots of all conceptualization—Being, *Sein*—had been misunderstood or neglected, forgotten. Rather than leaning to one side or the other of the antithetical conceptual pairs that have framed the tradition, Heidegger wanted to unearth the root of the antithesis—Being. This was Jaspers's method, too, once he had advanced beyond the *Psychologie der Weltanschauungen* with his ten-year self-education among the great philosophers. But Jaspers did not seek the single preconceptual (or as yet unthought) root of conceptualizing: he did not attempt a "fundamental ontology" in Heidegger's sense.

To put the matter in methodological terms, the two philosophers introduced a self-consciously dynamic mode of thinking that moves in and among different realms without reverting to a two-world theory; they avoided the mind-body duality, the subject-object split, the existence-essence opposition, the war between theists and atheists. Heidegger's philosophizing was—before and after the so-called *Kehre* (or "turn") of the late 1930s—concerned with the meaning of Being and man's estrangement from Being. This concern meant for Heidegger a critique of reason as conceived by the idealists. He viewed rationalism as thinking's adversary and irrationalism as this adversary's secret ally. Both rationalism and irrationalism neglect the crucial distinction between being (*das Seiende*) and Being (*Sein*); both begin from and never leave their orientation toward objects, things, beings, and their objectifying categories. Jaspers, too, avoided both traditional rationalism and modern irrationalism. But he did not seek a "meditative thinking" like Heidegger's, a thinking attuned to or receptive to Being. Rather, he gave reason (*Vernunft*) a different directedness and scope: he spoke of reason and Existenz as inseparable, dialectically related, and emphasized that "thinking is as the thinker does."[2] Jaspers's concern was ultimately not with the objects of thinking, or with nonobjectifying thinking, but with what reason does to the reasoner, how thinking illuminates the world and human situatedness in the world for the thinking person. "Philosophical thinking is a cast of mind that becomes part of a man's very nature."[3]

Jaspers's philosophizing is characterized by its illuminating movements and by its spaciousness. "There is," as von Hofmannsthal wrote, "no point in an individual taking a modest attitude in the intellectual sphere; the whole contemporary world, all the past included, is precisely the space he needs fully to exist.''[4] This was Jaspers's space. But he moved in it with a kind of philosophical modesty which he attributed, characteristically, to an orientation by existential contrasts, to a consideration of what thinking did to two human types:

> For a modest and honest philosophizing as we attempt it today, there is an orientation by two sides of humanity, both indispensable to the revelation of truth. On the one side we see the exceptions, the victims of their times, demonstrating in view of the abyss that the absolute is possible in human life. On the other side we see Goethe, this phenomenon and self-portrait of humanity on a single scale—of ideal normalcy, as it were—by way of a constantly changing reality of life. The exception fails; it seems constrained by the absolute with which it merges, perishing as existence. Goethe follows the road of "die and be born" [*stirb und werde*] into the utmost remorse and pressure of conscience; and after the break, after the dying, he is back and ready for a new, changing realization. Goethe chose to live a full, human life. He was no victim such as Nietzsche and Kierkegaard.[5]

Kant asking "what is man?" and Goethe seeking the "spirit of mankind" and Lessing indicating the freedom that is men's because they are not gods but, as it were, limited gods[6]—these were exemplary dwellers in what Jaspers called the atmosphere of reason and the atmosphere of *humanitas*.

Jaspers appealed ceaselessly for the atmosphere that prevails when people face reality squarely, aware of its possibilities and of its unlimited interpretability, ready to make fair judgments but free of dogmatic rigidities.[7] This atmosphere of reason and humanitas in which Jaspers was naturally at home did not blind him to the dark, to the world of the victims. Before the Second World War he said: "I hope to stand up for the kind of reason that does not ignore the irrational but seeks to illuminate it in thought."[8] But the challenge of the Third Reich, the war, and the bomb made the task of illumination far more compelling and complex. The eighteenth century's legacy, the

atmosphere of reason and humanitas, was—and still is—
threatened with extinction; we live in a situation in which all
men are potential victims.

> Civilizations have perished before. What is new today is that
> all mankind is threatened, that the menace is both more
> acute and more conscious, and that it does not merely affect
> our lives and property, but our very humanity.[9]

Jaspers constantly appealed for communication. For him the
atmosphere of reason is the atmosphere of dialogue and its
"loving struggle." In this Jaspers is the modern heir of Socrates, and his descriptions of Socrates's activity are keys to his
own endeavor.

> This is what is memorable and characteristic in Socrates:
> he carries his criticism to the extreme, yet never ceases to
> recognize the absolute authority, which may be called the
> true, the good, or reason. For him this authority represents
> an absolute responsibility. To whom? He does not know, but
> he speaks of gods. Whatever may happen in reality, this is
> the fixed point, which stands in a world of endless change.
> Socrates took over the reflection of the Sophists, but with
> it he did not seek to dissolve the human substance; rather he
> strove to actualize the substance of thought itself to awaken
> inner action.
> Here we find an imperative without fanaticism, the highest
> aspiration without ethical dogma. Keep yourself open for the
> absolute. Until you achieve it, do not throw yourself away,
> for in it you can live and be at peace.
> What made Socrates free was that in non-knowledge he
> had certainty of the goal toward which he had undertaken
> the venture of his whole life, and now of his death.[10]

Jaspers described the atmosphere of reason as "clearly evident
in unique individuals such as Lessing, individuals who—even
without substantial content—affect us as though they were
reason itself, and whose words we read just to breathe this
atmosphere."[11]

In Jaspers's own philosophizing—as with both Socrates and Lessing—there seems to be a lack of substantial content. But this is because, in Jaspers's own terms, the content of reason is unobjectifiable Existenz: "Existenz only comes clear through reason; reason only has content through Existenz."[12] To criticize Jaspers's philosophizing for lack of substantial content is to miss its dynamism; the content is what each reader experiences as he or she follows the thinking and reacts inwardly. On the other hand, the form of Jaspers's philosophizing is problematic. Jaspers's philosophizing is without formal or final system; there are networks of systemizations, approaches, thought-movements. As this study has attempted to show, each grows from a seed: a question, a contrast, a thinking operation.

Jaspers thought that the mobility and final insufficiency, or foundering, of this philosophy were incompatible with artistic forms. He emphasized the distinction between thinking and the products of thinking, between (on the one hand) the thinking which he identified with speech and (on the other) written works. But it does not follow from this important distinction that if one is going to write (as Socrates did not), artistic forms are not as capable of gesturing toward the nonobjective and reflecting mobility as the compact and continuous prose that Jaspers strove for, provided that they are not mistaken for the last word.

The aphorism, for one example, can be a heuristic device; it need not state facts or final conclusions. It is like the oracle which Heraclitus said neither reveals nor conceals but gives signs. Furthermore, it is a self-reflective form: it reaches out to touch reality and also reaches for the limits of its own medium, language. This self-reflectivity was characteristic of the German aphoristic masters, from Lichtenberg to Karl Kraus.[13] The aphorism is a fragment of a never-attained whole; hence it has been a key device for antisystematic thinkers like Nietzsche and Kierkegaard. Jaspers's works might have benefited from aphoristic foci, signs set within the ongoing motion. For a philosophy striving to speak popularly, such

signs would have provided an ingredient—memorability—
missing from vague introductory and summary systematic
statements.

As a second example: the dialogue would seem to be an appropriate form for a philosophy of communication. But even
though Jaspers held that "dialogue is the *reality of thought,
thought and speech are one*" and that "the dialogue form,
through the relation of the content to men and situations,
makes it possible to actualize the existential meaning of ideas
along with their logical meanings, he did not think that the
dialogue was finally the proper form for philosophy.[14]

> A true idea seeks a form and cannot find it, and the reader
> experiences the failure. . . . The utmost depth of humanly
> possible Existenz defies representation. . . . A dialogue may
> have a philosophical effect, but it is not the adequate form in
> which to convey philosophy. For it is impossible for philos-
> ophy to become entirely objective like the artist's figures.[15]

Whether or not the artist's figures are entirely objective is a
more open question than this indicates; indeed, the question is
so open that an entire philosophical tendency, hermeneutics,
has recently arisen to take it up.

Again, Jaspers's works might have benefited from dialogue
forms set within the ongoing motion. Among the formally most
effective parts of his work are those in which he engages other
thinkers directly (as in the portraits of Nietzsche and Kierkegaard in *Reason and Existenz*) or presents two figures in
dialogue (as in the debate between two Germans in *Philosophy
Is for Everyman*) or appeals directly to his audience (as in *The
Question of German Guilt*).[16] These parts of the works have
highlights and dramatic tensions lacking elsewhere.

Both aphorism and dialogue are effective vehicles for
philosophical irony: a double-edged irony that is at once (to
use Jaspers's terms) worldly in its orientation, existentially
elucidative, and playfully metaphysical. Irony might have
contributed to Jaspers's project: "we are indeed building up by
tearing down what we have built."[17] An ingredient of

irony—the mode so dear to the indirect communication of both Nietzsche and Kierkegaard—might have helped Jaspers present the paradoxical unity of the building-up and the tearing-down activities.

In general, as these examples imply, the form of Jaspers's works is problematic precisely because his two central existential concepts, communication and freedom, as existential concepts, reveal relations of one Existenz and another. Jaspers was certainly quite well aware that public discourse and debate cannot presume the endless, inconclusive loving struggle of one Existenz with another; that in the agora Socrates met not another Socrates but Callicles and Thrasymachus. How relationships between rational individuals bear upon the public realm and its plurality of actors is not clear. There is a fundamental tension in Jaspers's thought: reason is "the suprapolitical element" and yet reason is to grow in and from public exchange, where all control and correct each other. Having left behind the traditional image of the philosopher as a solitary and perhaps exceptional individual, removed from the world, Jaspers was confronted with the question of how the little communicative plurality of one and one can relate to the plurality of the many. His hope was clear: "What works in the smallest circles can become the supreme reality of an epoch and prove itself in the sequel. What has not yet reached the masses can permeate them in the future."[18]

The questions raised here about the form of Jaspers's philosophical writings are obviously not merely formal. The task of reaching beyond the circle of communicators is crucial; any philosophizing that *is* communication as loving struggle must consider those who will not or cannot struggle lovingly and those with whom loving struggle is not possible for the thinker. Before we turn back to the problem of political discussion, these questions can be put concretely by considering Jaspers's relationships with professional philosophers and with the one of his contemporaries in Germany who was, he felt, a philosopher of real greatness—Heidegger.

Jaspers and Heidegger met in 1921, at a birthday celebration for Edmund Husserl; each appreciated at once the other's freedom from the manners of the academic philosophers, and their subsequent meetings, at Jaspers's home in Heidelberg, were always at a remove from the world of their colleagues. Heidegger had begun even before the first meeting a careful study of Jaspers's *Psychologie der Weltanschauungen*, and he sent Jaspers a written review in 1921. Jaspers thought the review—appreciative but very strenuously critical—was unjust, though he admitted later to reading it with less care than he might have. When Heidegger's *Being and Time* appeared in 1927, Jaspers found it foreign to his own manner and method and did not offer Heidegger a written review. He did, however, begin to keep notes on the work, and these have now been published, along with the notes Jaspers kept about Heidegger and Heidegger's work for the next forty years, in a volume called *Notizen zu Heidegger*. His reaction to Heidegger's book is summed up in a three-word note: "communicationless—godless—worldless."[19]

The failure of the two philosophers to find a communicative mode for criticism was clear by the late 1920s, but neither pressed to discover what stood in their way. Jaspers trusted Heidegger sufficiently to dismiss rumors that Heidegger had publicly ridiculed Jaspers's 1923 essay *The Idea of the University* after he confronted Heidegger and heard his denial. But he did not question Heidegger deeply when far more disturbing signals of their lack of accord came. During a visit with Heidegger in March 1933, less than two months after Hitler became chancellor, Jaspers did not take seriously an oblique statement Heidegger made about the National Socialists: "one must get in step." When Heidegger came again in May, as the rector of Freiburg University, Jaspers was astonished by his fascination with the Führer and by his acceptance of the current anti-Semitic commonplace about international Jewish conspiracies. In part because Jaspers did not take seriously—despite the warnings of his student Hannah Arendt—the threat of National Socialism ("I was still convinced that National Socialism would never triumph in Germany"),[20] he did not come to terms with Heidegger's political opinions until the inevitable break in May 1933. In his notes, Jaspers described Heidegger as like a boy who has stuck his hand in the wheel of world history. But there was also, as Jaspers later admitted, an element of retreat from confrontation with the uncommunicativeness in their friendship: "I should have spoken with him. . . . I had failed this enthused and intoxicated Heidegger."[21]

After the war, Hannah Arendt, out of loyalty to Heidegger, who had been her first teacher, sought Jaspers's help; she felt that only Jaspers could save Heidegger from the mendacity of his university intellectual milieu, the banality of his home life, and his proclivity for pastoral romanticizing of rural life—that is, from all the facets of his life that left him isolated, communicationless. Jaspers vacillated, aware of the pain Heidegger had caused Gertrud Jaspers, a Jewess, during his last visit to their home and deterred by Heidegger's failure to make a public disavowal of his allegiance to the National Socialists. Jaspers did write in 1954–55 a chapter for his "Philosophical Memoir" on his friendship with Heidegger, which he then withheld at the urging of his wife and others, for fear that it would mortally wound Heidegger; and this chapter does end with a call for openness in future discussions. Jaspers had maintained his hope that he and Heidegger would produce a public exchange of letters to clarify their views—many of the notes in *Notizen zu Heidegger* were prepared for such an exchange—but he was disappointed. Specifically, he was disturbed when Heidegger issued in 1953 his 1935 *Introduction to Metaphysics,* which contained a statement about the "inner truth and greatness of that [National Socialist] movement (namely the encounter between planetary technology and modern man) . . ."[22] But generally he was disturbed by Heidegger's failure to speak out, to distance himself from National Socialism. By the end of his own life, Jaspers had broken his ties with Heidegger completely.

As Jaspers became more and more apprehensive about the political developments in postwar Germany, his own public statements about former Nazis became starker. In *The Future of Germany* he spoke against the tendency to dismiss as mistakes (rather than as moral collapses) the various degrees of allegiance to National Socialism of the German majority. Reflecting on Germany's ex-Nazi Chancellor Kiesinger in the 1967 postscript to *The Future of Germany,* Jaspers wrote against those Germans who would not admit that the state which had come into being in 1933 was criminal:

It [1933] was a breakdown—or a revelation of the character of the German majority. Considering the facts everyone could see, it was possible only if one would either deny the facts or treat them as non-existent. It took criminal untruthfulness. To fail to be absolutely, unreservedly anti-Nazi in view of the criminal facts, one had to be unimpressed by lawlessness and crime wherever apparent. Without profound inhumanity it was not possible.[23]

Before he wrote this passage in *The Future of Germany*, Jaspers had spent much time thinking about Heidegger's politics and about what in his philosophy might have left him vulnerable to the temptation of Nazism. As much as any element that was present, what was *not* considered by Heidegger troubled Jaspers: "The great questions are not touched upon: Sexuality, friendship, marriage—ways of living (*Lebenspraxis*)—vocation—state, politics—education, and so forth."[24] Before he wrote the passage from *The Future of Germany*, Jaspers also pondered what form a discussion with Heidegger should take. He planned statements entitled "Jaspers against Heidegger" and "Jaspers with and against Heidegger";[25] he wrote himself notes about the proper mode for *Kritik* or *Polemik,* and he adopted Nietzsche's maxim (from *Ecce Homo*): "He whom I attack, I esteem" (*ich ehre, wen ich angreife*).

This is the attitude that Jaspers maintained when he wrote about the great philosophers. He could, for example, outline with clarity the limitations of Plato's thinking—"Plato can be credited only with the idea of personal freedom based on philosophical reason, and not with the idea of political freedom"[26]—after having spoken with equal clarity of Plato's greatness. When he wrote about the great philosophers, Jaspers could see what in their very thinking activity could limit and blind them; his own attitude that philosophy is for Everyman is a strong—perhaps the strongest—antidote to the deformations of philosophers: to their concern with the philosophical few as opposed to the unreasoning many, to their world-alienation and capacity to become entangled in worldly institutions (academies, churches, schools of followers). The two central existential concepts in Jaspers's thinking— freedom and communication—are clearly posed *against* the philosophical *déformation professionelle* as well as *for* the possibilities of limitless reason and humanitas.

Jaspers was aware of how difficult it is to bring to bear upon a contemporary and a friend the attitude he maintained toward the great philosophers and toward the modern "exceptions," Nietzsche and Kierkegaard, who were both driven in their thinking toward stances Jaspers repudiated. But there is another dimension to this difficulty which, if we consider it, will bring us to Jaspers's relations with his critics—the second facet of our consideration of those outside Jaspers's circle of communication.

Like his 1931 *Geistige Situation der Zeit* (*Man in the Modern Age*), Jaspers's 1966 *Wohin treibt die Bundesrepublik?* (*The Future of Germany*) was a best-seller in Germany. Many of his popular works reached large audiences, and his books have been translated into more than a dozen languages (in Japan, interestingly, Jaspers's works have a very large popular readership). What these readers felt is, of course, unknowable, but there is abundant record of how his works were greeted among professionals—academics, journalists, politicians, scientists. Jaspers was far more often surrounded by controversy than by communication. Many of the controversies arose simply because Jaspers had hit upon what he called "life-lies," those desperately held illusions, falsehoods, rationalizations, which block experience of a boundary situation. But some arose because Jaspers, as he hit upon essential issues, over-stepped a line very difficult to locate: the line between appeal and announcement, moral discourse and moralizing, clarification and condemnation.

To take an example from a nonpolitical context first: Jaspers wrote this about love in his 1931 *Man in the Modern Age*:

> The exclusiveness in the love of the sexes unconditionally binds two people for the entire future. . . . There is no self-realization without strictness in eroticism. Eroticism becomes humanly meaningful only in the exclusiveness of unconditioned commitment.[27]

This is moralistic—in the sense that it establishes as universal a life practice which is not always accepted or aspired toward. And it contrasts sharply with what he says in "Goethe and Our Future":

> Of course we resent the old charge that Goethe was fickle in love and sooner or later unfaithful to every woman; we resent it because each of his loves is so essential and irreplaceable, because other lovers know and understand themselves in his words as in those of no other poet, because each of his partings occurred under pressure of his conscience, in a sequence that we cannot critically analyze. And how loyal he was to them all—how magnificently loyal throughout his life to Frau von Stein, despite her offensive conduct; how he worried about each beloved person, and how their unhappiness upset him![28]

In this passage, concrete and free of rigidity, the principle of unconditional love takes on meaning and exemplary power. There is willingness here to stand back and admit the limits of critical inquiry, of biography or characterization, and of abstract, external judgment upon people's existential choices and decisions.

In many respects, the contrast in these passages is representative of the difference between Jaspers's popular works before and after the war. The movements of Jaspers's thought did not change—and that is why they have been treated in this study without reference to historical setting—but the manner of his statements did. He did not often achieve forceful prose, but he did give his writing the power of example and concreteness. One of his most vehement critics, Theodor Adorno, wrote about Jaspers as a representative user of the "jargon of authenticity"—the lexicon of existentialism. Had Adorno, whose *Jargon of Authenticity* appeared in 1964, looked into Jaspers's postwar work, he might have hesitated to rebuke him for employing "the magic formula of existence . . . [to] disregard society and the psychology of real individuals which is dependent on that society." The hesitation might not have lasted long because the deeper difference between Adorno and Jaspers—which is more than a matter of jargon—had to do with the claim that the psychology of real individuals is *dependent on* society. But nonetheless there is a great difference between Jaspers's mode in these two statements about German education, the first from 1931 and the second from 1966:

Education will only be restored to its true level when the valuations of the masses (*Massenschätzungen*) are overridden by a distinction between teaching and discipline (*Lehre und Zucht*), between that which is comprehensible to all, and that which is attainable by an elite through disciplining of their inner actions.[29]

As children begin to mature, they need education in political thinking. They must be put in touch with political affairs, with the realities of the body politic. To prepare them for a life as voting adults with a share in personal responsibility for public affairs, they should begin in school to exercise what is now known as the "students' share of responsibility." They should undertake common tasks, meet, debate, confer, and make decisions about the things they encounter in school, the things that concern them.[30]

The terminology of the mass-elite largely disappeared from Jaspers's lexicon after the war, and he emphasized much more the possibility that disciplined inner action could come from action in the world, from participation with others in a common enterprise, as well as from a one-to-one situation. The first passage is vague and theoretical, the second clear and practical—but the same principle and concern motivated both.

What we can see by examining Jaspers's works in their historical contexts is his effort to bring the "how to think" lessons of his philosophizing in all its modes—world orientation, existential elucidation, metaphysics—into widely communicative practice. Near the end of his life, in *The Future of Germany,* Jaspers described the interplay of the modes in the practical terms which he developed as he considered how to meet his critics and, in the *Notizen zu Heidegger,* how to prepare for a discussion with, or critique of, Heidegger:

> Political education takes a way of thinking that must be trained, a kind of knowledge that must be acquired. It does not thrive in talk and in distracting discussions, only in the discipline of continuous application. The way of thinking I mean is a weighing, testing one in the flow of arguments and counter-arguments. If my mind is open I can hear what my opponent thinks and can even help him present his thoughts consistently and strongly. I can put myself in his place. I can tentatively suspend my initial position. I have the patience to develop all possibilities to the fullest extent.[31]

With this passage as a guideline, we can review the lessons in thinking that are explored in this study, emphasizing at each step the principle which preserves freedom.

Jaspers himself clearly recognized the problems of public debates and stated them in very simple language for his general audience:

> Discussions as a rule are not thorough. We bombard each other with poorly reasoned sentences. We frequently change

the subject. The sentences do not gravitate around a center. We get emotional. We are constantly at cross-purposes. We do not get results. We stop or give up.[32]

Unless discussions have a center, they flit from one surface issue to another. Discussants, as Jaspers pointed out, seldom know what they are aiming at. "Both [should] try to reduce the topic to the 'ultimate positions' and to point out the logical consequences by asking 'is that what you really want?' In this way, the disputants, in their common will for the truth, could reach the ultimate battleground where real forces come face to face through them."[33]

The first consideration in a public discussion should be how to reveal clearly what is aimed at, what is finally at issue. To do this, and to prompt it in discussion, a schematism like Jaspers's is needed to differentiate among the levels involved in a topic, whether political or philosophical. A schematism gives roadsigns, helps guide and orient thinking. For example, with the levels "Dasein," "Consciousness in general," "Geist," and "Existenz" in mind, one can avoid the simplifications and reductions that characterize so much of contemporary thought; these are starting points for recognizing that any theory or truth-claim which takes one level for all that is is bound to falsify. Biologism (or behaviorism, or a hybrid like sociobiology), psychologism, structuralism, and existentialism are examples of shells that foreclose possibilities. Similarly, the levels of phenomena or phenomena-as-ciphers warn against ideologies: naturalism, historicism (or historical determinism), subjectivism, rationalism, or religious absolutism. The first principle of Jaspers's "how to think" lesson is, simply: be aware of where you are, and do not mistake that place for the only place or the only ultimate position.

If a discussion stops at one level or fails over a conflict between levels, the basic dialectical procedure Jaspers used can be orienting. For example, if it is clear that there is a distinction as well as a relation between scientific knowledge and philosophical reflection—that philosophy without science is empty and science without philosophy blind—then the elements of fact and the elements of interpretation or opinion in a discussion can be sorted out. In our current national debate over the dangers and benefits of nuclear energy, to take a specific example, the difference between scientific or technological questions and philosophical questions is seldom clear; we seldom ask "is that what you really want?" in philosophical terms—at the level of existential elucidation, with regard to our way of life and human possibilities now and in the future. But any truthful discussion in such terms must be built on a factual context established and mutually recognized. The maxim here is simply: clarify dialectically the elements of a discussion.

If a discussion can be brought to a true confrontation of "ultimate positions"—not a battle of partial or rigidified isms on one level or another, but a true parity—what then? Suppose, for example, we distinguished between tactics or implementations, policies, and premises for policies in considering a political issue and were able to bring a debate to the level of premises—only to find them irreconcilable. If the premises are matters of doctrine, the procedure Jaspers used for cipher-reading can be orienting: detach the doctrine or the institutionalized revelation from the claim to reality that fortifies it. But to ask true believers or convinced nonbelievers to give up their attachment to the reality of their revelation or their doctrine—is that not next to impossible? It may be, as Jaspers believed, that "the disembodied ciphers cleanse the faith of free Existenz," but what is to be done about those religious warriors Max Weber said could not be fought with? We can state a maxim for the endless struggle of opposing faiths: find in your faith the path to communication with those of other faiths by refusing to attribute reality to the object of your faith. But how can the footpath of this maxim become what Kant called a broad highway?

What the metaphysics part of Jaspers's philosophizing can teach is the range and content of human belief and the varieties of man's ways of believing. But this lesson does not confront the question of what happens when ultimate positions come into conflict. It seems unrealistic to think of struggling to persuade someone, for example, to view the Ten Commandments as ten ciphers—as Jaspers actually tried to do in *Philosophy Is for Everyman*. But Jaspers's own question—"Is that what you really want?"—is a more worldly one to ask than "Is that how you really wish to hold your belief?" Once an ultimate position has been reached with the question "Is that what you really want?" it can be opened again: "Do you understand the consequences for you and others of really wanting that?" "Does the way you live accord with what you really want?" "Can you ask of others that they, too, want that?" and so forth. These questions can keep ultimate positions tied to the realms of existential elucidation and world orientation (in Jaspers's terms). Jaspers's three dimensions of philosophizing should not be engaged vertically or linearly: the freedom of his philosophizing would be lost if metaphysics was detached from the world, if the struggle of ultimate positions did not *grow out cf* worldly consequences and concerns and ceaselessly relate ɩo them. A discussion which keeps moving back and forth among these levels may be resultless or finally inconclusive, or it may fail in the face of ultimate conflicts; but it can keep open the space for communication beyond the one-to-one loving struggle of Existenzen.

Jaspers offered no definition of freedom. But there is an image that runs through the modes of the encompassing and binds them, and by which we can orient ourselves. Freedom comes to be when a space is opened and possibilities which come to light in the space are actualized. In the political realm space is opened in the give and take of discussion, possibilities are actualized in joint action. A thinking space is opened when fixed positions are abandoned and others—including the great philosophers—are engaged in communication. Objectively, political space is secured and protected by laws, and the thinking space is protected from arbitrariness and unclarity by method and methodicalness. Both are suffused with the freedom of Existenz as they allow that very freedom to come to be.

This image carries an imperative in it. Not an unconditional imperative but an imperative not to foreclose unconditionality. Keep yourself open and keep open the spaces in which you talk and act with others. It is not an imperative that invites relativism or "the dissolution of the human substance." More concretely, though again negatively, it is an imperative to reject intellectual absolutes and what Hermann Broch called "the earthly absolute," total enslavement, as the extreme opposites of motion and spaciousness. Communicate so that communication's space may come to be and be preserved; act so that action's space may come to be and be preserved: for you are truly free only if and as you communicate and only if and as you act.

# NOTES

## PREFACE

1. Karl Jaspers, "On Heidegger," *Graduate Faculty Philosophy Journal* 7 (Spring, 1978): 101.

2. Karl Jaspers to Hannah Arendt, 18 September 1946, Deutsches Literaturarchiv, Marbach, Germany.

3. A brief intellectual biography is available in German: Hans Saner, *Karl Jaspers in Selbstzeugnissen und Bilddokumenten*.

4. Such a study is available in English: Charles F. Wallraff, *Karl Jaspers: An Introduction to His Philosophy*.

5. Karl Jaspers, *Philosophical Faith and Revelation*, 295 (hereafter cited as *Philosophic Faith*).

6. Karl Jaspers, *The Way to Wisdom*, 37–38 (hereafter cited as *Wisdom*).

7. The comparison is not an arbitrary one: "For we can certainly say that the age of technology, the age to which we belong, is the most profound caesura in history to date. Outwardly, this is obvious. Henceforth the planet is one, and all human life depends on a planlessly man-made world. . . . To name but one symptom: the planet has been parceled out. Man can no longer emigrate as in past ages; the valve is shut, the pressure growing. But what happens inside man, due to and along with modern technology, remains wholly unclear. . . . Having lost a 'world' a man can perhaps remain erect as an individual in his independence, but the question is this: . . . how can he win a new world instead of an empty space?" (Karl Jaspers, *Existentialism and Humanism*, 36 & 90; hereafter cited as *Humanism*).

8. This passage is representative of Jaspers's sweeping and vague "introductory" style; each phrase is later unfolded, elucidated; each topic is approached again and again, from different angles. Such passages are germs or summaries. Jaspers was a masterful creator of schematics; the dramatic tensions in his thought are not usually, however, dramatically presented. There is clarity without traditional artistry, light without highlight; the crucial tool is the line *moving*

through space, as in action painting, an event. Karl Jaspers, *The Origin and Goal of History*, 2 (hereafter cited as *Origin and Goal*).
9. Karl Jaspers, *Philosophy*, 1:18.
10. *Philosophy*, 1:18.
11. *Philosophy*, 1:24, italics added.
12. *Philosophy*, 1:32.
13. Karl Jaspers, *Nietzsche: An Introduction to His Philosophical Activity*, 14 (hereafter cited as *Nietzsche*).
14. *Nietzsche*, 457.
15. Karl Jaspers, *Three Essays*, 238 (hereafter cited as *Essays*).
16. See the chapter entitled "Kant's Conception of Moral Freedom" in R. D. Miller's *Schiller and the Ideal of Freedom*.
17. Karl Jaspers, *The Great Philosophers*, 1:230.

CHAPTER ONE

1. *Philosophical Faith*, 69: this passage is a recapitulation of Jaspers's outline of "basic knowledge," *Grundwissen*. Jaspers, in his studies of Kant, placed great emphasis on Kant's doctrine of the ideas, on the "pleasure trips" (in Kant's ironic phrase) taken by imaginative reason in discovering and producing an ideational world. The important essay "Kant's Ideenlehre" in which this emphasis is clear was an appendix to Jaspers's *Psychologie der Weltanschauungen* (1919); it can be found in the recent collection *Aneignung und Polemik*.
2. Karl Jaspers, *Von der Wahrheit*, 231. (See Sebastian Samay, *Reason Revisited*, 13.)
3. *Philosophy*, 1:100.
4. Ibid.
5. *Philosophy*, 1:102.
6. *Philosophy*, 1:105.
7. *Great Philosophers*, 1:36 and 2:81.
8. *Philosophy*, 1:49. The interrelation of subject and object is expressed by Goethe: "Man knows himself only in so far as he knows the world; of the world he becomes aware only in himself, and of himself only in the world." Cited by E. Heller, *The Disinherited Mind*, 101.
9. *Philosophy*, 1:47.
10. *Philosophy*, 3:35.
11. Ibid.
12. *Philosophy*, 1:48.
13. Ibid.

14. *Philosophy*, 1:49.

15. Karl Jaspers, *Reason and Existenz*, 54.

16. *Philosophy*, 1:52. ("Consciousness at large" is E. B. Ashton's translation of *Bewusstsein überhaupt*. Ashton rightly points out that "consciousness in general" would overemphasize generality, which, for Jaspers, is only one aspect of *Bewusstsein überhaupt*.)

17. *Philosophy*, 1:52.

18. Kierkegaard, *Concluding Unscientific Postscript*, 109.

19. *Philosophy*, 1:55.

20. Kierkegaard, *Concluding Unscientific Postscript*, 545.

21. *Philosophy*, 1:57.

22. *Philosophy*, 1:53.

23. *Philosophy*, 1:55.

24. *Philosophy*, 1:48.

25. Ibid. This "positive way" is Jaspers's attempt to follow Schelling (and Kierkegaard) in the direction of "positive philosophy" without ending in "Gnosticism" or undercutting the possibility of philosophizing.

26. *Philosophy*, 1:56.

27. Hegel, *Phenomenology of Spirit*, 229.

28. *Philosophy*, 1:56.

29. *Philosophy*, 1:64.

30. *Philosophy*, 1:88.

31. *Philosophy*, 1:62. This statement is characteristic of Jaspers's approach to "semantic problems." For example, given the idea that the verb "to be" is grammatically misused in much speculation on "Being," Jaspers wrote: "Yet men do operate with the verb 'to be' as if it signified something beyond its grammatical meaning; and these operations have opened memorable paths pursued for thousands of years in the West, in India, in China. . . ." (*Philosophical Faith*, 167) Semantic analysis ("clearing up muddles") is helpful for eliminating pretensions to objective knowledge, but it does not touch the *existential* reality of the speaker's belief.

32. *Nietzsche*, 405.

33. Kierkegaard, *Concluding Unscientific Postscript*, 304.

34. Ibid.

35. *Philosophy*, 2:280, italics added. "Kant has said in the *Critique of Practical Reason* that God's unfathomable wisdom is as admirable in what it gives as in what it denies. For if God's wisdom in its majesty were always before our eyes, if it were an absolute authority, speaking unequivocally in the world, we should be puppets of his will. But

God in his wisdom wanted us to be free" (*Wisdom*, 46). In Cusanus's presentation of the *docta ignorantia* the following image occurs, which illustrates Jaspers's meaning: "There is a wall around the domain of the godhead, too high for us to climb over. Yet what lies behind the wall is active, present, underlying. We fail when we try to break through the wall, but in the process of coming up against it, we recognize it as the sign of the godhead" (*Great Philosophers*, 2:123). Paradoxically, this "foundering" is the "positive way" to being-in-itself.

36. *Philosophy*, 2:100, italics added.
37. *Philosophy*, 1:278.
38. *Philosophy*, 2:103.
39. *Philosophy*, 2:342.
40. *Philosophy*, 1:81.
41. Ibid.
42. *Philosophy*, 1:325.
43. *Great Philosophers*, 1:183.
44. *Philosophy*, 2:101.
45. Ibid.
46. *Philosophy*, 1:37.
47. *Philosophy*, 2:97.
48. *Philosophy*, 2:100.
49. *Philosophy*, 1:10. Communication or dialogue is central to the thought of several others whose names are linked with the word "existentialism"—Martin Buber, Gabriel Marcel, Franz Rosenzweig, Albert Camus—but only in Jaspers's thinking is communication equated with truth in the way here described.
50. *Philosophy*, 1:66.
51. *Reason and Existenz*, 52.
52. *Philosophy*, 2:57.
53. *Philosophy*, 3:50.
54. *Philosophy*, 2:110.
55. Ibid.
56. *Philosophy*, 1:57.
57. We see here another way in which the subject can be "desubstantialized," reduced to a demarcation or limit. If the idea of eternity is eliminated, the present becomes, so to speak, empty; this is what happens in Heidegger's scheme of *existentialia*. Between facticity, necessity, "having been thrown," guilt, and so forth, and care, death-begotten resolve, being ahead of one's present (projection), and

so forth, there is the moment (*Augenblick*), a point of tension between past and future. See Jonas, "Gnosticism, Existentialism, and Nihilism," in *The Phenomenon of Life*.

58. *Philosophy*, 3:181. For the present, until a full explication of the term "cipher" (*Chiffre*) is appropriate, we can think of it as a sign, for Transcendence, a linguistic mark for the ineffable. (See below, chapter 1, section 3.)

59. These concepts are presented in a preliminary way in chapter 1, section 3, and in detail in chapter 3, section 1.

60. *Nietzsche*, 350.

61. Rilke, *Duino Elegies*, ninth elegy (translation by C. F. MacIntyre).

62. *Philosophy*, 3:55.

63. *Origin and Goal*, 160–61.

64. *Great Philosophers*, 1:337.

65. *Philosophy*, 3:199; *Origin and Goal*, 160.

66. *Philosophy*, 2:105.

67. See *Philosophy*, 2:368: "The things which an objective observer sees changing and following one another are psychological characters, world images, modes of conduct, social and economic conditions, world historical situations and so forth; Existenz is always the same thing in another form. Not until I transcend and extinguish the historical side will a contemplation of history lead to the sense of historicity that assures me of being." This is an "end of history" obviously quite distinct from that posited in Hegelian-Marxist dialectics.

68. *Philosophy*, 2:91.

69. Cited by E. M. Manasse, "Jaspers' Relation to Max Weber," in P. A. Schlipp, ed., *The Philosophy of Karl Jaspers*, 375.

70. *Philosophy*, 2:328.

71. Ibid.

72. Karl Jaspers, *Man in the Modern Age*, 123 (hereafter cited as *Modern Age*).

73. *Modern Age*, 198. "Art originates as the elucidation of Existenz by an ascertainment that will let us visualize being in present existence. In philosophizing we treat being as thinkable, in art as *representable*" (*Philosophy*, 1:327).

74. Comparable to Kant's schemata of the ideas.

75. *Philosophy*, 1:79.

76. *Philosophy*, 1:332.

77. *Philosophy*, 1:327.

78. *Great Philosophers*, 1:373.
79. *Philosophy*, 3:34.
80. Kierkegaard, *The Concept of Dread*, 74n.
81. "Kierkegaard points in the direction of an absurd Christianity before which the world sinks away . . ." (*Reason and Existenz*, 48).
82. *Philosophy*, 3:95.
83. *Philosophy*, 2:17. Kant's categories are tabulated in the *Critique of Pure Reason*, A 80, B 106. The contrast between the categories and Jaspers's concepts is discussed in detail in chapter 3, section 1 below. As is often the case in Jaspers's thinking, the form or systemization comes from Kant and the content from Kierkegaard. In Kierkegaard's work there is an attempt to formulate existential categories on the basis of an understanding of existential time—such categories as repetition, contemporaneity, and the moment—but there is no systemization to his *Existential-Videnskab* (existential science).
84. *Reason and Existenz*, 67.
85. *Philosophy*, 2:177.
86. *Philosophy*, 2:178.
87. *Philosophy*, 2:180. Jaspers used Horace's claim that "should the world collapse, the pieces would hit an undaunted man" (*si fractus illabatur orbis, impavidum ferient ruinae*) to illustrate the stance of a man abstracting from *his own* situation, "lonely punctuality."
88. Ibid.
89. *Philosophy*, 2:178. Jaspers's debt to Kierkegaard in the elucidation of *Grenzsituationen* (particularly in *Psychologie der Weltanschauungen* and the *Philosophy*) is obvious; but Jaspers, unlike Heidegger, did not seek a new systematic philosophy, given the Kierkegaardian psychology.
90. *Philosophy*, 2:180.
91. Ibid.
92. *Philosophy*, 2:219.
93. *Philosophy*, 1:45. The notion that philosophizing starts with our situation, and that the question "what is being?" rises from our situation, is antithetical to Heidegger's position: "His questioning is directed toward understanding man in the perspective of Being, not the reverse of this, which he thinks has been a fundamental mistake of our philosophical tradition, that is, trying to understand being by investigating the human being." (J. G. Gray, "The New Image of Man in Martin Heidegger's Philosophy," *European Philosophy Today*, 33.)
94. *Philosophy*, 2:33.

95. *Philosophy*, 1:235.
96. *Philosophy*, 1:246.
97. Karl Jaspers, *Truth and Symbol*, 24.
98. Ibid.
99. *Truth and Symbol*, 35. In general, we can say that dialectical reversals within world orientation (as in example 1) move thinking into existential elucidation; while the reversals within existential elucidation (as in example 2) move thinking to metaphysics.
100. When Hamlet cannot find words adequate to his "heart of hearts" (it is the dilemma of Romantic poets generally) he is left with the hope that Horatio, his friend, will "in this harsh world" tell his story.
101. *Philosophy*, 2:62–63.
102. These "exceptions" are discussed in the first and fifth of the lectures in *Reason and Existenz*.
103. *Philosophy*, 2:247.
104. Ibid.
105. *Modern Age*, 159.
106. Ibid.
107. *Modern Age*, 158.
108. *Great Philosophers*, 1:362; see also *Origin and Goal*, xiv.
109. Jaspers pointed out the danger of this view in the following sentence: "Where an abstract freedom is made the goal, it becomes a phase on the way to some new tyranny." Jaspers wrote this in 1946 as a warning to advocates of a "New Europe" in his *The European Spirit*, 40 (hereafter cited as *European Spirit*).
110. Karl Jaspers, *The Future of Mankind*, 223.
111. This definition was given by Kierkegaard in *The Present Age*.
112. *Modern Age*, 57.
113. *Modern Age*, 79.
114. *Great Philosophers*, 1:302.
115. *Philosophy*, 3:58.
116. Ibid. With reference to Hegel's conception of absolute freedom, Jaspers wrote: "Nor am I truly free in an absolute freedom that would sublimate my Existenz into a generality and totality. It would not only make the subject and the object vanish; along with all antitheses it would annihilate Existenz itself" (*Philosophy*, 2:171).
117. *Philosophy*, 3:58.
118. *Philosophy*, 3:59.
119. *Philosophy*, 3:39.

120. *Philosophy,* 2:151.

121. Jaspers adopted from Kierkegaard the paradox of eternity intersecting time. For Kierkegaard, "the instant is that ambiguous moment in which time and eternity touch one another, thereby positing *the temporal,* where time is constantly intersecting eternity and eternity constantly permeating time" (*The Concept of Dread,* 80). Also for Kierkegaard, the moment is the moment of decision, of self-choice. (Kierkegaard thought that both Plato and Hegel made of the moment a "mute abstraction.") The paradox of eternity touching time is most fully developed by Kierkegaard in connection with Christ, the "Supreme Paradox," the "fullness of Time." Similarly, the permeation of temporal existence by the eternal in Goethe's *Parable* (*Märchen*), a *kairos,* is man's redemption; time is "the greatest gift of God" (*Wilhelm Meisters Wanderjahre*).

122. Cited by Heller, *The Disinherited Mind,* 101.

123. *Nietzsche,* 152.

124. Nietzsche found just such a correspondence in Goethe (see *Human, All Too Human,* vol. 7 of *Complete Works*), and contrasted it to Richard Wagner's virtuosity. It is interesting to note that Nietzsche thought awareness of limits to be a matter of taste.

125. *Philosophy,* 1:284.

126. *Nietzsche,* 298.

127. *Great Philosophers,* 1:263.

128. *Philosophy,* 2:224.

129. *Future of Mankind,* 209.

130. *Philosophy,* 1:45.

131. *Future of Mankind,* vii.

132. *Philosophy,* 1:2.

133. *Origin and Goal,* 263.

134. *Origin and Goal,* 263.

135. Ibid.

136. *Philosophy,* 3:30.

137. *Philosophical Faith,* 83. "Existence is made absolute in so-called pragmatism, biologism, psychologism and sociologism; consciousness at large in rationalism; the mind in 'erudition'; Existenz in existentialism (which becomes nihilism); the world in materialism, naturalism, idealism, and pantheism; Transcendence in a-cosmism." (This last term was used by Weber to describe the mystical perspective, as opposed to the cosmism of the Roman Catholic church.)

CHAPTER TWO

1. *Philosophy*, 1:197.
2. *Philosophy*, 2:9.
3. *Philosophy*, 2:285.
4. *Philosophy*, 2:256.
5. Aristotle, *Nicomachean Ethics*, 1139a16. In *Philosophy*, 2:258, Jaspers speaks of "Man, the only acting creature . . ."
6. *Philosophy*, 1:46.
7. *Philosophy*, 3:83.
8. *Philosophy*, 1:11. And cf. Karl Jaspers, "Was ist Existentialismus?" *Aneignung und Polemik*, 497–502.
9. See chapter 3, section 1 below, on Nietzsche's history of philosophy.
10. *Philosophy*, 1:6.
11. Richard J. Bernstein, *Praxis and Action*, 151.
12. Karl Jaspers, "Philosophical Memoir," *Philosophy and The World*, 278 (hereafter cited as "Memoir").
13. "Memoir," 278.
14. *Philosophy*, 1:13.
15. *Philosophy*, 1:34.
16. *Great Philosophers*, 1:328ff.
17. *Future of Mankind*, 218.
18. *Philosophy*, 2:9.
19. Ibid.
20. *Nietzsche*, 252.
21. *Modern Age*, 56.
22. "Memoir," 277.
23. *Future of Mankind*, 4.
24. Ibid.
25. *Modern Age*, 95.
26. *Future of Mankind*, 4.
27. *Future of Mankind*, 100.
28. Thus life under a totalitarian regime may be more imaginable for us reading a novel (*The First Circle*, for example) or a memoir (*Hope against Hope*, for example) than a work of "political science."
29. *Future of Mankind*, 282.
30. Nietzsche opposed real dialectic to the "traditional method of thinking dialectically by means of hasty surveys, which would amount to no more than a circular arrangement of the husks of the conceivable

within a large and vacuous medium" (*Nietzsche*, 394). Nietzsche's real dialectic is comparable to Kierkegaard's living through the "stages of life's way"; both are reactions against Hegel's dialectic of pure thought. See below, chapter 3, section 4, on Jaspers's *Psychologie der Weltanschauungen*.

31. *Great Philosophers*, 1:296.

32. *Philosophy*, 3:167.

33. *Modern Age*, 105 and 108.

34. *Modern Age*, 109.

35. *Philosophy*, 1:i. Jaspers consistently opposed political prophecy: "Prophets are as wrong today as ever. We can spot trends, but whether the trends materialize and bear out the predictions is uncertain and depends also on us." (Karl Jaspers, *The Future of Germany*, xiv.)

36. *Great Philosophers*, 1:129.

37. *Philosophy*, 3:167.

38. *Future of Mankind*, 275–76, italics added. Revelations are not subject to rational investigation, "reason cannot make a case for revelation" (*Philosophical Faith*, 27ff.). Ideologies are; and for Jaspers, the procedure for analyzing an ideology is to construct an ideal type (in Weber's sense) "not in order to mistake them for realities, but to check the realities against them, to see where the realities fit and where they do not" (*Future of Mankind*, 276). For an ideologist, for the "convinced protagonist," the ideology and the reality in which he is situated are identical, but "ideologies are products of thought; *reality is the* realm of action" (*Future of Mankind*, 275, italics added).

39. *Future of Mankind*, 221.

40. *Future of Mankind*, 284.

41. *Philosophy*, 2:255.

42. Instinctive and vital action characterize Dasein, whose truth is pragmatic; purposive action relates to the modes of subjective being Bewusstsein überhaupt and Geist, whose truths are functions of cogency and conviction. These types of truth are discussed below, chapter 3, section 3.

43. *Philosophy*, 2:257. In this passage, Jaspers's identification of immortality and eternity is adumbrated. The distinction between striving for immortality through great deeds and words and striving to transcend for impermanent world altogether, to contemplate the unspeakable eternal or to unite with it mystically, is taken up into the idea that: "This life—this is how the seeming paradox must be phrased—

decides in time about what is in eternity. The decision, made on the strength of love and at the bidding of conscience, is the manifestation of what already exists in eternity. The presence of eternity equals immortality. . . . Immortality is not an object of our knowledge; it is the spirit of love" (Karl Jaspers, *Philosophy and the World,* 138). The idea that immortality in this sense "exists as fidelity in action, as trustworthiness" (*Philosophy and the World,* 138) places immortality again *in the world,* in worldly action—eternity comes into the world in action.

44. *Philosophy,* 2:273.

45. *Philosophy,* 2:256.

46. Ibid.

47. *Philosophy,* 2:259.

48. *Philosophy,* 2:180.

49. Ibid.

50. Jaspers frequently contrasted the Stoic withdrawal from the world in boundary situations to the Jewish undespairing strength for reconstruction in the world—exemplified by Jeremiah ("and herein the Jews exemplify Europeanism"). See Karl Jaspers, *The Question of German Guilt,* 1222ff. and also *Wisdom,* 39.

51. *Future of Mankind,* 219. For the background of this discussion, see Max Weber, *Sociology of Religion,* 235ff.

52. *Future of Mankind,* 219.

53. Karl Jaspers, "Is Europe's Culture Finished?" *Commentary* 4 (1947), 521. See also *Philosophy and the World,* 62. One who surrenders to blind political will is one who "is discontented with his life, and complains of environing circumstances, regarding them, instead of himself, as the cause of the happenings of his life. He is inspired now with hatred, now with enthusiasm, but above all with the instinct of the will to power. Although he does not know what he might know if he would, and does not know what he really wills, he talks, he chooses, and he acts as though he knew. By a short-circuit, he passes abruptly from a quarter-knowledge to the license of fanaticism" (*Modern Age,* 96).

54. *Future of Mankind,* 248.

55. Ibid.

56. Ibid.

57. "Is Europe's Culture Finished?"

58. *Wisdom,* 34.

59. *Philosophy,* 1:148.

60. *Philosophy*, 2:331.

61. Ibid. Persuasion and suggestion are associated with the truth of empirical existence (Dasein), which Jaspers called "pragmatic," in distinction from rational argument, which is associated with the truth of consciousness at large, cogent truth (see below, chapter 3, section 3). Joint understanding comes from neither. It comes from conviction (the truth of Geist) and faith (the truth in communication of Existenz).

62. *Philosophy*, 2:256, italics added.

63. *Philosophy*, 1:87.

64. *Philosophy*, 2:55. We will return to this distinction below, chapter 1, section 3.

65. "Political freedom is intended to make all other human freedoms possible. Politics are directed toward the *ordering of existence as a basis, not as the final aim, of human life*" (*Origin and Goal*, 163).

66. *Future of Mankind*, 85.

67. Ibid.

68. For the relation between an idea and its incarnation, see *Origin and Goal*, 263, on the idea of mankind's origin, which Jaspers saw incarnate in the Axial Period. But "history shows us political freedom has only been tried in the West" (*Origin and Goal*, 153).

69. *Modern Age*, 89.

70. *Philosophy*, 1:111.

71. *Philosophy*, 1:148.

72. In distinguishing four spheres of mundane reality—inorganic matter, organic life, soul, mind—Jaspers is in agreement with H. Driesch and A. Wenz and also N. Hartman; the distinction between life and soul was particularly emphasized by Dilthey and Klages. Jaspers's distinctions are discussed in *Philosophy*, 1:187–96.

73. *Philosophy*, 1:147.

74. "Is Europe's Culture Finished?" 520.

75. The description which follows is based on *Philosophy*, 1:112.

76. *Philosophy*, 2:141.

77. *Future of Mankind*, 284.

78. *Philosophy*, 2:260.

79. Unconditional *ideal* action and *existential* action may coincide. But existential action may also "break through the idea"—it may, for example, call the idea of justice itself into question. See below, chapter 2, section 4, on breaking laws "with the positivity of Existenz-to-be."

80. *Philosophy*, 1:191. Thus the Greeks thought of the "barbar-

ians" as apolitical beings, not *polis*-dwellers, not freed from animal slavishness to physical necessity to become "social and historical beings" or to break with nature as acting beings.

81. *Modern Age*, 110.

82. Ibid.

83. *Philosophy*, 1:190.

84. *Modern Age*, 111. In 1931 Jaspers wrote: "It seems as if the characteristic feature of our situation was the breaking up of substantial education into an interminable pedagogical experiment. . . . One attempt is speedily abandoned in favor of another, the contents, aims, and methods of education being changed from moment to moment."

85. *Philosophy*, 3:26.

86. Ibid. This applies to both freedom in the political realm and freedom of thought. Education itself is a struggle: in "Socratic education" teacher and student ought to be on the same level, "engaged in a contest for truth." Socratic education is distinguished from scholastic education and apprenticeship, for example, where student and teacher are not on the same level. The latter are appropriate only for the young. Jaspers discussed these modes in *The Idea of a University*.

87. *Philosophy and the World*, 56.

88. *Philosophy and the World*, 116, italics added. *Great Philosophers*, 1:165: "Plato's political thinking lacks the idea of political freedom that has become a historic force in the Western world since the Middle Ages. . . . He did not conceive of a government based on the communication of all men. . . . He gave no thought to the means (e.g., representation) of creating a bond between the will of rulers and their elites. He did not find a way to overcome the rigidity of the laws . . . through laws susceptible of correction by legal methods which could themselves be corrected. . . ."

89. See *Origin and Goal*, 185: "Since such remarkable things have been achieved through planning within the realm of technology, the road leads from here, by intellectual thoughtlessness attendant upon fascination with technology, to the idea of a technocracy—the administration of technology by technology itself—which will put an end to every evil. . . ."

90. *Philosophy*, 1:147.

91. *Origin and Goal*, 187. See *Nietzsche*, 241, on how the machine furnishes patterns for community life.

92. *Origin and Goal*, 191.

93. *Origin and Goal*, 192.
94. *Future of Mankind*, 224.
95. "Memoir," 260.
96. "Memoir," 278.
97. *Future of Mankind*, 225. Leaders must arise, but *from* the people, as the people's representatives. Jaspers did not hold that the "possession of power corrupts the free judgment of reason inevitably" (Kant, *Perpetual Peace*); what is corrupting is isolation, removal from the "all control and correct each other, enhancing each other's reason" of shared power. As Jefferson asked Madison (Jefferson to Madison, 1787): "Say, finally, whether peace is best preserved by giving energy to the government, or information to the people. This last is the most certain, the most legitimate engine of government. ..." And (Jefferson to Judge Tyler, 1804): "I hold it certain that to open the doors of truth and to fortify the habit of testing everything by reason are the most effective manacles we can rivet on the hands of our successors to prevent their manacling the people with their own consent." (see M. D. Peterson, ed., *The Portable Thomas Jefferson*. Harmondsworth, England: Penguin, 1977).
98. Karl Jaspers, "Nature and Ethics," in *Principles of Moral Action*, ed. Ruth A. Anshen, 55.
99. *Future of Mankind*, 7.
100. *Philosophy*, 2:138 and 140.
101. *Philosophy*, 2:138.
102. *Great Philosophers*, 1:199.
103. *Philosophy*, 2:134.
104. *Philosophy*, 2:157.
105. Ibid.
106. *Philosophy*, 2:141. In Aristotle's terms, προαίρεσις, choice, is the efficient cause of all activity; such choice is not possible without desire and a λόγος ὁ ἕνεκά τινος, which, in Jaspers's terms, is purposesive clarity. That is, the existential clarity that Jaspers spoke of is beyond the bounds of Aristotle's analysis. (See *Nicomachean Ethics*, 1139a32ff.)
107. *Philosophy*, 2:139.
108. *Philosophy*, 2:140.
109. *Philosophy*, 2:141.
110. *Great Philosophers*, 1:199.
111. Ibid.
112. *Philosophy*, 2:159.

113. *Philosophy*, 2:174. *Philosophical Faith*, 234: "But I become in time what I am in eternity; this is the paradoxical formula for what already exists in itself, as a temporal phenomenon, but comes to appear in time, only by means of freedom. It is expressed in the maxim *'Become* what you *are'*—if I mean by this what I eternally am and never know."

114. *Philosophy*, 2:160.

115. *Philosophy*, 2:163.

116. *Philosophical Faith*, 45.

117. *Philosophy*, 2:141.

118. *Modern Age*, 98.

119. *Modern Age*, 97–98.

120. *Modern Age*, 98.

121. *Modern Age*, 98–99.

122. *Philosophy*, 2:33.

123. *Philosophy*, 2:332. Jaspers's *The Idea of the University*, written in 1946, *The Question of German Guilt*, and the essays collected in *Existentialism and Humanism* were presented in an effort to elucidate the ideas which had been all but lost during the war years. Max Weber's *Protestant Ethic and the Spirit of Capitalism*, as a contribution to understanding the manner in which ideas become effective forces in history, was a model for Jaspers's thinking.

124. *Philosophy*, 2:332.

125. *Philosophy*, 2:332.

126. *Modern Age*, 181.

127. *Modern Age*, 194.

128. *Philosophy*, 2:135.

129. Ibid., italics added. What Jaspers, following Kierkegaard, has here expressed in existential terms is, in political terms, appearance in public, being seen in action, participating in governance.

130. The distinction was made by F. Tönnies, *Gemeinschaft und Gesellschaft* (*Community and Society*, trans. C. P. Loomis. New York: Harper & Row, 1963); cf. Albert Salomon, "Max Weber," *Die Gesellschaft*, vol. 2, 1925, pp. 131–53.

131. This passage of Weber's is cited by Jaspers in *Essays*, 258, without the bracketed phrase. This phrase is an interesting clue to the importance for Weber of the George-*Kreis* with its ideal of a *Gemeinschaft* of high culture. See also Hofmannsthal's farewell letter to George in which he speaks of the need to turn to "small things" and to forego big words; as though, having lost touch with reality through

what Weber called *Entzauberung,* disenchantment, or demagication, the poets might regain reality by a more circumspect kind of magic which requires, in effect, a creation not of the cosmos, but of a microcosmos. On the relation of this to the ataraxic ideal and to Husserl's phenomenology, see below, chapter 3, section 4.

132. Weber distinguished ethical prophecy from exemplary prophecy—the former relies on commands and preaching and is functional, the latter is a showing of one's being (*Zuständlichkeit*).

133. M. Rheinstein, ed., *Max Weber on Law and Economy,* 323. See also Weber's *Basic Concepts of Sociology,* paragraph 8, on "The Concept of Struggle."

134. For example: R. Bendix, *Max Weber: An Intellectual Portrait,* 294 note 11, and Hannah Arendt, "On Violence," *Crisis of the Republic.*

135. Karl Jaspers, *Philosophy Is for Everyman,* 49 (hereafter cited as *Everyman*).

136. *Future of Germany,* 82–84.

137. *Future of Mankind,* 305.

138. *Future of Mankind,* 250.

139. Ibid.

140. *Future of Mankind,* 251.

141. *Philosophy,* 2:91.

142. *Philosophy,* 2:92.

143. *Everyman,* 52.

144. *Future of Mankind,* 7.

145. *Everyman,* 51.

146. *Humanism,* 25.

147. *Humanism,* 26.

148. *Humanism,* 33.

149. *Future of Germany,* 32.

150. *Humanism,* 41.

151. *Future of Germany,* 98.

152. *Philosophy,* 2:150.

153. Given two equally strong possibilities, one must become somehow stronger and must be realized by choice if anything at all is to happen, if men are not to be forever stalled between bales of hay, like Buridan's ass.

154. *Philosophy,* 2:145. Or one might say that here freedom of choice implies the necessity to choose. The emptiness of the *liberum*

*arbitrium indifferentiae* is perhaps most apparent in Descartes's philosophy: "Freedom of judgment, that is, freedom to affirm or negate or to suspend judgment is unlimited. . . . But this freedom is complete only in thought, that is, in the realm of *theory*. . . . In the realm of theory what counts is *compelling certainty*. . . . in action, on the other hand, what counts is *resolution*. . . ." (*Essays*, 88).

155. *Philosophy*, 2:147.

156. Ibid., italics added.

157. *Philosophy*, 2:148.

158. Ibid. *Wisdom*, 22: "The Stoic's perception of man's weakness is not radical enough. He failed to see that the mind in itself is empty. . . . the independent mind is barren."

159. *Philosophy*, 2:148.

160. Ibid. For Hobbes, the partner of pride is fear—of competitors, and ultimately, of sudden and violent death. On the dual train of Hobbes's consideration of pride (that it is Satanic self-love, provoking nemesis, and that it is a passion to imitate God like the medieval *sancta superbia*), see M. Oakeshott, "The Moral Life in the Writings of T. Hobbes," *Rationalism in Politics and Other Essays*.

161. *Philosophy*, 2:148.

162. *Great Philosophers*, 1:300.

163. Ibid.

164. Ibid. Kant stated (*Critique of Practical Reason*): "If pure reason is actually practical, it will show its reality and that of its concepts in actions, and all disputations which aim to prove its impossibility will be in vain."

165. *Great Philosophers*, 1:301.

166. *Philosophy*, 2:167.

167. Ibid.

168. *Philosophy*, 2:169. This is the thrust of Jaspers's argument against absolute freedom in the Hegelian sense. For Hegel, what confronts the individual in the world is not alien, not limiting; it is that wherein the individual finds himself, or regains himself, overcoming the state of "unhappy consciousness."

169. *Philosophy*, 2:168. See Max Weber's letter to Dr. Gross (cited by Mitzman, *The Iron Cage*, 281): "We can separate all ethics, whatever their material content, into two large groups. One makes principled demands on a man, which he is generally not capable of meeting, except in great highpoints of his existence, and which direct his striv-

ing into the infinite: the hero-ethic. The other is modest enough to accept one's everyday 'nature' as the maximum demand: 'average ethic.'"

170. *Philosophy*, 2:169.

171. *Philosophy*, 2:151.

172. Ibid. In 1931 Jaspers wrote: "Today there is beginning the last campaign against the nobility. Instead of being carried on upon a political and sociological plane, it is conducted in the realm of the mind. People would gladly turn the course of developments backward; would check that unfolding of personality which was regarded as fundamental to times which, though recent, are already forgotten. . . . Earlier revolts, political revolts, could succeed without ruining man; but this revolt, were it to be successful, would destroy man" (*Modern Age*, 208).

173. *Origin and Goal*, 169.

174. *Philosophy*, 2:332. Jaspers realized (*Origin and Goal*, 173): "It is true that ideas arouse motives, but they make their influence felt in the real course of events only on the condition that they are backed by the solid realities of power." But as we have noted, how ideas become associated with the solid realities of power is still a question.

175. *Philosophy*, 2:152. *Philosophical Faith*, 212: "Kierkegaard analysed this way of losing freedom more deeply than any before him. He showed how a desperate selfhood will want to be neither itself nor not itself, and cannot be both. I want to hide from myself and from others; I do everything to keep from revealing myself, and yet I may suddenly burst into helpless, desperate self-revelations—using these in turn as a facade for the seclusion I seek. It is the radical unwillingness to be transparent to myself that becomes the root of evil."

176. *Philosophical Faith*, 217.

177. *Philosophy*, 2:281.

178. *Philosophy*, 2:152–53.

179. *Philosophy*, 2:151.

180. *Philosophy*, 3:72.

181. *Future of Germany*, 89.

182. *Philosophical Faith*, 212.

183. Jaspers's criticism follows the lines of Weber's contrast of "ethics of principle" and "ethics of responsibility."

184. *Great Philosophers*, 1:299.

185. *Philosophy*, 2:169.

186. *Philosophy*, 2:313.
187. Ibid.
188. Ibid.
189. *Philosophy*, 2:315. Kant himself distinguished comparison of a statement with its object, testing with the intellect, to comparison of a statement with the subject, testing with conscience—intellectual truth and *Wahrhaftigheit*. A man may make true statements and even statements of belief without this self-reference—in which case he is deceiving himself as well as others. See *Philosophical Faith*, 252; *Philosophy*, 2:314; *Modern Age*, 182ff., on "the sophist."
190. *Philosophy*, 2:314.
191. *Reason and Existenz*, 41.
192. *Philosophy*, 2:287.
193. *Philosophy*, 2:288.
194. *Philosophy*, 2:289–90. A consequence of this distinction—which Jaspers did not indicate—is the need to distinguish, in political terms, between the solitary "conscientious objector" and a group of civil disobedients, who may be a communicative, "rational community." However, in *The Future of Germany*, 40 and 82, Jaspers indicated examples of "how reason can prevail by disobedience": "a rational people's hearts and minds can defy the irresponsibility of government and military." "A free citizen wants to make his political weight felt by his own activity. Singly, of course, he cannot be effective. He must promptly and principally form a group, establish an organization. We Germans do this in many fields, but rarely in politics."
195. *Essays*, 223, quoting Weber.
196. *Future of Germany*, 3.
197. *Philosophy*, 2:308.
198. *Modern Age*, 33.
199. *Modern Age*, 34.
200. *Modern Age*, 122.
201. *Philosophy*, 2:327.
202. *Modern Age*, 99.
203. *Modern Age*, 89.
204. "The will to the State or the sense of the State is the will of man to shape his own destiny, which never exists for him purely as an individual, but only in community formed by the succession of generations" (*Modern Age*, 90).
205. Ibid.

206. *Modern Age*, 91.

207. Von Humboldt, *Limits of State Action*, 12.

208. Von Humboldt, *Limits of State Action*, 28. See Hannah Arendt, *The Human Condition*, 29: "What all Greek philosophers, no matter how opposed to *polis* life, took for granted is that freedom is exclusively located in the political realm, that necessity is primarily a prepolitical phenomenon, characteristic of the private household organization, and that force and violence are justified in this sphere because they are the only means to master necessity—for instance, by ruling over slaves—and to become free."

209. Von Humboldt, *Limits of State Action*, 15.

210. Mill used the following quotation from Von Humboldt's essay (p. 16) as the epigraph to *On Liberty:* "The true end of Man, or that which is prescribed by the eternal and immutable dictates of reason, and not suggested by vague and transient desires, is the highest and most harmonious development of his powers to a complete and consistent whole. Freedom is the first and indispensable condition which the possibility of such a development presupposes; but there is besides another essential—intimately connected with freedom it is true—a variety of situations."

211. Ibid., 50.

212. Ibid., 51.

213. *Origin and Goal*, 160–61.

214. *Origin and Goal*, 161.

215. Hannah Arendt, *The Human Condition*, 28: "We find it difficult that according to ancient thought . . . the very term 'political economy' would have been a contradiction in terms; whatever was 'economic' related to the life of the individual and the survival of the species, was a non-political, household affair by definition." Von Humboldt is contrasted to Jaspers here because he clearly recognized this distinction—though in a historical context when the private sphere was considered the freest, the sphere for maximum human development, a consideration that stems from Rousseau and flourished with the Romantics.

216. *Origin and Goal*, 175.

217. *Origin and Goal*, 183.

218. *Origin and Goal*, 282.

219. Ibid.

220. Ibid.

221. *Modern Age*, 123.
222. *Modern Age*, 105.
223. *Modern Age*, 101 and 106.
224. *Origin and Goal*, 175.
225. *Origin and Goal*, 176.
226. *German Guilt*, 23.
227. *Origin and Goal*, 159.
228. *Modern Age*, 83.
229. *Origin and Goal*, 197.
230. *Modern Age*, 87.
231. Jaspers did not specifically distinguish these types; they are abstracted from his numerous discussions of authority (although the headings used here are Jaspers's own). See particularly *Philosophical Faith*, 288ff.; *Future of Mankind*, chapters 13–17; *Philosophy and World*, 33ff. ("Liberty and Authority"); *Philosophy*, 2:307ff. On the distinction of the authority of legality from the authority of tradition, revelation and "natural law," see Max Weber, *Basic Concepts of Sociology*, paragraph 7.
232. *Philosophical Faith*, 28–29.
233. *Philosophy and World*, 36.
234. *Philosophy and World*, 36–37.
235. *Philosophy and World*, 37, italics added.
236. *Philosophical Faith*, 29. Cf. Heidegger on the concept of *Ungeborgenheit*, unshelteredness.
237. *Philosophical Faith*, 30.
238. *Philosophy and World*, 33.
239. *Origin and Goal*, 7.
240. *Modern Age*, 132. Jaspers's sense of contemporaneity with the past, and particularly with the great philosophers, is itself an adoption of Kierkegaard's discussion of the disciple as one who is contemporaneous with Christ (see *Training in Christianity*). The "second coming" of Christ for each man is in his responsible decision. Kierkegaard also adopted the Greek concept of recollection into his notion of repetition (see *Repetition*). But instead of saying (as the Greeks did) that all that is has been, Kierkegaard asserted, "Existenz which has now been now becomes." See above, chapter 2, section 2, on the paradox of eternity in time.
241. *Philosophical Faith*, 34.
242. *Philosophy and World*, 50.

243. *Philosophical Faith*, 324.

244. The relation of faith and reason and Jaspers's concept of philosophical faith are discussed below, chapter 3, section 6.

245. See W. Ullmann, *A History of Political Thought: The Middle Ages*, 110ff. In Protestant countries, the tie of church and state took what Jaspers called a "cynical form"—that is, *cuius regio eius religio*, the religion of the king shall be the religion of the people (*Philosophical Faith*, 44).

246. *Philosophy and World*, 51.

247. Ibid.

248. *Philosophy and World*, 52.

249. *Philosophy and World*, 51–52.

250. *Future of Mankind*, 265.

251. *Philosophical Faith*, 358.

252. *Future of Mankind*, 308.

253. *Future of Mankind*, 309.

254. *Future of Mankind*, 297.

255. *Philosophical Faith*, 45.

256. *Future of Mankind*, 34.

257. *Future of Mankind*, 3.

258. *Memoir*, 266.

259. *Future of Mankind*, 148.

260. *Future of Mankind*, 149.

261. *Future of Mankind*, 97. Jaspers envisioned a confederation of *free* states. An initial confederation of the Western states would be augmented by non-Western states which had given up their aspirations to total rule and their colonies and by formerly colonial states once these had achieved their freedom. "Confederation can be made effective only by treaties between nations living under free conditions, with unlimited freedom of speech and the desire to preserve that freedom jointly" (*Future of Mankind*, 97).

262. *Origin and Goal*, 168. Jaspers expressed the same faith in the people (though not in the fiction of the sovereign people, who are "not wise or good, let alone divine") that is to be found in Montesquieu and Jefferson. Montesquieu spoke of virtue as "love of the republic; it is a sentiment and not *une suite de connaissances*. . . . When once the people have good maxims, they keep hold of them longer than what are called *les honnêtes gens*. . . . it is rare that corruption begins with them . . ." (Montesquieu, *Spirit of the Laws*, 5, 2).

263. *Origin and Goal*, 165.

264. *Future of Mankind*, 26. In de Tocqueville's assessment, the failure to maintain an independent judiciary was crucial to the course of the French Revolution: "Judicial customs had become in many respects the customs of the nation. The courts had spread the idea that every dispute may be argued and every decision appealed; they had made publicity customary and formality desirable, both of them things which ward off servitude. The subordination of the magistry to the government is, however, one of the triumphs of the Revolution. At the moment of proclaiming the rights of man, it destroyed their castle and paralyzed their defenders" (*The Old Regime and the French Revolution*).

## CHAPTER THREE

1. Nietzsche, *Complete Works*, trans. Levy, vol. 17, p. 24–25.
2. Ibid., p. 25.
3. *Nietzsche*, 330.
4. *Philosophy*, 1:100.
5. *Philosophy*, 1:101.
6. *Philosophy*, 1:107.
7. *Philosophy*, 1:108.
8. Ibid.
9. *Philosophy*, 1:117–18.
10. *Philosophy*, 3:16.
11. *Philosophy*, 2:167; cf. *Philosophy*, 1:79–80.
12. *Philosophy*, 1:77.
13. *Great Philosophers*, 1:365: "the reader who participates in Kant's thinking is 'compellingly' delivered from the prison of the phenomenality of existence."
14. *Philosophy*, 1:79.
15. Jaspers's distinction between objective and existential time was outlined in chapter 1, section 2, above.
16. *Philosophy*, 1:68: "Whatever we come to know in world orientation becomes both *an object* and *objective*, in the sense of general validity. The concept of objectivity covers both meanings."
17. *Philosophy*, 1:99.
18. Ibid.
19. *Great Philosophers*, 1:255.
20. *Philosophy*, 1:73.
21. *Philosophical Faith*, 64.
22. *Great Philosophers*, 1:255.

23. Ibid.
24. *Philosophy*, 1:240.
25. *Philosophy*, 1:227 and 235.
26. "Existenz does not claim to be generally valid. . . . Existenz is neither general nor generally valid" (*Philosophy*, 2:18–19).
27. *Philosophical Faith*, 66–67.
28. *Philosophical Faith*, 94. The presentation of "concepts of Existenz" in the *Philosophy* is introduced on pp. 17–18 of volume 1 and is developed in volume 2.
29. *Nietzsche*, 337.
30. *Nietzsche*, 339. The Kierkegaardian analogues to "states" are the "stages on life's way."
31. *Philosophy*, 1:17.
32. *Critique of Pure Reason*, B 183.
33. Ibid., A31.
34. *Philosophy*, 2:113.
35. Ibid. This same idea is expressed by Hans Jonas (*The Phenomenon of Life*, 270): "Thus it may well be that the point of the moment, not the expanse of the flux, is our link to eternity: and the 'moment' not as the *nunc stans*, the 'standing now' in which the mystics taste release from the movement of time, but the moment as the momentum-giving motor of that very moment. On the threshold of deed holding time in suspense, but not in respite from time, it exposes our being to the timeless and with the turn of decision speeds us into action and time."
36. *Philosophy*, 2:17.
37. Ibid.
38. *Nietzsche*, 130: *das noch nicht festgestellte Tier.*
39. *Philosophy*, 2:15.
40. Ibid., italics added.
41. *Philosophy*, 3:141.
42. Ibid.
43. *Philosophy*, 3:143.
44. *Philosophy*, 3:134.
45. *Philosophical Faith*, 92.
46. *Philosophy*, 3:134.
47. *Philosophy*, 3:135: "The eye of Existenz, contemplative imagination, makes it possible for me as I read the ciphers to have a sense of completion, of temporal fulfillment, for a vanishing moment. Imagination lets an Existenz find peace in being; the cipher transfigures

the world. All existence becomes a phenomenon of transcendence; in this loving imagination whatever exists is viewed as a being for its own sake. No usefulness, no purpose, no causal genesis defines its being for me. No matter what it is: as a phenomenon it will be beautiful because it is a cipher." In this passage Jaspers's adoption of the "Analytic of the Beautiful" of Kant's *Critique of Judgment* is most clear.

48. *Philosophical Faith*, 96.

49. *Philosophy*, 3:133.

50. *Philosophy*, 2:174. *European Spirit*, 38: "Our freedom is always dependent on something else, it is not *causa sui*. If it were, man would be God."

51. *Great Philosophers*, 1:363.

52. *Great Philosophers*, 1:370.

53. Karl Jaspers, "Philosophy and Science," *Partisan Review* 16 (1949), 875 (hereafter cited as "Philosophy and Science").

54. Descartes, *Oeuvres complètes*, ed. A. Adam et P. Tannery, 2:385 and 2:9.

55. *Essays*, 122.

56. "Philosophy and Science," 879.

57. Ibid.

58. See *Origin and Goal*, 83ff.; "Philosophy and Science," 873 ff.; *Essays*, 125ff.; *Modern Age*, 144ff.; *Philosophical Faith*, 50ff.

59. "Philosophy and Science," 874.

60. Descartes's ideal, *intellectum convincere*, to attain certitude comparable to that of geometry, implies rejection of probable knowledge, rejection of the so-called inexact sciences (like history), and rejection of such methods as, for example, the *Verstehen* of Dilthey and of Jaspers himself. Descartes's ideal also contradicted the notion "I know only what I can make." Vico contrasted his *inventio* to the Cartesian *demonstratio* (for the true and the made are convertible: *verum factum*). Descartes's approach involved him in an insoluble dilemma, of course, when he was unable to transform his "provisional ethics" into a deductive ethics.

61. Comte's arrangement, for example, proceeded from the science of least complex subject matter and greatest range (mathematics), through astronomy, physics, chemistry, and biology, to the science of the most complex subject matter and least range (sociology). The order was, Comte claimed, correct in historical terms, logical terms, and pedagogical terms.

62. *Philosophy*, 1:176.
63. *Philosophy*, 1:177.
64. *Philosophy*, 1:187.
65. The problem in this is that mathematical formulas can become untranslatable into conceptual language. The philosophical corollary to this radicality of inquiry is the thinking of the possibility that there might have been nothing at all; the question "why is there something rather than nothing?" was asked by Leibniz, Kant, Schelling, and Heidegger (*Introduction to Metaphysics*), as well as by Jaspers himself.
66. *Essays*, 133.
67. *Origin and Goal*, 87.
68. Ibid.
69. *Origin and Goal*, 125.
70. This distortion was implicit in Descartes's image of mechanics, medicine, and ethics as the fruitful branches (equally important) of the tree of philosophy. The tree's root was metaphysics, and its trunk was physics (*Oeuvres complètes*, 9, part 2, p. 14).
71. *Nietzsche*, 173.
72. "My knowledge of the given world rests upon discoveries; my knowledge of the made world upon inventions" (*Philosophy*, 1:112).
73. *Philosophy*, 1:109.
74. Jaspers spoke of three sources of philosophy: wonder (Plato, Aristotle), doubt (Descartes), and awareness of myself in my situation (e.g., Epictetus: "philosophy arises when we become aware of our own weakness and helplessness"). See *Wisdom*, 17.
75. *Philosophy*, 1:122.
76. *Philosophy*, 1:123.
77. *Philosophy*, 1:124.
78. *Essays*, 112.
79. Ibid.
80. Mathematics is the "archetype of cogent knowledge," but it is of "the least existential relevance" because it lacks substance, lacks contact with reality. "Wherever philosophy was comprehended in its existential function, it became the antithesis of mathematics" (*Philosophy*, 1:187).
81. The factor of change caused in an observed object by observation itself is, of course, the key to Heisenberg's "uncertainty principle" and to the more radical critique of von Weizsacher.
82. *Philosophy*, 1:124.

83. *Philosophy*, 1:125. Jaspers considered the "unintelligibility and elemental disorder of matter" (*Philosophy*, 1:125) as the limit of empirical research, the final barrier to the identity of theory and reality. "This is true even in physics, where laws are conceived as statistical" (*Philosophy*, 1:125). "We know no more about the movement of one atom than about the single outward act of a person who is a mere statistic" (*Philosophy*, 2:166).

84. *Philosophy*, 1:123.

85. *Philosophy*, 1:125.

86. *Philosophy*, 1:130.

87. *Philosophy*, 1:132–33. Cf. Borges's article "A Note on (toward) Bernard Shaw" in *Labyrinths:* "if literature were nothing more than verbal algebra, anyone could produce any book by essaying variations—a book is a dialogue, a form of relationship."

88. *Philosophy*, 1:133.

89. Ibid.

90. Ibid.

91. *Philosophy*, 1:141.

92. *Philosophy*, 3:114.

93. Karl Jaspers, *Myth and Christianity*, 22ff. (hereafter cited as *Myth and Christianity*).

94. From the preface to Poulet's work *The Interior Distance;* in this passage the spatial imagery is consonant with Jaspers's.

95. *Nietzsche*, 308.

96. *Philosophy*, 1:134.

97. Ibid.

98. *Philosophy*, 1:135.

99. *Philosophy*, 1:207.

100. *Philosophy*, 1:196.

101. *Philosophy*, 1:207.

102. *Philosophical Faith*, 56.

103. Karl Jaspers, *Reason and Anti-Reason in Our Time*, 31.

104. *Modern Age*, 146.

105. Mill, *Principles of Political Economy*, 3, i, 2.

106. Ibid.

107. *Nietzsche*, 186.

108. *Nietzsche*, 214: "Parmenides said: 'One does not think nonbeing.' Standing at the opposite extreme we say: 'whatever can be thought must surely be fictitious.' "

109. *Nietzsche*, 151.

110. *Philosophy*, 1:206–07.

111. *Philosophy*, 1:160. In his early work *The Psychology of World-Views*, 2, Jaspers spoke of prophetic philosophy which "confronts universal contemplation as essentially different because it gives *Weltanschauungen*, shows sense and meaning, and sets up tables of values as norms, as valid. This philosophy alone would deserve the name of philosophy, if the name were to retain its noble, powerful ring." Here Nietzsche's value creation is echoed; but in the *Philosophy* Jaspers left this position behind.

112. *Philosophy*, 1:160.

113. *Philosophy*, 1:161.

114. *Philosophy*, 1:162.

115. *Philosophy*, 1:183.

116. *Philosophy*, 1:170.

117. Ibid.

118. *Philosophy*, 1:207. The mind "carries in itself the freedom which we exercise in knowledge, as self-awareness, and in taking part in ideas; and that freedom is the premise and medium of existential freedom. For on this side the mind remains unclosed as the realization of its carrier, the possible Existenz."

119. A summary of the controversies generated in the social sciences over the notion of value freedom is given in A. Brecht's *Political Theory*.

120. *Modern Age*, 82.

121. *Philosophy*, 3:132.

122. Ibid., italics added.

123. "Philosophy and Science," 879.

124. *Modern Age*, 146.

125. When science is considered as an "end in itself," philosophy, being outside the province of science, may be considered as: "based on feeling and intuition, or imagination and genius; it is conceptual magic, not knowledge; it is *élan vital*, or resolute acceptance of death" ("Philosophy and Science," 872).

126. *Modern Age*, 151.

127. "Memoir," 261.

128. "Philosophy and Science," 877.

129. "In its political appearance a philosophy shows what it is. It was no accident that both National Socialism and bolshevism would regard philosophy as their deadly spiritual foe" ("Memoir," 278).

130. *Philosophy*, 1:167ff. Jaspers distinguished (*Philosophical*

*Faith,* 85ff.) the "skeptical eye" cast on all objective statements by the philosophizing man from the adoption of a skeptical position in the manner either of Cicero or of those whose skepticism ends in nihilism. Jaspers was in agreement with Nietzsche in holding that "true knowledge is a matter of method" (*Nietzsche,* 173); the antidote to skepticism is the "extreme circumspection" of one who is well aware of the consequences of lack of method. Jaspers also followed Nietzsche in recommending that all philosophers should have a grounding in at least one science (Jaspers's own grounding was, of course, in psychiatry and psychopathology and Nietzsche's in philology) so that they might know what method is.

131. *Philosophy and World,* 150.

132. Karl Jaspers, *Philosophy of Existence,* 36.

133. Jaspers called this level of truth "pragmatic," and it has features in common with Pragmatism's concept of truth. William James stated that the usual question for Pragmatism is: "Grant an idea or belief to be true; what concrete difference will its being true make in anyone's actual life? How will the truth be realized? What experiences will be different from those which would obtain if the beliefs were false? What, in short, is the cash value of the truth in experiential terms?" (*Pragmatism*). True ideas are those which can be assimilated, corroborated, verified. (Jaspers's pragmatic truth is not, however, strictly scientific.)

134. *Philosophy of Existence,* 36.

135. *Philosophy of Existence,* 37.

136. This adequation is the sole focus of a semantic theory of truth in the manner of, e.g., Tarski.

137. *Philosophical Faith,* 286. This distinction has been the basis for recent criticism of the claim, made by conceptual analysts, that the picture of man which emerges from analysis of our ordinary ways of thinking and speaking is true (see Wilfred Sellars, "Philosophy and the Scientific Image of Man," in *Science, Perception and Reality*). For Jaspers, *no* analysis (whether conceptual or empirical) is definitive; no analysis touches the being of Existenz.

138. *Philosophy of Existence,* 37.

139. See the Preface to Kant's *Critique of Judgment.*

140. *Philosophy of Existence,* 37.

141. *Philosophy of Existence,* 38. It is on the level of *Geist* that the identity of thought and Being holds, not on the level of Existenz. *Reason and Existenz,* 63: "The faith of *Geist* is the life of the individual

Idea, where Thought in Being ultimately is valid. The faith of Existenz [philosophical faith], however, is the Absolute in Existenz itself on which everything for it rests, in which *Geist*, consciousness as such, and empirical existence are found together and decided, where for the first time there is both source and goal; here Kierkegaard's proposition 'Faith is Being' applies."

142. *Philosophy of Existence*, 39.

143. The adequacy of language to the nonobjective is not argued; no proposition can embody the truth of Existenz, no "metalanguage" can comprehend the relation of objective speech and transcending thought. Jaspers was not alone in trying to distinguish levels or types of truth: Marcel distinguished profane or scientific knowledge from sacred or metaphysical knowledge; Scheler distinguished (in *Die Wissenformen und die Gesellschaft*, 1926) *Leistungswissen* (achievement knowledge), *Bildungswissen* (cultural knowledge) and *Erlösungswissen* (knowledge of salvation). But both of these thinkers hold a much broader conception of "knowledge" than Jaspers and blur the distinction between science and philosophy.

144. *Philosophy*, 2:361.

145. *Philosophy*, 2:362. Jaspers often illustrated this distinction by contrasting the responses of Bruno and Galileo to persecution. Galileo's truth was scientific; Bruno's was a matter of philosophical conviction: "we do not see struggles of faith waged for rational consistency as a private law, not even for the cogent empirical certainty of a Galileo . . ." (*Philosophy*, 1:264).

146. *Philosophy*, 2:363.

147. *Philosophy*, 2:372.

148. Ibid.

149. *Philosophical Faith*, 201.

150. *Philosophical Faith*, 204.

151. *Philosophical Faith*, 201.

152. *Critique of Pure Reason*, B 1x.

153. *Great Philosophers*, 1:368.

154. *Philosophy*, 2:366: "Reality does not appear alike to each original Existenz. The question is *who* sees it *as what*, and from any knowledge there is always a leap to the answer. . . . As an object of cogent cognition in world orientation, of course reality is universal, but as such it never comes to be the full reality of my experience and my actions."

155. *Philosophy*, 2:179.

156. *Philosophy*, 2:18.
157. Karl Jaspers, *Allgemeine Psychopathologie*, 5th edition, 24. Dilthey distinguished between "descriptive" and "dissecting" psychology, and Spranger spoke of *geisteswissenschaftliche* psychology in terms similar to Jaspers's *Verstehen* psychology.
158. *Allgemeine Psychopathologie*, 5th edition, 259.
159. L. B. Lefebre, "The Psychology of Karl Jaspers," in *The Philosophy of Karl Jaspers*, ed. P. A. Schlipp, 478. In his 1921 review of Jaspers's book, Martin Heidegger pointed out that although Jaspers's *verstehende Psychologie* addresses the problem of the psychologist's own preconceptions as an observer it does not really explore these. For Heidegger, the *primary* question must be directed to the questioner himself. (Heidegger's review is available in Hans Saner, ed., *Karl Jaspers in der Diskussion*, 70–100.)
160. *Philosophy*, 1:252.
161. *Philosophy*, 1:253.
162. Ibid.
163. A world view can be approached from the subjective side and from the objective side. An attitude (*Einstellung*) is a formal possibility, a pattern of behavior. Jaspers discussed attitudes under three headings: objective (examples of which are rational, scholastic, experimental, dialectic), self-reflective (the attitude of immediacy, *Augenblick*, which was the focus of Kierkegaard's *Either/Or*, is an example), and enthusiastic. Correlated to attitudes are *Weltbilder*, which Jaspers discussed under the headings: sensory-spatial, psychical-cultural, and metaphysical (including mythological and philosophical views). *Weltanschauungen*, as fusions of attitudes and world-pictures, are mobile; they are totalities in motion. The motion is lost if the *Weltanschauung* becomes a shell; as nihilism, individualism, rationalism, romanticism, skepticism, and so forth. Inside a shell, a man is protected from the boundary situations which provoked his withdrawal originally.
164. In *The Great Philosophers*, Jaspers classed Nietzsche and Kierkegaard, along with Pascal and Lessing, as "the radical awakeners." The *Psychologie der Weltanschauungen* is Jaspers's own radical awakening.
165. *Reason and Existenz*, 97.
166. *Reason and Existenz*, 98.
167. *Philosophy*, 1:270.
168. *Nietzsche*, 121.

169. *Philosophical Faith*, 157–58.

170. That the company of others should be a sign of decline is completely the contrary of Jaspers's idea of communication; Heidegger's "Self" is atomistic, freest in isolation, freest in contemplation.

171. *Philosophy*, 2:368: "But if my contemplation, instead of keeping me universally ready for existential searching, makes me pile up images of man in his history and in his possibilities, it is not myself that is in touch with what I have seen. As a feeling for diversity, this erudite contact may carry universal contemplation to the very borderline of existential concern and yet be abysmally apart from it."

172. *Philosophy*, 2:358.

173. *Philosophy*, 3:61.

174. *Philosophy*, 3:63.

175. Ibid.

176. *Philosophy*, 3:66.

177. Sophocles, *Oedipus Rex*, line 1272.

178. *Philosophy*, 3:67.

179. Karl Jaspers, *Tragedy is Not Enough*, 77. (This is a translation of one section of Jaspers's *Von der Wahrheit*.)

180. *Philosophy*, 3:73.

181. *Philosophy*, 3:74–75.

182. *Philosophy*, 3:78.

183. *Philosophy*, 3:81.

184. *Philosophy*, 3:84.

185. *Philosophy*, 3:90.

186. *Philosophy*, 3:96.

187. Ibid.

188. Ibid.

189. Ibid.

190. *Philosophy*, 3:103ff.

191. *Philosophy*, 3:106.

192. *Philosophy*, 3:111.

193. *Philosophical Faith*, 284.

194. *Humanism*, 47. The main critic of Jaspers's "Goethe and Our Future" was the literary historian Ernst Robert Curtius. But after Curtius published his strenuous, bombastic review "Goethe or Jaspers?" there was a great wave of articles in German newspapers, almost all of them critical of Jaspers in very nationalistic terms. The level of the discussion was so disappointing to Jaspers that he began to feel that the mendacity and intellectual violence of the Nazi era had

not receded at all. See Hans Saner, ed., *Karl Jaspers in der Diskussionen*, 58–59.

195. *Great Philosophers*, 1:129.

196. *Philosophy*, 3:107.

197. *Great Philosophers*, 1:128. Jaspers cited Plato's *Gorgias* (428B), where Socrates claims that it is better that all men disagree with him than that: "*being one*, I should be out of harmony with myself and contradict myself." Kant's third commonsense maxim—"always think in agreement with yourself"—is similar.

198. Jaspers followed Nietzsche in adopting Pindar's demand "become what you are!" But not in his definition of creation as freedom without transcendence; see *Nietzsche*, 155.

199. *Philosophy*, 2:283.

200. *Philosophy*, 2:284.

201. *Philosophy*, 3:120.

202. *Philosophy*, 3:115.

203. *Philosophy*, 3:116.

204. Ibid.

205. Ibid.

206. Ibid.

207. On Van Gogh, see Jaspers's early monograph *Strindberg und Van Gogh*.

208. *Philosophy*, 3:121.

209. Ibid.

210. *Philosophy*, 3:119.

211. Ibid.

212. Kant, *Critique of Judgment*, part 59.

213. *Philosophy*, 3:121–22.

214. Nietzsche, *Will to Power*, 1041.

215. *Philosophy*, 3:37.

216. *Philosophy*, 3:38ff.

217. *Philosophy*, 3:60.

218. Ibid.

219. Ibid. See also *Philosophy*, 3:35: "We ascertain the philosophical idea of God as thinking fails us, and what we grasp in this failure is *that* there is a deity, not *what* it is."

220. *Philosophy*, 3:60.

221. *Reason and Existenz*, 59.

222. *Philosophical Faith*, 135.

223. *Great Philosophers*, 1:306. Kant spoke of a "Chiffre-Schrift"

in the Critique of Judgment (section 42) as that *"wodurch die Natur in ihren schönen Formen figürlich zu uns spricht,"* through which Nature speaks to us figuratively in her beautiful forms. It is in this section that Kant links aesthetic judgment and moral feeling.
224. *Philosophy*, 1:335.
225. *Philosophy*, 3:119–20. In temporal terms, *Philosophy*, 3:191: "To Existenz, eternity is present, athwart its present temporality—but again in temporal ciphers only, as decision, resolve, probation, fidelity."
226. *Philosophy*, 3:21.
227. *Philosophy*, 3:31.
228. The latter two of the three paradoxical formulations are indications of the view of the Kantian *intellectus archetypus* which "contains in one what for us is divided, what we cannot in any way unite:—the universal and the particular . . . , possibility and reality . . ." (*Great Philosophers*, 1:291).
229. *Philosophical Faith*, 23.
230. *Philosophical Faith*, 24.
231. *Philosophical Faith*, 25.
232. Ibid. Jaspers objected to what he took to be the Lutheran element in Bultmann's theology; he objected to the juxtaposition of a faith free of orthodoxy and a faith based on commitment to the event of God's redemption through Christ, to the juxtaposition of a free faith and an exclusive one. "For a philosopher this is the most alienating, the most outlandish of beliefs—this Lutheran dogma with its terrible consequences scarcely seems any longer denotative existentially" (*Myth and Christianity*, 50).
233. *Philosophical Faith*, 25.
234. Ibid.
235. As distinguished by Plato and Kant and by Spinoza (who, however, reversed the traditional terms *intellectus* and *ratio*); on the distinction between *Verstand* and *Verstehen* in Jaspers's psychology, see above, chapter 3, section 4.
236. *Great Philosophers*, 1:190.
237. *Philosophical Faith*, 27.
238. Ibid.
239. *Philosophical Faith*, 321.
240. *Philosophical Faith*, 340.
241. Ibid.

242. *Myth and Christianity*, 86.

243. *Philosophical Faith*, 34.

244. *Philosophical Faith*, 47.

245. *Philosophy*, 3:24.

246. *Philosophy*, 3:24.

247. *Philosophy*, 3:23.

248. *Philosophy of Existence*, 44.

249. *Philosophy of Existence*, 47.

250. *Philosophy of Existence*, 44.

251. Ibid.

252. *Philosophy of Existence*, 45. See Jaspers's article "Kierkegaard" in *Cross Currents* 3, 3(1952), and also in *Aneignung und Polemik*, 296–311.

253. *Philosophy of Existence*, 46–47.

254. *Philosophy of Existence*, 51.

255. *Philosophy of Existence*, 55 and 56.

256. Thus Jaspers considered himself a Christian in that he was born into "the historic Christian space" and in that he lived "by the biblical faith" (which "requires no revelation"). He accepted neither Kierkegaard's view that there are no Christians nor the view that church authorities and theologians may pronounce who is and who is not a Christian: "in the world, he who considers himself a Christian ought to be deemed one" (*Philosophical Faith*, 20–21).

257. *Philosophical Faith*, 21.

258. Ibid.

259. *Philosophical Faith*, 338.

260. *Philosophical Faith*, 339.

261. For an English translation, see Lessing's *Theological Writings*, selected and translated by Henry Chadwick. On Lessing's relation to Reimarus and the tradition of distinguishing the historical and the mythical or doctrinal Jesus, see Albert Schweitzer's *The Quest of the Historical Jesus*.

262. Karl Jaspers, *The Perennial Scope of Philosophy*, 100 (hereafter cited as *Perennial Scope*).

263. *Perennial Scope*, 99–100. See also *Philosophical Faith*, 343f., "Tensions peculiar to the biblical religion."

264. *Philosophical Faith*, 341.

265. *Philosophical Faith*, 345.

266. *Philosophical Faith*, 352. "Unlike the Catholic priest, the

Protestant pastor is no official functioning as the impersonal purveyor of grace (*ex opere operato*). He is an individual personality, depended on to realize his faith for the orientation of others. He is an equal among equals, a shepherd of souls and a thinker of unshakeable honesty'' (*Philosophical Faith*, 352).

267. *Philosophical Faith*, 103.
268. Ibid.
269. *Philosophical Faith*, 104. That is, embodiment strengthens our will, but not our "grand will."
270. *Reason and Existenz*, 96.
271. Ibid.
272. *Reason and Existenz*, 48.
273. *Philosophical Faith*, 349.
274. Ibid. For Jaspers's critique of the theology of Karl Barth, see *Philosophical Faith*, 109–15.
275. *Reason and Existenz*, 37.
276. *Reason and Existenz*, 46.
277. *Reason and Existenz*, 48.
278. *Reason and Existenz*, 137.

## CONCLUSION

1. *Everyman*, xvii.
2. In his 1950 *Reason and Anti-Reason in Our Time*, Jaspers announced his preference for describing his work as *Philosophie der Vernunft* rather than *Existenzphilosophie*. In part, the terminology distinguished his work from Sartre's and protected it from charges that it was subjectivistic; but the shift also underscored Jaspers's concern with how reason and Existenz relate.
3. *Everyman*, xvii.
4. Hugo von Hofmannsthal, "The Books of Friends," *Selected Prose*, 358.
5. *Humanism*, 58.
6. See Gottfried Lessing, *Theological Writings*, 99.
7. *Philosophy of Existence*, 60.
8. *Philosophy*, 1:19.
9. *Humanism*, 83–84.
10. *Great Philosophers*, 1:20, 31, 25, 25 (respectively).
11. *Philosophy of Existence*, 60.
12. *Reason and Existenz*, 57.

13. Lichtenberg characterized his work by saying: "I have thrown out seed ideas on every page, and if they fall on fertile ground, yea chapters even dissertations can grow from them" (*Gedankenbücher,* 86).

14. See *Philosophy*, 2:101–03, on the form of philosophy.

15. *Philosophy*, 2:102.

16. *German Guilt*, 15: "What we have thought as individuals, or heard in conversations here and there, may partly be objectivized in a reflective connection. You want to participate in such connected reflections, in questions and attempted answers in which you will recognize what lies already within yourselves or is already clear. We want to reflect together, while, in fact, I expound unilaterally. But the point is not dogmatic communication, but investigation and tender for examination on your part. . . . Brainwork is not all that this requires. The intellect must put the heart to work, arouse it to an inner activity which in turn carries the brainwork. You will vibrate with me or against me, and I myself will not move without a stirring at the bottom of my thoughts. . . ."

17. *Philosophy*, 1:34.

18. *Everyman*, 121.

19. Karl Jaspers, *Notizen zu Heidegger*, ed. Hans Saner, 31 (hereafter cited as *Notizen*).

20. *Philosophy and the World*, 68.

21. Karl Jaspers, "On Heidegger," *Graduate Faculty Philosophy Journal* 7 (Spring 1978), 118. (And see also Saner's foreword to *Notizen*.)

22. Martin Heidegger, *Introduction to Metaphysics*, 199.

23. *Future of Germany*, 167.

24. *Notizen*, 261. Jaspers's own meditation on sexuality, friendship and marriage (for a popular audience) is in the lecture called "Love," in *Everyman*.

25. *Notizen*, 129 and 139.

26. *Great Philosophers*, 1:55.

27. *Modern Age*, 205 (translation emended).

28. *Humanism*, 48.

29. *Modern Age*, 116.

30. *Future of Germany*, 90.

31. *Future of Germany*, 91.

32. *Everyman*, 46.

33. Ibid.

# CHRONOLOGICAL LIST OF
# SELECTED WORKS BY JASPERS

*Allgemeine Psychopathologie.* Berlin: J. Springer, 1913. (*General Psychopathology.* Trans. J. Hoenig and M. Hamilton. Chicago: University of Chicago Press, 1963.)

*Psychologie der Weltanschauungen.* Berlin: J. Springer, 1919.

*Strindberg und van Gogh.* 2nd rev. ed. Berlin: J. Springer, 1926.

*Die geistige Situation der Zeit.* Berlin: deGruyter, 1931. (*Man in the Modern Age.* Trans. E. and C. Paul. New York: Doubleday, 1957.)

*Philosophie.* Berlin: J. Springer, 1932. (*Philosophy.* Trans. E. B. Ashton. Chicago: University of Chicago Press, 1969.)

*Vernunft und Existenz.* Munich: Piper, 1935. (*Reason and Existenz.* Trans. W. Earle. New York: Noonday, 1955.)

*Nietzsche: Einführung in das Verständnis seines Philosophierens.* Berlin: de Gruyter, 1936. (*Nietzsche: An Introduction to the Understanding of His Philosophical Activity.* Trans. C. Wallraff and F. J. Schmitz. Tucson: University of Arizona Press, 1965.)

*Descartes und die Philosophie.* Berlin: de Gruyter, 1937. (*Three Essays.* Trans. R. Mannheim. New York: Harcourt, Brace and World, 1964.)

*Existenzphilosophie.* Berlin: de Gruyter, 1938. (*The Philosophy of Existence.* Trans. R. Grabu. Philadelphia: University of Pennsylvania Press, 1971.)

*Die Idee der Universität.* Berlin: J. Springer, 1946. (*The Idea of the University.* Trans. H. Reiche and H. Vanderschmidt. Boston: Beacon Press, 1959.)

*Nietzsche und das Christentum.* Munich: Piper, 1946. (*Nietzsche and Christianity.* Trans. E. B. Ashton. Chicago: Henry Regnery, 1961.)

*Die Schuldfrage.* Heidelberg: Schneider, 1946. (*The Question of German Guilt.* Trans. E. B. Ashton. New York: Dial Press, 1947.)

**219**

*Vom Europäischen Geist.* Munich: Piper, 1947. ("Is Europe's Culture Finished?" *Commentary* 4 (1947). *The European Spirit.* Trans. R. G. Smith. London: SCM Press, 1948.)

*Von der Wahrheit.* Munich: Piper, 1947. (Two extracts: *Tragedy Is Not Enough.* Trans. H. Reiche et al. Boston: Beacon Press, 1952. *Truth and Symbol.* Trans. J. T. Wilde et al. New York: Twayne, 1959.)

*Der Philosophische Glaube.* Munich: Piper, 1948. (*The Perennial Scope of Philosophy.* Trans. R. Mannheim. New York: Philosophical Library, 1949.)

*Philosophie und Wissenschaft.* Zurich: Artemis, 1949. ("Philosophy and Science." Trans. R. Mannheim. *Partisan Review* 16 [1949].)

*Vom Ursprung und Ziel der Geschichte.* Munich: Piper, 1949. (*The Origin and Goal of History.* Trans. M. Bullock. New Haven: Yale University Press, 1953.)

*Einführung in die Philosophie.* Munich: Piper, 1949. (*The Way To Wisdom.* Trans. R. Mannheim. New Haven: Yale University Press, 1954.)

*Vernunft und Widervernunft in unserer Zeit.* Munich: Piper, 1949. (*Reason and Anti-Reason in Our Time.* Trans. S. Godman. New Haven: Yale University Press, 1952.)

*Rechenschaft und Ausblick.* Munich: Piper, 1951. (Essays from this volume in: *Existentialism and Humanism.* Trans. H. E. Fischer. New York: R. F. Moore, 1952.)

"Kierkegaard—Leben und Werk." *Der Morat* 3 (1950/51), pp. 227–36. ("The Importance of Kierkegaard." *Cross Currents* 2 [1952].)

"Nature and Ethics." Trans. E. T. Gadol. In R. A. Anshen, ed., *Principles of Moral Action.* New York: Harper Brothers, 1952.

*Die Frage der Entmythologisierung.* Munich: Piper, 1954. (*Myth and Christianity.* Trans. N. Guterman. New York: Noonday, 1958.)

*Schelling, Grösse und Verhängnis.* Munich: Piper, 1955.

*Die Grossen Philosophen.* Munich: Piper, 1957. (*The Great Philosophers.* Trans. R. Mannheim. Ed. H. Arendt. New York: Harcourt, Brace and World, 1962.)

*Die Atombombe und die Zukunft des Menschen.* Munich: Piper, 1958. (*The Future of Mankind.* Trans. E. B. Ashton. Chicago: University of Chicago Press, 1961.)

*Philosophie und Welt.* Munich: Piper, 1958. (*Philosophy and the World.* Trans. E. B. Ashton. Chicago: Henry Regnery, 1963.)

*Der Philosophische Glaube angesichts der Offenbarung.* Munich: Piper, 1962. (*Philosophical Faith and Revelation.* Trans. E. B. Ashton. New York: Harper and Row, 1967.)

*Hoffnung und Sorge: Schriften zur deutschen Politik, 1945–1965.* Munich: Piper, 1965.

*Kleine Schule des Philosophischen Denkens.* Munich: Piper, 1965. (*Philosophy Is for Everyman.* Trans. R. F. L. Hull and G. Wels. New York: Harcourt, Brace and World, 1967.)

*Wohin treibt die Bundesrepublik?* Munich: Piper, 1967. (*The Future of Germany.* Trans. E. B. Ashton. Chicago: University of Chicago Press, 1967.)

*Schicksal und Wille.* Munich: Piper, 1967.

*Philosophische Aufsätze.* Frankfurt: Fischer, 1967.

*Aneignung und Polemik.* Munich: Piper, 1968.

*Chiffren der Transzendenz.* Munich: Piper, 1970.

*Philosophische Autobiographie.* rev. ed. Munich: Piper, 1977. (Chapter added to revised edition: "On Heidegger." Trans. D. Ponikvar, *Graduate Faculty Philosophy Journal* 7 [1978].)

*Notizen zu Heidegger.* Ed. H. Saner. Munich: Piper, 1978.

# GENERAL BIBLIOGRAPHY

Adorno, Theodor. *The Jargon of Authenticity*. Trans. K. Tarnowski and F. Will. London: Routledge and Kegan Paul, 1973.

Allen, E. L. *The Self and Its Hazards: A Guide to the Thought of Karl Jaspers*. London: Hodder and Stoughton, n.d.

Arendt, Hannah. *Eichmann in Jerusalem: A Report on the Banality of Evil*. New York: Viking Press, 1963.

———. *The Human Condition*. New York: Anchor Books, 1969.

———. *Crises of the Republic*. New York: Harcourt, Brace and Jovanovich, 1972.

Aristotle. *Nicomachean Ethics*. Trans. W. D. Ross. New York: Random House, 1966.

Bendix, Reinhard. *Max Weber: An Intellectual Portrait*. New York: Doubleday, 1960.

Bernstein, Richard. *Praxis and Action*. Philadelphia: University of Pennsylvania Press, 1971.

Blackham, H. J. *Six Existentialist Thinkers*. London: Routledge and Kegan Paul, 1961.

Bollinow, Otto F. "Existenzphilosophie und Geschichte." *Blätter für Deutsche Philosophie* 11 (1938), pp. 337–78.

———. "Existenzerhellung und philosophische Anthropologie." *Blätter für Deutsche Philosophie* 12 (1939), pp. 133–74.

Brecht, Arnold. *Political Theory: Foundations of Twentieth Century Political Thought*. Princeton, N.J.: Princeton University Press, 1960.

Brecht, Franz Joseph. *Heidegger und Jaspers: Die beiden Grundformen der Existenzphilosophie*. Wuppertal: Marees-Verlag, 1948.

Chadwick, Henry. *Lessing's Theological Writings*. Stanford: Stanford University Press, 1959.

Collins, James. "An Approach to Karl Jaspers." *Thought* 20 (1945), pp. 657–91.

———. "Karl Jaspers' Philosophical Logic." *The New Scholasticism* 23 (1949), pp. 414–20.

————. *The Existentialists: A Critical Study.* Chicago: Henry Regnery, 1952.

Cowan, Marianne, ed. and tr. *Humanist without Portfolio: An Anthology of the Writings of Wilhelm von Humboldt.* Detroit: Wayne State University Press, 1963.

Descartes, René. *Oeuvres complètes.* Ed. Adam and Tannery. Paris: J. Vrin, 1956–57.

De Waelhens, Alphonse. "Un véritable existentialisme: La philosophie de Karl Jaspers." *Orbe* 2 (1946), pp. 11–25.

Dufrenne, Mikel, and Ricoeur, Paul. *Karl Jaspers et la philosophie de l'existence.* Paris: Editions du Seuil, 1947.

Ehrlich, L. H. "Philosophical Faith and Mysticism: Karl Jaspers." *Bucknell Review* (1967/70), pp. 1–21.

————. *Karl Jaspers: Philosophy as Faith.* Amherst: U. of Mass. Press, 1975.

Fischer, Hanns. *Karl Jaspers' Trilogy.* New York: Russel F. Moore, 1951.

Gabriel, Leo. *Existenzphilosophie von Kierkegaard bis Sartre.* Vienna: Herold-Verlag, 1951.

Gray, J. Glenn. "The New Image of Man in Martin Heidegger's Philosophy." In *New European Philosophy.* Ed. G. Kline. Chicago: Quadrangle Books, 1965.

Hartt, J. N. "God, Transcendence and Freedom in the Philosophy of Jaspers." *Review of Metaphysics* 4 (1951), pp. 247–58.

Hegel, G. W. F. *The Phenomenology of Mind.* Trans. J. Baille. 2nd ed. London: George Allen and Unwin, 1961.

Heidegger, Martin. *Introduction to Metaphysics.* Trans. R. Mannheim. New York: Anchor Books, 1959.

Heller, Erich. *The Artist's Journey into the Interior.* New York: Random House, 1965.

————. *The Disinherited Mind.* New York: Barnes and Noble, 1971.

Hersch, Jeanne. "Une philosophie de l'existence: Karl Jaspers." *Lettres* 3 (1945), pp. 56–63.

Hommes, Ulrich. *Die Existenzerhellung und das Recht.* Frankfurt am Main: Klostermann, 1962.

Hyppolite, Jean. "Jaspers." *Dieu Vivant* 1 (1945), pp. 63–80.

————. "Situation de Jaspers." *Esprit* 16 (1948), pp. 482–96.

James, William. *Pragmatism.* New York: Meridian Books, 1969.

Jonas, Hans. *The Phenomenon of Life.* New York: Delta Books, 1969.

Kant, Immanuel. *The Critique of Practical Reason.* Trans. L. W. Beck. New York: Library of Liberal Arts, 1956.
———. *The Critique of Pure Reason.* Trans. N. K. Smith. New York: St. Martin's Press, 1965.
———. *Perpetual Peace,* trans. L. W. Beck. New York: Bobbs-Merrill, 1957.
Kierkegaard, Sören. *The Present Age.* Trans. A. Dru. New York: Harper Torchbooks, 1962.
———. *Concluding Unscientific Postscript.* Trans. D. F. Swenson and W. Lowrie. Princeton, N.J.: Princeton University Press, 1964.
———. *The Concept of Dread.* Trans. W. Lowrie. Princeton, N.J.: Princeton University Press, 1967.
Krell, David Farrell. "Toward Sein und Zeit." *Journal of the British Society for Phenomenology,* vol. 6, no. 3 (1975), pp. 147–56.
———. "The Heidegger-Jaspers Relationship." *Journal of the British Society for Phenomenology,* vol. 9, no. 2 (1978), pp. 126–29.
Lichtenberg, G. C. *Gedankenbücher.* Ed. F. Mautner. Heidelberg: Lothan Stiehm, 1967.
Lichtigfeld, Adolph. *Jaspers' Metaphysics.* London: Colibri Press, 1954.
Mill, J. S. *Principles of Political Economy.* New York: D. Appleton, 1894.
Miller, R. D. *Schiller and the Ideal of Freedom.* Oxford: Oxford University Press, 1970.
Mitzman, A. *The Iron Cage: An Historical Interpretation of Max Weber.* New York: Knopf, 1970.
Montesquieu. *The Spirit of the Laws.* Trans. T. Nugent. New York: Hafner, 1959.
Nietzsche, F. *Complete Works.* Trans. O. Levy. New York: Macmillan, 1924–.
Oakeshott, M. "The Moral Life in the Writings of Thomas Hobbes." In *Rationalism in Politics and Other Essays.* New York: Basic Books, 1962.
Patri, A. "Jaspers et la foi philosophique." *Monde Nouveau* 9 (1953), pp. 62–64.
Peterson, M. D., ed. *The Portable Thomas Jefferson.* Harmondsworth, England: Penguin, 1977.
Piper, K., ed. *Offener Horizont: Festschrift für Jaspers.* Munich: Piper, 1953.

Poulet, Georges. *The Interior Distance*. Trans. E. Coleman. Baltimore: Johns Hopkins University Press, 1959.

Rheinstein, M., ed. *Max Weber on Law and Economy*. Cambridge, Mass.: Harvard University Press, 1954.

Ricoeur, Paul. *Gabriel Marcel et Karl Jaspers*. Paris: Editions du Temps Présent, 1948.

Rilke, R. M. *Duino Elegies*. Trans. C. F. MacIntyre. Berkeley: University of California Press, 1963.

Samay, Sebastian. *Reason Revisited: The Philosophy of Karl Jaspers*. South Bend: University of Notre Dame Press, 1971.

Saner, H. *Jaspers in Selbstzeugnissen und Bilddokumenten*. Hamburg: Rowohlt, 1970.

————, ed. *Karl Jaspers in der Diskussion*. Munich: Piper, 1973.

Saner, H., and Piper, K., eds. *Erinnerungen an Karl Jaspers*. Munich: Piper, 1974.

Schlipp, P. A., ed. *The Philosophy of Karl Jaspers*. New York: Tudor Publishing, 1957.

Schrag, Oswald. *Existence, Existenz, and Transcendence: An Introduction to the Philosophy of Karl Jaspers*. Pittsburgh: Duquesne University Press, 1971.

Sellars, W. *Science, Perception and Reality*. New York: Humanities Press, 1963.

Smith, Ronald G. "Karl Jaspers on Theology and Philosophy." *The Hibbert Journal* 49 (1951), pp. 62–66.

Tilliette, Xavier. *Karl Jaspers: Théorie de la vérité, Métaphysique des chiffres, Foi philosophique*. Coll. "Theologie." vol. 44. Paris: Aubier, 1959.

Tocqueville, Alexis de. *The Old Regime and the French Revolution*. Trans. S. Gilbert. New York: Anchor Books, 1955.

Ullman, W. *A History of Political Thought: The Middle Ages*. Baltimore: Penguin, 1968.

Von Hofmannsthal. *Selected Prose*. Bollingen Series. New York: Pantheon Books, 1952.

Von Humboldt, W. *The Limits of State Action*. Trans. J. W. Burrow. Cambridge: Cambridge University Press, 1969.

Wahl, Jean. "Le problème du choix: L'existence et la transcendence dans la philosophie de Jaspers." *Revue métaphysique et morale* 41 (1934), pp. 405–44.

Wallraff, Charles. *Karl Jaspers: An Introduction to His Philosophy*. Princeton, N.J.: Princeton University Press, 1970.

————. "Jaspers in English: A Failure of Communication." *Philosophy and Phenomenological Research* 37 (1977), pp. 537–48.
Weber, Max. *Sociology of Religion.* Trans. T. Parsons. Boston: Beacon Press, 1963.
————. *Basic Concepts of Sociology.* Trans. H. P. Secher. New York: Greenwood Press, 1969.
Wisser, Richard. *Verantwortung im Wandel der Zeit: Einübung in geistiges Handeln: Jaspers, Buber, v. Weizsäcker, Guardini, Heidegger.* Mainz: Hase and Koehler, 1967.

# INDEX

Action: instinctive, 46; purposive, 46, 51–52; vital, 47; unconditional, 47, 48, 52; political, 51–59; technological, 53; educational, 55

Aquinas, Thomas, 151–52

Arendt, Hannah: *On Revolution,* 67; *Eichmann in Jerusalem,* 78; mentioned, ix, 169, 196n135, 200n208, 200n215

Aristotle: on men acting, 37, 194n106; mentioned, viii, 18, 39, 116, 151

Ataraxy, 48, 130, 153, 186n87, 191n50, 195n131, 197n158

Augustine, 151–52

Authority: of faith, 70, 81, 91, 92; of legality, 70, 81, 91, 92–94; of reason, 89, 153; societal, 89; of cogency, 120

Axial Period, 31, 41, 91–92, 95

Being-in-itself, 3–4, 5, 27. *See also* Transcendence

*Bewusstsein überhaupt:* defined, 1, 3, 4, 100, 103, 155, 183n16; and authority, 89; and objectivity, 107, 148; and science, 111, 116; and truth, 125–27

Bolshevism, 26, 58, 63

Boundary situation: defined, 20–22, 131–36; mentioned, *passim*

Bultmann, Rudolf, 153, 214n232

Ciphers: and politics, 44, 97, 160; and science, 122; Jesus as cipher,

157; mentioned, 13, 18, 23, 31, 48, 92, 106–08, 129, 144–49, 213n223

Cogency: types of, 112–16; mentioned, 120, 210n154

Common sense, 49–50

Communication: and truth, 7, 9, 127; and freedom, 49, 75; educational, 55; and rational community, 68, 80, 155, 168; and lying, 79; and authority, 92, 157; as Existenz concept, 105–06; mentioned, xii, 62, 121, 133, 167, 184n49

Comte, Auguste, 108–09, 123, 205n61

Conscience, 44, 199n189. *See also* Evil

Contemplation: as inner action, 36; active, 107; mentioned, 212n171

*Dasein:* and society, 82; and authority, 89; and time, 102; and truth, 126; mentioned, 1, 43, 100, 155

Descartes, René: on science, 108, 111, 205n60; mentioned, 1, 39, 196n154, 206n70, 206n74

Determinism, 71–73

Dialectic: as method, ix, 109, 119, 185n67, 189n30

Dialectical reversals: examples of, 21–23; mentioned, 11, 77, 177

Dostoyevsky, Feodor, 25, 94

Education, 55, 193n84. *See also* Action

Ethics: of principle, 80; of responsibility, 80, 160, 197n169, 198n183

**229**